MISSION: SAUDI ARABIA

On the road below us, big black shapes rumbled by, with the jerks and mindlessness so peculiar to tanks. This was it. We had been in ambush in North Yemen since nightfall.

The flares burst in the sky over the road, brilliant white. I recognized Russian T-62's, the first time I had ever seen them except in photographs.

I took direct aim at a tank and squeezed the rubber-covered firing lever of the LAW . . .

MERC:
The Professional

FRANK CAMPER

A DELL BOOK

Published by
Dell Publishing
a division of
Bantam Doubleday Dell Publishing Group, Inc.
666 Fifth Avenue
New York, New York 10103

ISBN: 0-440-20215-9

Printed in the United States of America

Published simultaneously in Canada

January 1989

10 9 8 7 6 5 4 3 2 1

OPM

For the real Recondos—
May we live to spend it.
Vive la mort!
Vive la guerre!
Vive la sacre mercenaire!

CONTENTS

In the Interest of Accuracy

The conversations in this book are condensed approximations of what was actually said based on my best recollection and do not represent verbatim accounts.

Finally, to those of you who personally participated in these incidents and recognize a little judicious obscuring of facts, please remember that some techniques, and some people still living and working, have to be protected.

PREFACE
Mercenary Motives

The "National Soldier," in the service of his country, must fight the foe of the day and the enemy of the hour, as dictated by the politicians who control his job.

Tomorrow that enemy might be an ally, and today's ally tomorrow's antagonist.

To me, being a government soldier is the definition of death for hire. As a mercenary, I could choose my enemy, and if I thought a certain job was wrong, I could refuse.

I find it ironic that mercs are generally considered amoral because they fight for pay as opposed to patriotism. Critical citizens *don't* consider the fact that the merc is hired to do the things their own government can't, or won't, do . . . but things that still must be done.

It is a social hypocrisy only.

Sure, I've known a few mercs who were genuine cutthroats, who would kill for money only. There are no standards in this line of work, but there are averages.

I've told my story as openly as possible despite the security restrictions on it. Some names and details have been changed, and I regret that some missions don't even appear here.

The route I took in making a profession of being a hired soldier and my reasons and motives are in this book. I have no apologies. I have lived by my own standards, not by those of others.

CHAPTER ONE
Prisoner

---

22 January 1968: Crystal River, Florida

The spotter plane had us pinned down, and I could hear the signal horns of the dog teams as they closed in from both sides.

I raised my 98k Mauser rifle out of the palmetto bushes and aimed at the flimsy aircraft. It was circling us, guiding the dogs our way. I was exhausted, angry, and trapped. The powerful Mauser could shoot the little plane out of the sky.

I had been back in the United States only six months, and I was in combat again, but now my enemy was my own government. I was using all I had learned in Vietnam to escape and evade it.

I glanced at my partner, George Larkins. His face was a sweaty mask of tension, eyes desperately searching for the dog teams. He held his pistol ready.

"I'm going to bring that son of a bitch down," I said, and released the Mauser's safety.

How I came to be in that palmetto thicket takes some explanation.

---

7 June 1967: Oakland, California

I had just returned from Vietnam and spent a day processing in at the Oakland Army Terminal in California. I was to be on a 707 home to Birmingham, Alabama, the next morning. My orders gave me leave until the end of August and a new assignment to Fort Gordon, Georgia.

I had gone to Vietnam as a nineteen-year-old private first

class, with a brigade-level intelligence and operations (S2–S3) shop. After arriving, I had transferred into the infantry and been promoted, getting my combat experience as a squad leader.

Following that, I joined our newly formed LRRP (Long Range Reconnaissance Patrol) platoon, putting me back with 2nd Brigade Headquarters of the 4th Infantry Division.

The 5th Special Forces took operational control of our LRRP platoon, and some of our missions began to be for the Special Operations Group.

By then I had turned twenty.

The LRRP/SOG missions had been incredible, our small teams infiltrating and raiding deep into Cambodia and remote parts of Vietnam.

I never even had an R&R, pulling missions until just a few days before I left Vietnam.

Coming out of combat so quickly was a shock. In the Philippines, during a refueling stop, I had looked out the window of my plane and wondered briefly why the runway wasn't lined with gun bunkers facing the tropical treeline, before I thought.

As we rode from one side of the Oakland Army Terminal to another, a soldier dropped a sliding window of the bus, and the rapid clatter of the ratchet lock sounded like a machine gun, making me flinch, thinking for an illogical instant we were being ambushed from the side of the road.

At first, being back home was wonderful. I had all I could eat, I could sleep without interruption, and having my friends and family so considerate and interested in pleasing me was novel.

But it couldn't last. They had lives to lead, and daily business soon took them back onto the rails of their routines. I found myself avidly watching the news about Vietnam each day on television, trying to catch a word about my unit or see someone I recognized on the news tapes.

July 1967: Malaria

I had been instructed to carry a small bottle of antimalaria tablets home and take them. When they ran out, I developed malaria. I had actually had it for a long time, but taking the tablets in Vietnam had kept it suppressed.

The disease made me ill-tempered, took away my appetite, and, during the worst attacks, robbed me of leave time by reducing me to a bed patient. I fought it stubbornly.

George Larkins and I had grown up together in Birmingham, having been friends since grammar school. We had been closer than brothers. In the summer of 1967, George was tall, lean, and his thick, black hair was graying prematurely at the temples.

I spent a lot of time with George while on leave. I found him divorced from his wife (I had introduced them) and living a lonely life in a one-room apartment, working by day and going to college at night. I talked George into joining the army. It seemed to be a way out for him.

---

31 July 1967: Post Hospital, Fort Gordon, Georgia

I had a serious attack of malaria the day I arrived at Fort Gordon and was hospitalized even before I could get my orders processed for my new assignment in Headquarters Company, United States Army Training Center.

I was put in the contagious-diseases ward, a roomful of beds filled with basic trainees who had hepatitis, but they didn't seem to be severely ill. I was fading in and out of a fevered sleep, dreaming jumbled, disjointed nightmares.

The hepatitis patients talked, walked, played music, and generally acted like a bunch of restless young soldiers. They disturbed me greatly, and if I could have gotten to my feet, I would have run the whole group to another ward.

---

8 August: Recovery

The first few days in the ward had been a blur. Now I knew when the interns came and took my blood samples, and I had enough strength to argue back at the nurses who came by with carts of milkshakes and fruit, insisting I eat, believing me to be one of the hepatitis patients.

10 August: ETV

I left the hospital to prepare for duty in the stateside army.

My new job was as an illustrator for the Army Educational Television Unit, after Headquarters Company discovered I could draw—very different duty from long-range patrols in the jungle.

By the end of the month, I had been paid, rented an apartment off post, and sent for my wife, Mavis, and two-year-old son, Barret.

We had been married at eighteen, just prior to my joining the army. She had long dark hair and the square jaw and straight nose of the Cherokee, who were her distant ancestors. I was very much in love with her, and surviving Vietnam had been important to me because of her and my son.

I went to work daily at ETV, illustrating in an office managed by a civilian. My job had little to do with what I thought of as the army, and I began to realize this was how many career soldiers spent their entire enlistments.

George Larkins called me with the news he had finished his basic training at Fort Benning, near us in Georgia, and was being assigned to Fort Gordon.

George loaned me his old 1963 Volkswagen sedan when he arrived, and told me to keep it while he was in training.

15 November: 75th Rangers

Orders assigning me to the 75th Rangers at Fort Rucker, Alabama, appeared in my mailbox at Headquarters Company. The personnel office on main post apparently had discovered my real job in Vietnam, and there was a critical shortage of long range patrol troops.

Furthermore, the 75th Ranger Company was preparing to go to Vietnam.

I took the news home to Mavis, telling her I had to go and

she would have to stay behind until I knew what my disposition would be with the Rangers at Fort Rucker. I packed my duffel bag, loaded it into the VW, and left for south Alabama, half a day's drive.

At the 75th Rangers' company headquarters, I was not welcomed. They were in the process of a major inspection and felt that trying to get a new man moved in would disturb the neat, military atmosphere of the barracks. The company sergeant suggested I report in after the weekend, when the inspection was finished. That suited me fine. I started home that night.

The drive back from Fort Rucker to Fort Gordon was tiring, and I was in the dark, lonely farm country of central Georgia.

It was just before dawn. I was sleepy, the weather was freezing, and the VW had a rusted-out heater system.

Somewhere past Macon, carbon monoxide fumes from the heater overcame me. I nodded at the wheel and vaguely remember the headlamps shining out into the night sky, because the car was flying off an embankment. I don't remember the impact.

I awoke lying on my face in the grass. I was very calm. I knew there had been a wreck. I also knew I was hurt, because I could not move, yet I felt no pain.

I wondered in how many places I was opened up.

I knew something had to be done if I was bleeding, but I was powerless. George's car was on fire. I could see the flickering light from the flames. I wondered how close to it I was lying.

I tried to crawl, to get to my hands and knees. That brought the pain. It was the most agonizing thing I had ever felt, but I couldn't scream. I could barely breathe.

I rolled over and saw the car was upside down, fire from the engine compartment coming up between the rear wheels.

I passed out again and came to when someone spoke to me. A man was asking how I felt. I told him I couldn't move and in a detached way asked if I was bleeding, and said I thought I was going into shock.

When the ambulance crew lifted me onto a stretcher, the pain knocked me out.

The next morning, I awoke in a military hospital at Warner Robbins Air Force Base, Georgia.

There was a cast on my left leg from toe to hip. I was told my left ankle was broken. My neck was in a brace. The doctor said I had cracked vertebrae in it. My back was out of commission, with massive muscle damage.

I had been lucky. I was not dead.

I hurt all over, but worried about my new duty station, asked the air force hospital staff to contact the Ranger company.

Mavis came on Thanksgiving day with Wally Burns, a friend of mine from Fort Gordon who had a car, and they drove me to Fort Gordon, propped in the backseat with my stiff, plastered leg outstretched.

The hospital in Fort Gordon examined me and put me on an outpatient basis where I could recuperate at home, and come back on post for treatment.

10 December: Arrested

I had written the Ranger company, addressing my letter to the company commander, and asked what I should do, since I was temporarily out of action.

Mavis answered a knock at our front door a week later, and there stood two military police officers.

They told me I was under arrest and waited while I got out of bed, dressed, and went on my crutches to their car. I told Mavis I would get some word to her as soon as I could. The arrest made no sense to me.

I did not know the 75th Rangers were carrying me as AWOL (absent without official leave), a serious offense. The air force had not notified them. When the Rangers received my letter, they had promptly called the Military Police.

I was taken to the stockade. The MP sergeant there told me to give him my shirt. I propped the crutches against the desk and unbuttoned my shirt. He took it and began cutting the insignia off, hard-earned insignia like my combat infantry badge.

On the left sleeve he had a soldier sew a white armband, signifying I was a prisoner. From there, I was locked in a nearby cell, thinking of my CIB and other patches thrown on the floor.

Soon an MP arrived with an officer. The officer looked at me, shook his head in disgust, and left. The MP unlocked the cell door. "Come on," he said, "we're moving you to the hospital."

* * *

My accommodations at the hospital were barely better than the stockade. The orderlies shoved a bed for me into a large closet.

A doctor told me to take off my uniform and put on a hospital gown. I did it slowly, my back muscles still sore, hanging my uniform on a wall rack.

Outside the closet was a guard, an MP with a pistol, sitting on a stool. He said I was not allowed to talk to him, and shut the closet door.

I lay on the bed, looking at the white armband on my shirt. I was a prisoner. I had been arrested, processed, and jailed. I could not believe it.

When my wife found out where I was being held, she came to see me. She was scared and confused. I tried to explain that sometimes the military made mistakes like this, but I was having trouble convincing myself.

Having a high-level security clearance automatically "flagged" my records. Since I had been reported as AWOL, procedure was for me to be held until cleared by Military Intelligence for possible security violations.

I lay alone on that bed in the closet, staring at the white prisoner armband on my shirt, which hung on the wall rack at the foot of the bed. I had fought for my country, but to the clerks of the stateside army, it didn't matter.

Even the officers were only ranking clerks.

I had no tolerance for such treatment. I was still in a state of war inside. Maybe if it had all happened later I would have been more able to take the indignation like a good, soulless, mindless minion. But there was no time, no later.

I knew what it was to fight and to take risks, and my sense of self-worth was too strong.

My twenty-first birthday had just passed in October. Even as I came to legal age, the politicians, clerks, and bureaucrats that made up my government lost me. I was no longer their property.

I broke with the army then, lying in that closet. I realized those who hurt me were my enemy. Those who helped me were my friends. It was a basic truth.

Having made the decision, I was now on my own.

After a week, I was ordered to leave the hospital and be returned to the 75th Rangers. I was driven by the military police back to my apartment just off post, and told to get my baggage and take a bus to Fort Rucker.

I broke the cast off my leg with a kitchen knife. My ankle was tender and had no strength at all. As I painfully worked at trying to walk, I told my wife to pack a bag for me, because I had to get away.

I went to the bus station and took a bus to Atlanta, to hide.

I needed time to think and plan. My goals were short range: simply to escape and evade first, then try for something permanent. It was not logic that drove me. It was a survival instinct.

The Atlanta rooming house I stayed in was drab and dirty. To get up to my room, I had to climb several flights of stairs, and it was agony with my ankle. I could make it only by firmly holding the handrail and taking one step at a time.

I watched the streets from my room window. Below were the slums of Atlanta, where the poor wandered and drunks lay in the gutters. It was a view that matched my mood.

I sat in my dingy room, a military fugitive. I knew now I had to make my own fortune, without the blessing or dictates of my government or society.

Below, on the sidewalk in front of a bar, the police were dragging a drunk toward a police car, beating him with nightsticks. Inside the bar he had probably been fierce, but now, outnumbered and hurt, he was only managing to cover his head with his arms as they hit him.

"Just let me go home," screamed the drunk, "please, just let me go home!" It was my feeling exactly.

Mercenary Plans

After a week, I took the bus back to Fort Gordon. At home, I talked with my wife and my friend George. I told them I was finished with the military. My plan was to find a hideaway until I could get to Central America or the Caribbean Islands, where I could hire on with a local government or guerilla group as a trainer.

George said he wanted to go with me, but I told him there was only trouble ahead so he should stay where he was.

"No, we've been together too long," George said. He had no

one else; his mother and brother dead many years from an automobile accident, his father remarried into a family he did not love, and his own wife and children gone, lost by divorce.

I could not refuse him.

I bought an old bolt-action 98k Mauser rifle and some field equipment. I had chosen a swampy, remote part of central Florida to use as a refuge. It would do for a month, allowing Mavis to resettle with her family in nearby Orlando.

1 January 1968: Crystal River

A friend drove George and me to Florida and let us out on a back road just south of Crystal River, near the small towns of Wildwood and Inverness.

George carried the Mauser. I had a small .22-caliber automatic pistol, one I had originally bought for my wife to keep at home.

We walked into the swamp, our packs filled with canned food and bags of rice, and left civilization behind.

Camp was on high ground among the many streams that webbed into Crystal River. We erected a tent, made a firepit, and established a daily routine of patrolling and camp improvements.

There was a small store an hour's walk from our camp, and we used it to buy provisions.

In the cold nights of January, as George and I huddled close to our campfire, I could stare into the coals and plan for my new life as a hired soldier.

My patriotism had proven to be naïveté. America was expending its young men in Vietnam with no intent of victory, while the public bickered, the politicians argued, and the weapons manufacturers made money. I was only a survivor.

I shot and killed an alligator one day as it kicked off its bank and swam toward George, who was waist-deep in murky swamp, fording to the embankment where I waited.

The powerful bullet from the Mauser blew the alligator's head completely off, and the body rolled belly up, squat legs still kicking. The head fell back to the water and was quickly covered with scavenger turtles, ripping and biting at the flesh as it sank.

Living in the swamp was hazardous. Trying to wade or swim was risky because of the poisonous snakes, quicksand, and alligators, so George and I found an old abandoned boat and used it to paddle around in the river tributaries.

We were floating quietly down a stream a few days later, the sun filtering through the overhead mass of tangled tree limbs and vines, when I saw a lethal cottonmouth moccasin coiled on a branch almost exactly level with my face. The boat was taking me on a collision course with it.

"Back up!" I called to George, who had the paddles, but it was too late. The snake and I were coming rapidly at each other, and I could see the white inside its open mouth that gave the reptile its name.

I aimed my pistol at the snake, trying to squeeze the trigger carefully so I didn't pull the sights off alignment. The cottonmouth reared its head back, looking me in the eye. We were less than a meter apart when I fired.

The bullet went through the snake under the lower jaw and killed it instantly.

The reptile relaxed, uncoiled off its branch, and dropped into the water. The turtles struck at it as they had the alligator, taking the carcass to the bottom to tear it apart.

---

21 January 1968: Pursuit

George and I had walked to the small country store, coming at it from the swamp side. George waited beside the rowboats tied in the inlet while I approached the building from the rear with the rifle.

I glanced around the corner of the store at the road and froze.

There were police cars and a milling crowd of sheriff's deputies carrying shotguns.

I looked back at George. He was sitting near the boats, unaware of the pending disaster. I ran back to him, my heart pounding.

"They're here!" I said. "Must be a dozen cops!"

We sprinted back to camp through the cattails and gnarled vines.

I had to assume the police were just behind us. We tumbled into camp and grabbed the rest of our ammunition, the last can of food, and a canteen each and ran out again. The stop only took seconds. We left our tent, blankets, rice, and packs behind.

When we had dashed far enough away from the camp to stop and rest, I checked my pockets. "Do you have the compass?" I asked George.

He felt through his field jacket and trousers. "No!" he said.

I knew where it was. The compass was still with our equipment in camp. It was my fault. I shouldn't have let something as vital as the compass be left behind just because we were in a hurry.

"We're going east, back toward the store," I told George. "We'll go around them, toward the interstate highway. They'll probably be expecting us to go west into the swamp."

We started through the swamp to the store, moving slowly. I walked as pointman, the Mauser loaded. I didn't want to shoot any of the police, but I would fire in self-defense. My restraint ended if my life was in danger.

I had a mental map of the area, and I could tell direction by the sun or moon. I knew I could get us out. I wanted to get to Interstate 75, due east of Crystal River.

The interstate was miles away, and half the distance was treacherous swamp, teeming with natural booby traps like the snake and alligator I had killed.

"There's the store," I whispered to George, pointing through the trees.

"Hey! HALT!" a man from our flank shouted.

I dove. George crashed down behind me. "Stop!" the voice cried. Others joined in the yelling, coming at us. I looked up and saw several of them, about twenty-five meters away, all uniformed Florida state troopers.

I jumped to my feet and raced into the swamp, George with me every step of the way. I expected shots, but there were none. I damned myself for not taking a wider path past the store.

Unexpectedly, we stepped out onto a sand road. I stopped so suddenly George almost collided with me. I crept forward and, as I turned the first bend, came directly on a parked police car.

I jerked the Mauser to my shoulder, but the car was unoccupied. I had broken a rule we had in LRRP: *If you want enemy contact, get on a trail.*

I dodged off the narrow road and reversed directions. "What are you doing?" George hissed.

"This place is crawling with cops," I said. "It's too easy for them to move around here. We're going back west and cutting north, toward the river."

Every move I made was pure caution. I could have been back on the Cambodian border, tiptoeing through North Vietnamese positions. We would not be surprised again.

Many hours later, we were deep into the worst of the swamp. Winter daytime temperatures could be mild in Florida, but as it became night, the cold returned.

Exhausted, soaked, and chilled from crossing the swamp, George and I sat down back to back to rest. "We can't risk a fire," I said. "We don't know if we've lost them yet."

George agreed. We talked in low tones, about how far we had come, what the terrain would be like ahead, and what we should do next.

We slept sitting up, still back to back. I awoke sometime during the night. My wet clothes felt like ice. While I was trying to go back to sleep, a large wild boar walked up to investigate us.

George was asleep. I couldn't have cared less about the boar's presence. I was angry and frustrated enough to kill one with my bare hands.

Come dawn, the cold was intolerable. I felt stiff and ill. A noise brought me to life. It sounded at first like a low-flying plane, but in a moment I identified it.

There was an airboat looking for us.

The police had small flat-bottomed boats that skipped and dashed across the surface of the swamp, mounted with aircraft engines driving huge propellers covered by wire screens to prevent the boat pilot or passenger from getting injured. The damn boats could go almost anywhere.

George and I were shivering. I knew I had to make a fire. It was a matter of survival. I told George to endure for another few minutes, that I was going to get us warm, and began to dig out a firepit in the damp soil.

"Won't they see the smoke?" George mumbled, almost too cold to talk.

"Not this one," I said.

Over the firepit, I built a wide baffle of wet leaves on a stand of sticks. The baffle dispersed the smoke enough so it was not a rising column. It was a Vietcong trick.

With a hot fire between us, we warmed our clothes and boots. There was no coffee or tea to make. That was also in camp with the compass.

The airboat buzzed past, a hundred meters out. I knew we were on ground too solid for them to come this way.

"They're really running that river," George said, his hands near the flames, rubbing circulation back into his fingers.

"Let them, they're just burning fuel," I said, trying to catch a glimpse of the boat through the trees and vines. Their own sophisticated equipment limited them. They could only search where the boat could go.

When we felt capable, I buried the fire, scattered the baffle. Weapons ready, we moved on.

Every step we had taken the day before to get into the swamp was distance we had to retrace to go back toward the interstate.

The morning began to warm as the sun rose over the jungle, and I welcomed it. Our progress was steady, and I counted paces to estimate the distance we traveled.

I faced the sun as we walked, guiding us eastward toward Interstate 75, which ran north and south, making it impossible for us to miss, even if we strayed a bit off course.

We sloshed across waist-deep mud, forded more streams, made our way across quicksand ponds by walking over cypress roots or grass clumps, and pushed through brambles and thorn bushes. The Florida jungle was every bit as nasty as some of the places in Vietnam.

I knew we could reach the interstate in a day or so, if we maintained our progress. I would also call my wife and make pickup arrangements for George and me. It occurred to me as we walked that my friend who drove us to Florida might have been the one who turned us in.

We began to encounter a network of sand roads at midday and, while crossing from one to the next, saw a dark-blue truck we could have almost touched, carefully camouflaged with tree branches. The truck bore the gold crest of the State Police K-9 unit. That meant tracker dog teams were somewhere close.

I quickened the pace, the sun now high, the morning's warmth becoming noon heat. I unzipped my field jacket.

The drone of a light plane came to us on the wind, and we stopped, heads upturned. The sound of the engine became more distinct.

"Spotter plane!" I said, and George and I ducked into the bushes.

The little plane flew over us. It was a fabric-covered type, with a fully enclosed cockpit, overhead wing, and fixed landing gear.

The plane circled lazily and banked away. It hadn't spotted us. "Let's go," I said, and trotted out of the bushes. I led us from tree to tree. We could no longer use open areas. It made movement more demanding of our time and energy.

The country was becoming drier. We were leaving the swamps along the river, and getting into the grasslands. Soon the terrain would be open and rolling, without convenient concealment.

For now, we still had islands of palm trees and thick foliage, connected by stretches of sharp "Spanish bayonets," dense groups of palmettos growing out of the sand.

We heard the plane this time only a few seconds before it roared over the treetops. George and I dove into the palmettos, trying to get under the splayed clusters of heavy, pointed blades. The palmettos cut like knives.

The pilot knew what he was doing, coming in low and fast, so we wouldn't have advance warning of the engine noise.

"I think he knows we're here," George said.

The bleating of air horns became recognizable. It was the dog teams coming our way. The plane was still overhead.

We couldn't stay where we were because the dogs would find us, and we couldn't get up and run because the plane would see us.

We lay sweating in the palmettos. The plane was our chief problem.

George and I were anxious, nerves stretching with the waiting, the signal horns of the dog teams coming closer. There was a team on our right flank and one on our left. We were beginning to hear the dogs themselves.

It was being trapped that made me raise the rifle. I knew a bullet through the cockpit windscreen would drive the aircraft away. A hit or two in the engine might bring it down.

I calculated my aim, warning George I was about to fire.

"Wait," he said, "I think I see them!"

I lowered the Mauser. He was right. There was a team about a hundred meters to our north. The dogs were barking and whining, pulling at the handler. Men in hunters' camouflage jackets with weapons followed the dogs.

Judging by the horns, the team to our south was almost even with them. We lay in the middle. The north team stopped and appeared to be discussing what to do next.

"If they get too close, I'll kill one of the dogs," I said to George. "They'll take cover, and we can run."

The dogs caught our scent. Coming our way, the handlers began to sound their horns again. The hounds were bellowing now, sensing they were closing in on their prey.

I knew I had to make a precise shot that would kill a dog and not a man.

The dogs leapt into the palmettos, now only fifty meters away. The howled as they pricked and stabbed themselves, but they didn't stop.

The handlers tried to enter the waist-high palmettos, but they were ripping them badly as they struggled with the dogs.

Cursing and yanking, the handlers pulled the dogs out of the palmettos by their leashes. The spotter plane was now circling on farther west.

The handlers forced the dogs westward as well, and in a moment they had picked up another scent and went chasing it. The men had not wanted to fight through the palmettos, probably believing the dogs were tracking a false scent.

The horns sounded weaker, diminishing with the distance as they left us. I flipped the safety back on the rifle.

We rested in the palmettos and walked east when I felt it was safe to move. We had penetrated their search line.

The trek out of the swamps into the yellow grasslands began, the sun now behind us. I wanted to bring us out on the interstate near the Wildwood exit, because there was a truck stop and restaurant there.

The escape of the day before and the harried evading of the

morning had seriously fatigued us. We had not eaten in two days, since yesterday's meal was forgotten in the rush. Our diet for the last three weeks had been mostly rice and beans, rationed out once a day.

Our body reserves were depleted. By midafternoon we were dragging, forcing each footstep.

George questioned me about how far we had to go, and when I tried to explain our route, he began to doubt if I was taking us the correct way.

"I think we're going south," George said.

"No, we're not," I assured him. "There's a national forest south of us, and a paved road we'd have to cross to get to it."

"But maybe we crossed the road and didn't know it," George said.

I knew when he said that his condition was serious. The exhaustion and lack of food were wrecking his ability to think clearly.

I had our one can of pork and beans in my field jacket pocket, and we would have to eat it soon. I began to worry about water as we continued, since we had found no streams or ponds. We each had a canteen. Mine was almost full. George's was half full. I resolved then we had to stop drinking until we found a source of water, and said so.

Our senses were dulling. It had become too much of an effort to move off the straightest possible line of march. I realized we were taking chances by not using the concealment of the clumps of trees across the open grasslands.

In the late afternoon, we collapsed in a ditch and I cut the top off the pork and beans can with my knife. We shared the food and then rested, actually able to feel strength spreading back through our bodies, and walked out of the ditch refreshed.

As yet, there had been no water to find. We discovered some old concrete water troughs set out for cattle, but in the bottom of them had only been thick, green scum. We passed it by, hoping for better.

The sun was going down, and the air was beginning to cool. It seemed as if we had been walking forever.

"Did you hear that?" George asked suddenly.

"What?" I asked.

"A truck, I think I heard a truck! We must be getting near

the interstate!" he exclaimed. We kept walking. Night was coming quickly, the shadows dark under the trees.

I knew we were coming back to civilization when we found our way blocked by a barbed-wire fence. We climbed over it. Soon we hit another one. The sound of cars was distinct now.

The interstate was below us. We had made it.

I gave George a drink of my water and waited there while he walked south down the highway to locate the truckstop and make the calls.

George returned with sandwiches and the news we were only two miles away from the interstate exit I wanted. His call to Mavis did get through, and she was sending her brother, Larry Evans, from Orlando to get us the next morning.

We slept that night on a rise beside the highway, hidden in the trees on a bed of pine needles, shivering in the cold. After sunup, we buried the rifle and ammunition under a log.

Larry arrived on time, and we drove away from Crystal River, leaving the dog teams and the police to continue their search.

---

28 March 1968: Capture

I was alone at my sister's house in a rural suburb of Orlando. George was working with a group of fruit pickers in the orange groves.

The police came and surrounded the house, their pistols drawn and ready for a fight. They caught me bodily as I went out the back door, wrestling me to the ground.

I was taken to jail and questioned by the Federal Bureau of Investigation while waiting for the Military Police to arrive. I told them nothing.

The car that came for me was from the air force. They took me to McCoy Air Force Base outside Orlando and locked me up, and I waited there for a week to be taken back to Fort Gordon.

Just before the army prisoner bus arrived for me and several other AWOLs who had been arrested in the Orlando area, George Larkins was delivered to our jail.

George told me he had been arrested the same day as I while in the groves with the orange pickers.

George and I had been living with my sister and her family, trying to decide what to do next. Obviously the police had talked to her or her husband and they had agreed to turn us in.

George and I were handcuffed together on the bus trip north, and we spent the first night on the road in a marine brig in Jacksonville, Florida.

The marine guards were especially sadistic to army prisoners. They went out of their way to intimidate us by striking at our elbows and knees with their nightsticks.

George was taken off the bus at the next overnight stop. He would be accepted back to active duty and sent to Vietnam, serving with the 9th Division in the rice paddies of the delta, where he would receive a Silver Star for bravery.

Once I was back at Fort Gordon, they threw me in the stockade, cut my hair, and questioned me almost every day, demanding to know where I had been and what I had done.

After a while, I began to learn the system. There was a low-security unit called SPD (Special Processing Detachment) where prisoners who had committed no criminal offenses were billeted. It was the next step to a release to duty.

I played their game after that, subduing my resistance. I told them I was ready to cooperate.

They assigned me to the Special Processing Detachment.

1 April 1968: Going South

I escaped, leaving the barracks after I had taken a shower, eaten a meal, and decided how I could get off base without being spotted.

I took a bus to Orlando and told my wife I was leaving the country. I picked Jamaica because it didn't require a passport for a U.S. citizen to enter and it was a gateway to trouble spots in the Caribbean.

Mavis gave me the money for a ticket. I said I would send for her once I was established. She was living with her parents in Orlando.

3 April: Kingston Town

The flight south from Miami to the island nation of Jamaica was directly over Cuba. I looked at its fields and road network with some interest.

From out of Cuba, the Soviets were pushing revolution in the Caribbean and onto Central and South America.

Jamaican Customs allowed me through with no more explanation than I was there on holiday. I found a taxi, told the driver I needed a place to live, and he drove me to a private boarding house in Kingston.

I rented a small room there and talked to the brothers in the family that ran the house. I told them I was a combat veteran of Vietnam and had come to their country to find work as a mercenary. They told me about a bar in town where I might meet men in the mercenary business, but their opinion of mercenaries was poor, thinking of them as hired guns for drug runners, or worse.

The next morning I set out walking in Kingston and located the Cherry Bar. It was made of bamboo and sheet tin, with an open patio shaded by palm trees.

The black customers were friendly and listened avidly as I described combat in Vietnam. After several glasses of rum and cola, I found many of them had been in the Jamaican military or police, and some had experience contracting out as independents.

One of the men said he had worked for the Cubans, and they would probably talk to me. It was good my drink was on the table and not in my hand or I might have dropped it. I maintained my composure while the Jamaican said he'd pass along the word that I was available to his Cuban friends. I had to talk to the Cubans out of morbid curiosity, if nothing else.

4 April: The Cuban Connection

I returned to the Cherry Bar the next day and met with a representative of the Cuban Embassy. The man was polite but cautious. I was equally cautious, making it a short meeting.

He said there was a possibility Cuba would be interested in

me, but he could make no promises. We left it at that, agreeing to talk again.

I would not have actually gone to work for communist-Cuban interests, but I had an idea I might be able to somehow arrange to be accepted by them, and then make a deal with the CIA to work as an agent *against* the Cubans, from the inside.

Being totally estranged from my country was hard on me, and such a desperate idea at least had the appeal of giving me hope I might eventually come to coexistence terms with my own side.

I was in my room at the boarding house after dinner that evening. There was a knock on the door just after 7:00 P.M., and one of the women in the family said, "King is dead." I didn't fully understand her, and opened the door. The family was huddled around a radio.

The news was from the United States. Martin Luther King, leader and prime mover of black Americans in their fight for racial equality, had been assassinated.

5 April: Confrontation

I walked into Kingston, several stops on my agenda. I planned to visit the Emigration Office and ask about the requirements of residence status, and I had another meeting scheduled with the Cuban.

I noticed quickly there was something wrong in town. Many businesses were closed, there were milling crowds on street corners, and I was drawing cruel glances from the blacks. There were no other white faces on the streets, not even locals.

As I walked deeper into town, people began to shout hostilities at me, some from out of windows, others from across the street. The words were unclear, but I understood the threatening message.

I changed course, passing an idle group of black workmen, when one of them yelled an obscenity at me. I kept walking.

The laborer yelled again, then crossed the street, coming at me. His friends followed him, carrying wine bottles and digging tools, staggering as they approached. They were drunk and dangerous.

The laborer shattered his bottle against a wall and came at me with tears of rage in his eyes. I began retreating as far as I could along the sidewalk, until blockaded by more blacks.

I was pushed against the locked doorway of a store, and the workmen surrounded me. I watched the sharp glass of the broken wine bottle flash in the morning sun.

The screech of a siren turned the heads of the crowd. I looked past the mob leader and saw a small police car with a roof-mounted light stopping beside the curb.

There was one black police officer in the car. He was dressed in a British-style uniform of tan shorts, short-sleeve shirt, and cap. He jumped from the car, shouting at the crowd to disperse, pushing through the workmen to get to me.

The mob leader dropped his broken wine bottle, and the policeman pulled me to his car, reaching under the driver's seat to get a Webley .38-caliber pistol he had to unwrap from an oilcloth.

"You lucky I come by," he said. "That bunch they likely to do anybody white great harm."

He guarded me with the Webley while I climbed into the little Ford, then drove me out of the area, letting me go with a warning to get back to my boarding house. The man had saved my life.

I took a long, safe route home, avoiding any more confrontations with bloodthirsty mourners.

That afternoon, a team of police with sidearms came to the boarding house and arrested me. Not given a chance to pack, I was driven directly to the Immigration Building and left in a guarded office.

An Immigration official said I was to be deported immediately back to the United States, but offered no explanation.

A VW bus took me and my guards to the airport, along Port Royal Road beside the bay.

Following our bus was a Mercedes sedan, not trying to pass. The driver and passenger of the Mercedes were white men dressed in business suits, wearing sunglasses.

I wondered if they were American CIA, but it didn't matter. I was on my way out of the country. Someone had turned me in.

At the airport, the Jamaican officer walked me to the boarding ramp for the Miami flight and apologized for the necessity of his presence. He said perhaps I could return to his country one day under better circumstances.

We landed briefly in Montego Bay, the routine stop after leaving Kingston, and I was amused to see several squads of armed soldiers conspicuously spread out between our aircraft and the airport building. The soldiers were there to make sure I didn't get off the plane.

I expected the FBI to be waiting for me at the airport in Miami, but for some reason, they were not.

20 April: Recapture

I saw Mavis in Orlando briefly, then left for the underground. There was a flourishing network of antiwar groups that sheltered military AWOLs and deserters. The groups were run by political liberals and leftists, and peopled by teenagers who were told they were part of a new generation of peace. They called it the Age of Aquarius.

The youth of America embraced one premise without question. All they needed was love to overcome adversity.

I did not take drugs, or grow my hair long, or wear bizarre clothes. I wasn't part of the hippies. I was a desperate man with nothing but the clothes I wore, staying a few days with one group and then another, constantly on the move.

On 20 April I was caught by the FBI while visiting my parents' apartment house in Birmingham, turned in by family again.

The FBI gave me to the police who gave me to the military.

I was taken back to Georgia and locked in solitary confinement as an escapee.

My cell was in the isolation building in the stockade compound, and I was interrogated by Military Intelligence frequently.

They knew I had been in Jamaica, but seemed to know little of what I had done there, and I wasn't about to tell them. They'd never believe my motive about the Cuban, about what I'd had in mind.

They questioned me in teams, using techniques for which I

had seen training programs while working at Fort Gordon. I told them I knew how the interrogation sessions were supposed to go, often knowing what they were going to say before they spoke.

I was locked back in my cell while they decided on another method of breaking me.

---

1 June: Over the Wall

I used a pencil given to me by a guard to reach so delicately outside my cage door with my fingertips and open the latchbolt. It was often not securely fastened, but I could do nothing until I had a tool like the pencil. If it had not been a new pencil with its full length, it would not have worked.

I went out the back door of the isolation building, threw my blanket over the top of the stockade barbed-wire fence, and climbed over it. I knew they would find the blanket in the morning, but by then it would be hours too late.

I threw away my plain green prisoner's uniform, stole civilian clothing off the backyard line of a private home, and hitchhiked out of Georgia, going to Florida.

I surprised Mavis when I arrived. I told her I had to have a place to hide, so she rented me a small furnished apartment in a residential suburb of Orlando very near where she lived with her parents.

The little apartment was sterile and impersonal. I did not dare go outside to walk around the neighborhood, because I knew I could be recognized, so I stayed indoors.

---

6 June: "Kennedy Is Dead"

I was half asleep on my bed, the television playing in the next room, when I heard an announcer say that Kennedy had been shot.

That sounded puzzling. Of course Kennedy had been shot. I was in high school then, it had been 1963, five years before. But then I came fully awake. The television was talking about *Robert* Kennedy. Someone named Sirhan Sirhan had shot and killed him at a political rally. It was just another stroke of insanity.

The daily television news from Vietnam was somber. Weekly totals of American dead were in the hundreds. Thousands were being wounded. Television coverage had helped a majority of previously undecided Americans revolt against the war.

The public had finally cracked under the pressure of the news media and the antiwar protests. My country was morally and politically defeated. The enemy knew it, and our politicians knew it.

Every kilometer I had walked, every bullet I had shot, every hour of fear or uncertainty I had spent in combat had been in vain. The body bags, the medevac helicopters, and all the bandages were for men wasted to no end result except to fill graves.

My days and nights in the apartment seemed endless, broken only by clandestine visits from my wife, who would bring me food. Our marriage was severely strained. I noticed Mavis was wearing more makeup and dressing more attractively for her job. Her visits to me became shorter and less frequent. Confined in the apartment, the pressure on me was becoming intolerable. The worst part of it was not knowing what to do next.

Mavis and I argued and fought, reducing her visits even more. Finally, in the heat of a vicious argument, she threatened me with exposure. She said she had met another man, and he would protect her from me.

I was stunned. She left me alone in the apartment, knowing I could not follow. The stress of my private war with the military had finally taken its ultimate toll.

Later Mavis did return, but it was to make sure I was leaving. She had signed what financial assets I had left over to her mother, and she told me she would not pay the rent again for another month at the apartment. I had to get out of her life.

25 June: Military Police

I was at Mavis's parents' house the morning of the twenty-fifth, driven out of my apartment by grief and anger. I was there to demand she give me enough money for a weapon.

While I was in the house talking to her, an unmarked car with two MP's dressed in civilian clothes arrived. They had known when and where to come.

Stockade, Fort Gordon, Georgia

I was swiftly taken back to Fort Gordon and locked into solitary confinement again, but this time in a cell so small I could almost touch both sides and the roof while standing in the center. The only furnishing was a toilet and a wooden bunk bolted to the wall. There was no sink. The walls themselves were covered with sheet metal, painted yellow. A spotlight shone through a heavy screen wire above the metal door. It was never turned off.

The door itself had narrow top and bottom ventilation slots, covered with layers of the same type of heavy screen wire that protected the spotlight.

I noticed the door lock when they put me in the cell. It was a pivoting drop bar attached to the outside wall and dual brackets on the door. To lock the door, the bar was lowered into the brackets.

It was hot in the cell. In Georgia in July it was normally near 100 degrees Fahrenheit, and in the solitary confinement barracks there was no air conditioning and little ventilation. Living in the small cell under the spotlight was like being in an oven.

There was no water allowed us except at mealtimes. I was lucky. I was not on the cereal and water diet of the other prisoners. I got regular meals from the stockade mess. I was also allowed to keep my clothes. The other prisoners were stripped, wearing only underwear.

The reason I was treated differently was the staff at the Fort Gordon Stockade didn't know exactly why I was being held, except that 3rd Army Headquarters said to keep me in strict confinement, with no incoming or outgoing communication.

I didn't care that I couldn't call or write anyone. My wife and family had tired of me and delivered me to the authorities when I became a problem in their lives and routines. I was the product of an unpopular war, unable to stop fighting, and no one at home wanted me. They didn't want the trouble.

My wife's admission she had begun to see another man had shattered me, and she had done it just when I needed her most. It was the last thing I had expected, but it taught me about loyalty. I had fought beside men who would and did die to help save each other. Now my own wife had renounced me because I was inconvenient.

My country had not been loyal to those of us it had sent to Vietnam, with no definite idea of what we were to do once there.

Loyalty, by and large, was a lie. It was a tool used by some to gain control over others.

I could have broken down mentally in my cell. I did not. I would not be broken by the actions or attitudes of my family or my government. I had only myself now. I had to survive.

I searched the cell a millimeter at a time, looking for a weak spot, an opportunity. I ran my fingers along the walls, feeling, rubbing, until I found the smallest of things under my bunk. It was the head of a nail, not quite flush in the sheet metal.

I took off my issue brass belt buckle and used the edge of it to work the nail out. It was slow going but it came.

I then bent the nail like a hook and tied it to the end of one of my boot laces. I worked a hole large enough in the finer screen wire of the door's upper ventilation slot to push the nail through, and dropped it out like a fishing line. When I felt the nail hook the lock bar, I pulled on the boot lace. The bar lifted and I quietly pushed open the door, elated at the simplicity of the feat.

After looking both ways in the hall, I put my nail and boot-lace in my pocket and slipped to the rear door of the barracks.

I was out of solitary, but I was still in jail.

The stockade library was the only place I could think of to go, and I went there hoping none of the guards would recognize me. I relaced my boot and kept the nail.

Because it was daylight, I could not go over a wall. I was not much better off than before. My ultimate decision was to go back to the solitary barracks, but I couldn't resist taking several books with me. I was bored in the little cell and badly wanted something to read.

I went to the front of the barracks and knocked on the door. The guard opened it and gawked as he recognized me. I calmly walked past him into the barracks.

"What—what are *you* doing *out* there?" he stammered.

He nearly ran me down the hall and shoved me inside my cell again. I still had my books.

I replaced the nail in its hole under the bunk for future use, and lay down to look at my books.

The lock bar outside my cell door swung up with a metallic

rattle and the door was jerked open, the confinement officer and two MP's standing outside.

"How in the hell did you get out of here?" the officer demanded.

"I was bored, I wanted something to read," I said.

The officer was visibly agitated. He tried to get me to confess how I had done it, but I would not.

"Will you not do it again if we let you go to the library?" he asked in full seriousness.

"Sure," I said, and with an angry, confused expression, he slammed my door and went away.

After that, I had library privileges, plus the nail if I needed it.

---

12 July: Deception

Two Military Police had taken me out of the Fort Gordon stockade to the airport and flown with me to Fort Campbell, Kentucky, where the army maintained a modern maximum security prison. I was to be jailed there, instead of in a stockade.

On the flight, regulations forbade me from being handcuffed, and when one of the MP's left his seat to go to the lavatory while the other beside me was napping, I quietly slipped my confinement orders from their briefcase and put it into the seatback pocket in front of me.

When we exited the aircraft in Kentucky, the MP's never knew what they were leaving behind.

Once we arrived on post, the MP's delivered me to the provost marshal's desk, and were puzzled when they could not produce the paperwork on me from their document case.

The officer in charge told them he needed a confinement order to put me in his prison. The provost marshal allowed them to telephone Fort Gordon, but they could not reach anyone there who knew anything about my transfer because it was late Saturday afternoon.

The discussion ended with the provost marshal ordering the MP's to release me to him, and sending them away. He then had me taken to SPD.

I was only there a few hours, just long enough to organize myself and steal clothing to get off post.

Two days later I was back in Alabama because I had nowhere else to go. My wife was still in Florida, but she didn't matter anymore. My family in Birmingham made it clear they did not want me near them, but grudgingly agreed to help as long as I stayed away as much as possible.

It was the lowest point of my life. I was on the street, a fugitive, with no money and nowhere to turn. Nothing that I tried had worked. The government seemed too big to fight, and so far I had only succeeded in losing my wife and family and getting deeper into trouble.

I lived from day to day, sleeping and eating where I could. It was during that time I met Jim Vines, who would later work with me on an FBI operation in 1970. But in August of 1968, Jim was just a new friend who gave me shelter in a suburb of Birmingham. That alone meant a great deal.

When Mavis learned I was in Birmingham, she arranged to call me at my grandmother's house. She told me she was sorry and wanted us to get back together. She traveled from Orlando to Birmingham, and I met her, but with suspicion and doubt.

She apologized for what she had done in Orlando. I considered all she said, but in my heart, I could not accept her again. I had lost trust.

The fact remained I had a son just barely three years old. I did not want him raised in a broken home. I either had to leave Mavis for good or stay with her for the sake of my boy. I told her we would try and stay together, but it was with reservations and provisions, because our marriage had suffered the kind of damage I felt it could not survive.

On 13 August 1968 local police came to arrest me. I went without resistance. I had to use different tactics now.

---

16 August: Prison

The Fort Campbell maximum-security military prison was a world apart from the wooden barracks and barbed wire of the stockades.

Fort Campbell prison had steel and concrete cells, barred doors that locked electrically from a master station, and many other refinements technology had brought to penal quarters.

I was assigned to a sixteen-man cell and shown the procedures of life there. My bunk was a steel rack bolted to the wall. I had a mattress, sheets, pillow, and blanket. By day the bunk had to be kept clear, with the mattress rolled and the sheets, pillow, and blanket folded.

Inside each cell was a communal shower and latrine with a row of exposed toilets. This was built so the guards could look directly into it from the hallways outside the cells.

We were awakened each morning at 0445 hours, to hurriedly dress and fall out in the exercise yard. The compound was surrounded by high wire fences and gun towers, with banks of spotlights shining inward.

After roll-call inspection and physical exercises, we marched into the messhall for breakfast. The food had to be eaten fast, and there was no talking allowed.

After chow, we were searched for stolen spoons or forks as we reentered the cell blocks.

The workday began then, with details sent around the post to paint, pick up garbage, or dig ditches. I was not sent out on work details. I was classified as an escape risk, and confined to the prison.

Life in prison was monotonous. The walls were gray, the uniforms olive drab, and the faces of the inmates pale. We were identified by numbers, not names. I was 105.

Naturally, there were fights between the prisoners, but a more serious problem was developing. The black and the white prisoners were separating, congregating only with each other. Animosity was growing, and in prison, where matters that might be dismissed in the outside world brewed and seethed, and violence was the rule rather than the exception, I knew I was in another combat zone.

The blacks were angry. It was a time of race riots in the United States, a time of black struggle to gain a better position in life. They wanted to show their group strength.

The prison command did not know how to handle the dangerous unity of the blacks because no one had ever seriously challenged the system within the prison before.

We were heading for a riot.

Violent incidents became more frequent, mostly sharp, fast physical assaults by small gangs of blacks on lone whites, at times when there were no witnesses.

The threat was real. Several of the white guards who specialized in harassing prisoners were marked by the blacks for revenge.

One morning as I was issued some supplies, I was standing near the sallyport, the gateway into the supply and administrative section of the prison, when there were frantic shouts from down the cellblock hall.

I turned to see two prisoners rapidly dragging a bloody guard toward the sallyport. The guard was limp. The men's faces showed their fear. The guard was almost dead. He had been attacked at the far connecting hall of the two long cellblocks, and he was literally cut to pieces.

His shirt hung off him in tatters, and his flesh was open in uncountable crimson slashes. I clearly saw his lower lip hanging off his face, swinging as they pulled him toward me. He had been cut by razor blades.

Wide-eyed guards pushed open the barred sallyport gate, took the bleeding guard from the prisoners, and slammed the door closed in their faces.

The prisoners, black and white, were preparing for war. They were taking razor blades, heating them with matches, and embedding them into the handles of toothbrushes, making a kind of improvised straight razor. It had probably been the same kind of weapon used on the guard.

It was time to fight to take revenge, time to vent the rage at being imprisoned.

Riot

That evening, after a long, tense day, the loudspeakers announced all prisoners were to report to the chapel, and the doors automatically unlocked and opened. Silently, we came out of our cells and walked down the hall.

I could feel the charged atmosphere as clearly as my heart beating.

It didn't take long for the prisoners to fill the chapel seats. No one was speaking. Keys rattled loudly in the lock of the armored door between the chapel and the administrative side of the prison. A nervous Military Police officer entered, the door held open behind him by an armed guard.

He told us not to make trouble. He said a unit of riot troops was standing ready and they would do whatever was necessary to keep order. Then he and the guard turned abruptly and left, the guard carefully locking the door behind them, leaving us all in the chapel.

The prisoners were encouraged. They were accustomed to rigid authority, but in the face of challenge, the authority was showing fear.

A lone white guard opened the main door for us to return to the cellblock, then ran down the hallway toward the sallyport.

A group of blacks leapt over the chapel benches and chased him. I jumped, too, to try to catch the guard, but not to hurt him. I had a vague idea that I might be able to keep him from being killed, but I didn't know how.

For a mad moment, the guard was racing down the long hall, the blacks on his heels, screaming and shouting. Guards at the sallyport were yelling for their man to make it to safety, and I was mixed in the bloodthirsty mob of blacks, running for all I was worth. For a moment I thought the guard would make it.

The blacks caught the guard near the sallyport, and he fell, rolling against the wall, trying to cover his head with his arms. I collided with the blacks, pulling at them, hearing the thuds of their feet slamming the guard. We were right beside my cell.

They were kicking the man to death, splattering blood up the wall. I could see it all clearly, the booted feet hammering him down, the faces of the blacks leering with murder.

A sallyport guard fired a pistol shot. I couldn't tell if it was at us or up into the ceiling, but it was loud. I sprinted into my cell, sour fear in my throat, expecting a barrage of bullets to sweep the hall.

Somehow, in the moment of surprise following the shot, a

band of guards burst through the sallyport door and grabbed their unconscious friend. Prisoners were running to their cells.

Cell 3, the next down from mine, housed the blacks that had beaten the guard. They were ripping apart bedsheets and lashing their cell door to the barred walls to prevent the MP's from entering. I heard crashes as they smashed their porcelain sinks and toilets to make sharp, throwable missiles.

Smoke began drifting into my cell. Mattresses from other cells down range were being burned in the hall. The prisoners in the row starting with Cell 3 were all ranting, creating an incredible din.

From my position in Cell 2, I could see the riot police at the sallyport. They had clubs.

The hallway lights were protected by glass in steel cages, but bits of broken toilets thrown from out of the cells soon had many of the light housings shattered. Water was splashed on the exposed bulbs from cigarette-butt cans kept in each cell, bursting the hot bulbs, darkening the hallway.

The smoke from the burning mattresses was getting thicker. I could see the glow of flames on the hallway walls.

The sallyport gate opened, and the riot police charged into the hall. As they passed my cell, a hail of sharp ceramic shards from between the bars of Cell 3 hit them, bringing blood from impact wounds on the arms and faces of the surprised guards.

The door to Cell 3 was tied securely shut. The MP's could not open it while being hit with the fragments of broken toilets and sinks.

A firehose crew tried to get down the hall, high-pressure water aimed at the burning mattresses, but they too were stopped by the ceramic bombardment.

MP's who tried to untie the bedsheets holding Cell 3's door closed had their hands slashed with toothbrush razors.

The riot troops were in disorder. Several of them were hit in the head with large chunks of ceramic and knocked unconscious, having to be dragged back to the sallyport.

Other cells down the hall were forced open, and Military Police waded into hand-to-hand combat with the prisoners, nightsticks against fists and feet.

The men in my cell were almost hysterical. The battle was happening right in front of them, but they were not part of it. I was glad. I didn't want any part of it. Our cell floor was awash with water from the firehose.

Somehow, the MP's ripped the sheets off the door of Cell 3 and rushed the prisoners. We could not see into the cell through the solid wall that separated us, but the sounds were incredible.

The hall echoed with the curses and blows of men in wrestling, bashing combat. I could hear cries of fury, cries for mercy. The impact of police clubs on bone made a cracking sound. MP's retreating to the sallyport with open gashes in their faces and hands passed fresh reinforcements coming in, their blood staining the starched uniforms of the new men.

There was now also a steady stream of wounded prisoners staggering or being carried back to the sallyport.

The firehose was turned on the prisoners in Cell 3 after all of the MP's had been thrown out of the cell. At close range, the high-pressure water from the hose had tremendous impact. Prisoners' shouts were stopped short as the water smashed them to the cell floor.

The water in our cell was over our ankles now.

The prisoners used mattresses to shield themselves from the water so they could keep throwing pieces of toilets at the firehose crew. Many of the police had lost their clubs to prisoners in the hand-to-hand fighting, and the prisoners were bashing back at the guards with their captured weapons at new attempts to drag them out of their cells.

More MP's were pouring through the sallyport. I knew the resistance in the cells could not last much longer.

In the end, it was the firehose that decided the battle. It had the power to knock a man into a wall, mattress shield or not. The firehose crew used the water like a machine gun, cutting down opposition in cell after cell.

With all the cell doors finally open, and most of the prisoners stunned and awash on the flooded floors, the MP's moved in to corner and beat the diehards.

I stood beside my steel bunk and bowed my head as the howls of the final fights vibrated in the hall. It no longer sounded like men. The snarls and shrieks of surrounded prisoners making their last stands were like cries from hell.

When the guards had finally withdrawn from the cellblock, there was nothing left but the smell of smoke, the cold water on the cell floors, and muffled whimpers and whispers.

Many of the hallway windows were broken, and the night air was cold.

In an unexpected interview by one of the legal officers at the prison, I was told I might be tried for *treason.* The officer had no details to give me and himself seemed surprised at the charge.

Treason was as serious as murder, and even carried the death penalty.

All I could presume was that because I had been AWOL and left the country while holding a security clearance, someone was assuming I had disclosed classified information. Obviously my brief meeting with the Cuban figured in it.

The threat of the charge should have scared me to death, but it didn't. Maybe by that time I was just past caring.

I was summoned to the counseling office a few days later and told the army treason investigation against me was over, and I had been cleared.

The officer also told me the reason I had not gone to trial for AWOL was 3rd Army had my records during the investigation, and I had been in technical limbo. He said he was going to get my court-martial arranged soon, because I had already been in jail just days short of half the maximum sentence of a special court-martial.

24 October: Court-Martial

I was called to the sallyport gate and told when I reported there I was on my way to trial. I went in prison fatigues.

The court-martial was held in a nearby barracks office. A panel of officers sat behind a table, facing me. I was told to sit at a table with my defense counsel, an officer I had never seen before.

The whole trial took only minutes. The charges specified against me were simple: Absent Without Official Leave. My counsel pleaded me guilty.

The judge said I was to be fined $73 a month for three months and sentenced to three months' confinement, and suspended the entire sentence in the next breath.

I was taken out of the office and driven back to the prison. I packed my clothes, said my good-byes, and the next day I was out.

All I wanted to do now was finish the rest of my time in the army with the least amount of trouble. At twenty-one, I was a very tired, bitter young soldier.

CHAPTER TWO
Ranger School

The day I left the prison, I was placed temporarily in the Fort Campbell Special Processing Detachment to wait until I was sent on to regular duty. That assignment came on 26 October 1968, sending me to the "Old Guard," a 3rd Regiment unit that did little besides provide dress and honor guards, escorts, and military funeral personnel at Fort Campbell and other locations.

The funerals became my detail, and I did enough of them to learn too many were a mockery of the sincerity I felt should have been part of such occasions. Few of us on the funeral detail carrying the coffins, standing to guard, or firing salutes with blank cartridges wanted to be there. Sometimes, not even the ceremony we put on was adequate. Too many of our buglers were inexperienced, and from the traditional, just-out-of-sight position from where they played, we often would endure a halting, note-by-note massacre of taps.

The families of the men in the government-issue coffins wept genuine tears, but most of us supporting the service were interlopers in their grief. The majority of the dead we buried on my details were aged, infirm veterans of earlier wars, men we didn't feel an immediate connection with. Forced by the army to be there, we just wanted the detail to end. Other details buried Vietnam casualties.

When I received new orders in December to report to Fort Benning, where I would be with a regular infantry unit, I was almost as happy as if I had received a discharge.

December 1968: 197th Light Infantry

The 197th was located on Sand Hill at Fort Benning, arrayed in a complex of modern barracks. Its mission was to support the Officer Candidate School (OCS) and the Ranger School. OCS did all their training at Benning, while the Rangers did only some, having a swamp school in Florida and a mountain school in North Georgia, all locations where 197th personnel pulled duty.

Vietnam veterans made up a large part of the 197th's troops, so combat infantry badges and healing wounds were common. Many men limped as they walked, and in the platoon showers, the dimples of bullet wounds, seams of surgery, and sunken, freshly skinned-over gaps in muscle tissue were always evident.

A lot of those men were on medically ordered profiles of light duty and held jobs suited to their incapacities, such as driving if they could not walk, clerking at a desk if they could not stand. Some were just left in the barracks, doing nothing but existing between surgeries to remove metal fragments from their bodies or operations to straighten arms and legs.

John Sabo, a friend I made quickly, was a perfect example of the walking wounded of the 197th. His job was to keep our "D" company dayroom dusted and organized. He had been shot in the head in an ambush in Vietnam, and he was waiting to go back to surgery to have a plate installed to cover the gap in the top of his skull. A stretch of scalp covered the hole, but Sabo was almost totally bald now, so we could see how his soft spot would sink in when he sat up and bulged out when he lay down, as his brain moved. In his dayroom job, he couldn't stand on a chair to dust the tops of the window blinds, because he had no balance. He was just twenty years old.

Being healthy, I was on field duty. My issue was an M14 rifle with blank adapter, a gas mask, and cold-weather boots and parka hood for the north Georgia mountains. Like the other men on my roster, I would go to the company bulletin board every afternoon to see what assignment I had for the next day.

Supporting the OCS and Ranger programs usually involved sending a group of us to a field training range where we acted out a simple course scenario, such as sitting in a camp and letting the students recon our position, or maybe letting them win a mock ambush or raid.

We were each given a twenty-round box or two of blanks for our rifles, and told to shoot a few to make noise before the students took their by-the-numbers victory. I was at once amazed at the simplistic nature of the field exercises and terrifically bored with them.

The students were usually clumsy as they playacted their missions, in fear of the scoring instructors. It was possible they thought that particular part of their training was as poor as I did.

I had to do something about it, just to make life on the ranges bearably interesting. At first I started small, working only on my own. I began taking a few CS tear-gas cannisters and explosive-artillery and grenade simulators out with me; and instead of one rifle magazine, I took a basic load of five, all loaded, with extra boxes of blanks in my pockets. Some of the men would willingly give me their blanks, because they didn't want to shoot their rifles and have a harder time cleaning them later. Blank powder is dirty.

When we would reach a training site, I'd let the rest of the group perform the scenario, and I would leave the camp and go after the students myself. Nothing like this was in the schedule, and when I hit student recon squads or raided one of their ambushes, the trainees would go all to pieces, not knowing exactly what to do. In the confusion, I'd get away. This spiced up my life, made the students more careful, and I discovered if I didn't absolutely wreck the program, even the training officers didn't mind.

It was not long before some of my new friends in the 197th wanted in on the action. I began taking one man with me, then two, and it grew from there. To my surprise, the NCO's and officers in my company seemed to like this more aggressive action and supported me.

Even though I had no real rank, I could ask for men for a raid or sortie and get them, really starting to make the Ranger and OCS cadre earn their pay. I developed a steady team with the unofficial title of "Camper's Commandos."

A few of the best were men like Ed Lodor, who had also served in the 4th Division in Vietnam and had returned with only four toes on one foot and horror stories about North Vietnamese flame-thrower attacks on hills 881 and Mile High, and McKay, a veteran of the 9th Division in the delta rice paddies. We even had

McDonald, a green kid right out of training, who liked to fool around too much with his rifle and was always scaring the hell out of us around the campfire by firing off a surprise burst of blanks, bad nerve treatment for veterans. One day McDonald somehow got an overloaded blank and blew his rifle apart, scaring the hell out of him but improving his manners.

There were others, like dour Robbins the Drunk, and young Rich Wyziak, who went off to Vietnam later and was wounded by our own artillery.

Bounty Hunters

Captain Allgood, commanding officer of my company and himself a wounded Vietnam veteran, told us in formation one morning before we left on a large-scale training support operation that from then on, he would give a three-day pass to any of us who brought in an OCS student as a prisoner. I was happy to hear that. Imagine a *bounty* on students! Of course it wasn't all glad tidings. Taking a grown man back when he knows you can't actually kill him (plus knowing he will later suffer greatly at the hands of his instructors or be penalized in his grading) is a difficult thing. It was going to require technique.

I modified my rifle's blank adapter so it was dangerous, spurting a jet of muzzle blast out ten feet, with the power to blow the bark off trees. I also started carrying parachute cord to tie hands and feet. After my infantry and long range reconnaissance patrol experience in Vietnam, slipping up on a few careless officer candidate students would be easy.

With my M14 on full auto, I would leap into one of their small positions, blasting leaves, bark, pine needles, and ration boxes into the air, taking back with me any of them too slow or confused to escape. I also stunned outposts with grenade simulators, tied up my choice of prisoner and dragged him away, breaking contact with the recovering squads or platoon with well-placed CS cannisters. From the day the bounty was set, I had so many prisoners I often gave some away to my friends so they would get passes too.

On some training missions, prisoner-taking was not allowed, so we had to amuse ourselves in other ways. A classic example of introducing the student to confusion and disruption was what happened at a position my team prepared at Fort Benning. The scenario was simple, as usual. OCS students in a company-sized force were to recon and then attack our squad as we lounged near our truck beside a stream and campfire in the forest. Instead of taking it easy, we dug pits and made booby traps all over the area, and I sent Lodor and our machine gun out of camp to nest in a protected thicket of trees uphill from us, so it could give better overall fire.

An hour after we had heard their recon teams come and go, the students finally attacked. At the first shots, I grabbed my M14 and ran to cover so I could watch the assaulters using the crude log bridge we had built across the stream. It had a smoke grenade booby-trapped to it, and as the first student across tripped it, he glanced in surprise over his shoulder and then fell into the deep, dead-leaf-camouflaged, water-filled pit to which the bridge led.

We had figured the OCS students, fastidious lot that they were, wouldn't want to get their feet wet and would use our bridge. We were right.

The smoke was so thick from the grenade, two more of them fell into the pit before the first man, crawling out, could yell and make his warning understood. That arm of the attack floundered.

In the only other seemingly clear area along the stream, another student dodged between the trees, point for another arm of the attack. He fell in another flooded and camouflaged pit, holding his rifle far over his head and wondering in astonishment what to do next. His spit shine and starch creases were ruined.

More fire and movement were coming from upstream, so I jumped the water (the way the students should have) and scurried up a hill to escape being overrun in the camp. I came head-long into a charging platoon of students just as I reached the crest. They were shocked to see me, perhaps thinking I was part of a larger force.

I fired a burst at them and changed directions, running to my right, down the hill parallel to the stream. They chased me, firing and shouting, and, son of a gun, I ran into another attack-ing platoon's flank.

They fired on me too, and I emptied my magazine at them and changed directions again, heading back into camp. Behind me, a fierce battle exploded, with much shooting and yelling of orders. The platoon pursuing me had taken the platoon I had run into as my men, and vice versa, an easy enough thing to do. For the next few minutes, the OCS students burned up their ammo on each other.

I jumped the creek again and decided to die gracefully so I could watch the rest of the booby traps happen.

The student acting company commander, a tall, authoritative black soldier who would have made a perfect recruitment poster, was walking backward through our camp. He was shouting commands and gesturing heroically at his men when he sank one highly polished boot into an ankle-deep foot trap and fell on his ass, his helmet rolling away.

Students were everywhere, the camp was taken, and the shooting stopped. It was warm weather, and we had known some of the men would be thirsty, and, being garrison soldiers, they would want to fill their canteens from a water can, not the stream. Under our five-gallon water can we had buried a smoke grenade, pin out and handle up, so when the can was tilted it would pop. It worked perfectly.

Turning over our "dead" truck driver to search him for documents, a student froze as a smoke grenade under the body rolled out and went off, adding more mortifying haze to the camp.

"Didn't you check that man out first?" yelled a student acting platoon leader to the hapless, guilty student who had done it.

"But he *told* me he was dead, sir!" the wide-eyed student said, realizing how ridiculous he sounded as soon as he spoke.

Now the platoons were forming to move out, much pride hurt and a few uniforms wet and muddy. Someone was loudly ordering the students to watch where they stepped and not to touch anything. The acting platoon leaders got their men into formation, the acting company commander standing before them, all like rows of pop-up targets.

Our M60 machine gun just above them in the thicket opened up as soon as their dress-right-dress formation was made.

The OCS instructor and the 197th officer who had come out with my team were doubled over with laughter. My "commandos" had again cost the students time, pride, and points.

There was a serious side to it, of course. Most of the blushing faces in the startled student formation were going to Vietnam to lead troops. I hoped to God we had taught them something.

* * *

Another memorable action was the day I searched the band of our PRC-25 radio until I found the students' frequency, just prior to a large-scale helicopter assault they were making against us in big CH-47 Chinooks. I monitored until I learned their call signs, and when I saw the Chinooks flying over my position near the landing zone, I used their commander's call sign and ordered them all to abort the mission and stay on the helicopters, *and they did.*

Soon the actual commander began to shout over his radio for them to get the hell out of the Chinooks, which were all parked on the LZ, doors open and rotors churning. The loads of terribly confused students slowly offloaded.

I stayed on the frequency for the next half hour, alternately telling the students not to believe anything they were receiving over the radio, since the frequency was compromised, then giving stern orders contradicting the actual commander. The running, backtracking, circling students trying to set up an LZ perimeter defense didn't know what to do.

Cobra Six, the commander, was berating some platoon leader whose people were scattered and disorganized (my own work), until I overrode the exhausted and frantic student's reply and said, "But sir, I can't *control* my men!"

Do you think that officer candidate graduated?

Do you think any of the men on that training operation ever took the field radio as the inviolate voice of authority again?

A last OCS war story (and probably one that shouldn't be mentioned in case participants who still hold grudges read this) concerns the day my commandos discovered an unguarded student ammo dump and sabotaged it.

The small dump was near a road location where the students were going to converge for chow, a briefing, and resupply. We carefully untaped the smoke and CS grenade shipping cannisters, removed the safety pins out of the fuses, and resealed the containers. The spring-loaded arming handles remained snug in the unarmed position until someone pulled the grenade out. The fuses only had a nine-tenths second time, guaranteeing ignition as soon as ammo resupply started.

We were not in the woods watching when the students arrived, but we heard about it later. A few ranking staff officers from the OCS headquarters drove to the site to coolly observe the troops during that break, and were there basking in their own wonderful spit-shined authority when the tear gas grenades began to pop all around them.

War is hell.

The Mountain Ranger Camp

Our assignments were to either Eglin, Florida, for the swamp phase of the Ranger School, or to Dahlonega, Georgia, where the camp was secluded far back in the north Georgia hills. There the students were learning how to patrol in mountainous terrain, how to rappel, and about small-unit combat in rugged country. I went to Dahlonega.

The winter cold, snow, ice, cliffs, and valleys conspired with the busy Ranger training schedule to really teach more about enduring hardship than anything else.

I found the course scenarios to be as fixed and stale as at Fort Benning, and I couldn't have that. Dulled, half-frozen Ranger students were even easier to confuse and agitate than intimidated, harassed OCS students. There was some problem with independent action in Dahlonega, since we were directly controlled by the Ranger course cadre, but that just meant I had to work at it harder.

Anti-Ranger Operations

The killing cold of the Blue Ridge Mountains was no ally to anyone. In a long predawn ambush one night, literally up to my neck in snow, one of my feet *froze*. Much later, when I got my artic-grade insulated boot off, there was actually a film of ice over my foot and between my toes.

One night an M60 machine gun blew up in my hands from a cold-induced malfunction, and the feed cover flew off and almost brained me.

Our C-rations froze, and if not rotated while being heated before a fire, one side remained iced while the other half burned. The water in our canteens froze into solid quart-size lumps of ice.

I am telling all this to reinforce the fact of the winter cold in Dahlonega and the Blue Ridge Mountains. It was serious.

At least the snow did make it easy to track their patrols. I actually joined files of slogging Ranger students at night enough times to make me wonder if they really knew who the tail gun on their team was supposed to be, because many times it was me, wearing a Ranger patrol cap and preparing to do them harm.

My commandos outfoxed the stumbling, exhausted Ranger students in frequent ambushes and harassed their overnight positions with probes and CS-artillery simulator attacks. One night Lodor and I captured an M60 machine gun and its student crew, who had blundered and set up their gun in *front* of my ambush, facing away from us. Their mission was apparently to provide blocking force fire for the raid their main unit was going to conduct against our camp up the hill.

We used the gun to break up the raid when it came assaulting out of the treeline. The Ranger student raid leader blew his whistle for his people to fall back, failing to even count his men and note he was light one gun and crew.

That was a bit too much. You don't run off and leave your people like that. I yelled to the student to check his men. He couldn't see me, but he abruptly yelled he *had* all his people, and started to go back into the trees himself.

It just so happened the assistant Ranger camp commanding officer was sitting in a jeep not far behind me at a frozen stream. He was there to observe and had seen it all.

He descended on the student that instant, taking him out of the course for the night. I never knew for sure, but I hope the officer failed him.

My slim margin of respect for the ability of most Ranger students—who might one day be released with Ranger qualification tabs on their shoulders—hit its lowest level when McDonald, our worst team member, went out of camp one night to take a piss and came back with a captured Ranger student. It was no real feat, explained McDonald. He had discovered the student lying against a log trying to get a recon on us, and the struggle in the slushy snow to see who would get who was over quickly.

"He couldn't find his rifle"—McDonald grinned— "because he was standing on it."

* * *

The peak of the absurd came on a late afternoon in the spring of 1969, all my frustrations with the training wrapped up in one incident. I had placed my team on a small, rocky, brush-covered hilltop the students would cross over. Most of the time the patrols went from position to position as if on rails, making my self-appointed job of dealing them misery easier.

My idea was to hit and run, since we only had rifles and there were five of us to the dozen or so students we were expecting. We went down in the rocks, placed to give each other supporting fire. On time, the students trudged up the hill into the ambush, and were right in the middle of us when we opened up. Some of the students ran back down the hill, and some of them went to cover in the rocks, splitting themselves up nicely.

In the ensuing firefight I realized that the students couldn't even get back together, much less overpower us. A couple of their assault attempts cracked and left them worse off than they were before. They could have backed up, sacrificed their honor, and gone around the hill. The patrol leader's desperation was apparent in the commands he shouted, trying to unify his people. To make it worse, we kept answering for his own men, trying hard not to laugh.

The patrol was stalled on the hill for almost an hour before the cadre instructor with them yelled to us: "Hey, let these guys go by, will you? We have to get to training area Bravo in fifteen minutes!"

We ceased fire, and as the student patrol walked past us, one of them said, "Jesus, there's only five guys up here!"

I swore to myself that if I ever ran my own training program, I would never make the mistakes I was witnessing at Ranger School.

If I told you that one afternoon, Lodor and I met a two-man Ranger student road outpost, told them we were "off duty," asked where the trucks were going to park to pick everybody up, walked past them to their perimeter camp and, from a safe place in the trees, convinced the student commanding officer we had his road outpost hostage and actually got some C-rations and ammo in "exchange" for them, would it make you laugh?

The students didn't think it was funny, once they found out

what we'd done to them. Obviously a lack of a good sense of humor.

27 June 1969: ETS

The day finally came, as all days seemingly too far in the future to be real do in fact come, that the military let me go. I had already been in the army almost a year too long because of my AWOL.

Between breakfast and lunch, I had my separation papers, and even though they were inaccurate in places, I didn't argue. The clerk processing me out even failed to list my combat infantry badge from Vietnam in my awards and decorations, but I didn't want accuracy, I wanted out. I went back to my company, packed my duffel bag, said a heartfelt good-bye to my unofficial "commandos," told them to keep harassing Rangers, and signed out in the orderly room. Under "DESTINATION," I wrote ETS (expiration of time in service), with much satisfaction.

A friend drove me off post from Fort Benning to the bus station in Columbus, and I was on my way home to Birmingham that afternoon.

I was too happy at the time to worry about it much, but in the back of my mind, I was wondering, as uncountable discharged soldiers have wondered on their way home, *what to do next.*

CHAPTER THREE
Communist Party of America

We waited in ambush in the night. I lay, concealed in the shrubbery, with a .30-caliber carbine in my hand.

The other men in the ambush were spread out beside the house and fence, armed with shotguns and pistols. They were making no noise, tense in the autumn darkness.

It was not Vietnam.

It was a black neighborhood near Birmingham, Alabama. The ambushers were not soldiers but black militants, waiting to murder one of their own who had defied them.

They called themselves the Alabama Black Liberation Front. They had been created by the Communist Party of America.

I saw the victim's car as it turned the corner coming toward us. The headlights were very bright on the dark street.

The car parked, and the driver's door swung open. I lifted myself up on one elbow, finger on the carbine safety, trying to get a better look.

Slightly drunk, the victim stepped out of his car and closed the door. He staggered toward the back porch of his house, directly toward the ambush.

Muzzle flashes and shattering blasts rocked the yard as the shotguns and revolvers fired. I knew I had to fire too, to prove afterward I had been involved. I squeezed off a few shots at the ground.

The victim staggered but did not fall. He screamed in pain and pulled a pistol from his pocket.

Now, with the ambushers' weapons empty, the victim began blazing at the bushes with his pistol. The night came alive with dodging black militants, tripping over each other, shrubbery, and fences.

As revolutionaries they had a long way to go, and they were depending on me to take them there.

Spring 1970

After leaving the army, I returned to Birmingham and was presented with the immediate problem of finding employment. I tried many jobs, all of them mundane. I wasn't happy in the civilian work-a-day world, finding myself longing for the demands of combat where the senses all had to work at peak and every move was critical.

I had even applied for employment and been hired by Pinkerton's Detective Agency, one of the largest private security firms in the United States, until Pinkerton's called the FBI, checking my background. Then they had shown me the door.

I felt I had fought for my country and done the best I could. Now, because of an air force clerical error and my reaction to it, at twenty-four years old, I was an outcast. The army had even issued me a letter saying I was barred from holding a security clearance again and was ineligible for reenlistment.

It was a special time in U.S. history. Our country was being ripped apart by dissent, much of it originated by communist agents. Every issue that could be was exploited, tearing bleeding wounds in the flesh of America. Organized protesters demanded the United States get out of Vietnam. Racial hatred, women's liberation, and civil strife were inflamed by demonstrations, riots, and bombings. Children rebelled against their parents. Colleges were forcibly shut down by protesters. Police and soldiers openly fought with masses of civilians in bitter street conflicts. Homes and businesses were looted and burned.

It was the United States of 1970. I had gone from one phase of the Vietnam war to another.

Early in 1970 I was plodding through the motions of a job as an insurance salesman in a black neighborhood of Fairfield, a suburb of Birmingham, when I accidentally encountered the Communist Party of America. I was soon to get the action I thought I wanted.

The leader in the Alabama Chapter of the Party was a young white student sort who drove a late-model VW sedan. He and the other Party members did not dress or act like the typical "hippie" of the late 1960s and early 1970s. They did not wear their hair long and dirty, dress in rags, and take drugs. They controlled the people who did that.

They looked like reasonably clean, conventionally dressed citizens. In private, as I would later learn, one of them admitted that after a socialist victory, the hippies and other rabble, including the chronic unemployables, would have to be "eliminated," because in a productive workers' paradise there was no place for them.

The first time I saw their leader, he was visiting some other whites, also young and idealistic, who lived in Fairfield. They were VISTA (Volunteers in Service to America) volunteers, a domestic Peace Corps organized by the U.S. government to take knowledge and assistance into poverty-stricken areas of the United States via middle-class college student volunteers.

The fact that I was a veteran of Vietnam, shunned by my own government, and also drove a VW (the VW was an antiestablishment symbol) seemed to endear me to the VISTA volunteers.

The leader was open with his Party activities, being known at the Birmingham steel factories for handing out antimanagement leaflets, sponsoring socialist lectures, and trying to organize student groups at the universities. I had fought Russian-backed communists in Asia and was surprised by his blatant pro-Soviet attitude, but I concealed it. Instead I deliberately tried to cultivate him by stressing my past in the "antiwar" movement, my army court-martial, and my genuine bitter feelings about the war.

As soon as I was sure I was getting close to the Party leadership I made my decision. It was very similar to my idea about joining the Cubans in Jamaica in order to compromise them to the CIA, and for the same reason—to try to reestablish, on my own terms, some kind of relationship with my country.

I called the Federal Bureau of Investigation. It was an absolute blind move on my part. The FBI had been the chief agency that had pursued me in 1967 and 1968. To my mind, they were still potential adversaries.

I told the agent who answered the phone who I was, and who I had met. He asked me a few questions and asked if I would meet personally with another agent. I agreed.

I understood the communists. My decision to oppose them

wasn't a simple reactionary one. I had seen the cutting edge of one of their revolutions. I knew they considered the means to be justified by the end.

The Marxist-Leninist theory of "from each according to his ability, to each according to his needs" had a poetic ring to it, but did not reflect the honest nature of people, which is to want to personally reap the rewards of their efforts and be able to keep it, and do with their profits as they wish.

Meeting with the Federal Bureau of Investigation agent initially made me uneasy. All the FBI agents I had known before had been chasing me. This man was almost classic. He was tall, imposing, dressed in suit and raincoat, and had a bullet scar across one temple that stretched the skin of that eye back slightly.

His name was Muggavin, and he told me he had been a street cop and was a combat veteran of World War II. He took the time to gain my confidence and establish a personal relationship with me. I told him I believed the Party members would accept me on their perception I was a renegade and opposed to the United States government.

Muggavin and I met often after that, him teaching me what to do to best effect a penetration of the Party. He told me to act like a subordinate, to seem a little less intelligent than everyone else, but work harder. Hard workers, Muggavin said, would always be picked for better jobs because they could be depended on, and the leadership gratefully bestowed responsibility to a capable worker. Together in restaurants, coffeeshops, or sitting in Muggavin's car, I began to absorb an education in spying.

I used my friendship with VISTA to get an invitation to a meeting. It wasn't an actual Party meeting but a black citizens' group in Fairfield being helped by VISTA. I recognized the real communists there. They were the whites who tossed in provocative statements, often helping the angry blacks to reach a conclusion, then applauding them as if there had been no assistance rendered.

I smiled a lot and frequently nodded my head to the suggestive phrases used by the communists, each one aimed at making the blacks more dissatisfied with their lives. It would seem the key to equality and freedom was strikes, protests, and most important, more meetings, if the whites in the assembly were to be believed. Black fury was encouraged. By the end of the meeting, several of the younger black men were shouting, promising to strike back at the system that had kept them repressed.

In Asia, I would have called them the Vietcong. In Fairfield, Alabama, they were simply disaffected, desperate citizens, being professionally directed in how to vent their hate. Only then did I fully understand how guerrilla warriors were created.

In my social visits to the VISTA volunteers, I made sure they understood my past, because I knew they were talking about me to their friends, several of whom were close to the Party leadership. The ploy worked. I received more invitations to meetings, some at private homes and some at schools or churches, but all conducted with the guiding hand of one or more communists.

The subjects were always the same—poverty, unemployment, welfare, and racial tension. Solutions for the problems were offered as socialist parables, and they came from the mouths of white faces, straight out of the book of Marx and Lenin.

I made myself available, offering to give people rides to meetings. As time passed, I felt I was being accepted.

Muggavin and I met once a week to discuss my progress. He critiqued me on my errors and gave me advice on how to handle different situations. I was drawing cash payments from the FBI for my time, the money delivered to me in bank envelopes.

I changed jobs, becoming a commercial artist, working by day in an office with advertising people. By night I was in the underground, attending meetings and helping with the making of signs and posters for VISTA or a group named the Young Worker's Liberation League, a youth branch of the Communist Party and an organization used to train and test potential members.

I could not join the Party directly. That took years, and many careful steps in loyalty tests and indoctrination. I could, however, join the YWLL, and on Muggavin's advice did so after attending several of their meetings. In March of 1970, I was presented with my Young Worker's League membership card, and paid my membership dues (with FBI cash) through to the end of the year.

Carrying the card made a difference. I was entitled to attend training sessions and meetings where strategy and tactics were often decided. Actual Communist Party members controlled the

YWLL, and they conducted training classes for it on Marxist theory. I went once a week to YWLL education classes to be taught how a socialist economy functioned.

I maintained my militant image, frequently speaking in bitter terms about the United States involvement in Vietnam and how I wanted to get even with the government because of their treatment of me.

I went to a leftist rally in Birmingham on 15 April 1970. I was to be a speaker there so the YWLL could show off their "defector" from the establishment.

> *NEWS ITEM: 16 April 1970* The Birmingham News *DEMON-STRATIONS PROTEST WAR, RACISM AT MORATORIUM DAY by Mike Lewis*
>
> *Moratorium Day demonstrators marched Wednesday outside the Birmingham local Internal Revenue Service and listened to speakers attack the war.*
>
> *A neatly dressed ex-GI, Frank Camper, called the war useless and said brave men die without glory. Being killed in Vietnam, he said, is "like being slaughtered in a stockyard."*

The demonstration had been planned to take place in the park as people downtown were leaving work. The newspapers and television studios were called to make sure there would be news coverage. There was nothing spontaneous about the demonstration. It was well planned, coordinated, and what each of us as speakers had to say was approved in advance by the leadership.

The YWLL decided to take advantage of my military experience by introducing me to the Alabama Black Liberation Front, which was exactly the opportunity I had been waiting for.

The Alabama Black Liberation Front was mainly composed of seething, violence-prone blacks, most of whom wore bushy Afro hairstyles, carried knives or pistols, and hated white people regardless of politics.

The local party leader and his white friends did not stay too long in the company of the worst of the ABLF. Instead, the ABLF was indirectly controlled by other blacks, who had stronger ties with the Party than with their blood kin.

I was recommended to the ABLF as a potential military trainer and sent to meet them at a mixed affair where some of the ABLF would be visiting with leaders from other leftist groups—a coalition gathering. I wore an old army uniform shirt and carried a fighting knife on my belt, sitting in the meeting room and watching the ABLF distributing cheaply printed magazines from the Black Muslims, illustrations of blacks brandishing communist AK-47 assault rifles on the covers.

The ABLF members swaggered about, barely listening to the coalition speakers, making sure their independence and power were noticed. Most of them were street toughs who would have been with a ghetto gang if they were not revolutionaries. I noticed several of them watching me. They knew I was the white who was supposed to come and train them in combat tactics. I stared back, openly examining them, and made sure my combat-knife sheath visibly protruded from under my jungle shirt.

The Alabama Black Liberation Front was going to be very interesting.

Muggavin warned me about the ABLF. He told me I could not be protected when I was alone with them and that he wouldn't blame me if I refused the operation.

He told me my going into the ABLF was risky in other ways. I was exposing myself to arrest because if I participated with the ABLF in anything illegal, the FBI could not cover for me.

I told Muggavin I wanted to keep going with the penetration, and he raised my pay. We also made a deal. Officially, Muggavin could not advise me to undertake anything illegal or have me report to him about anything illegal that was going to take place that would compromise me, because it would then be his duty to report it. What I would put into my reports to him would concern only what he could cleanly or legally turn in to his superiors.

If I were forced to do anything that a law enforcement agency might want to prosecute me for later, it was best that I not incriminate myself in my own reports. To help me, Muggavin said he would let me know about any other undercover agents who might cross my path, especially those from local law enforcement organizations.

My first meeting alone with the ABLF happened at night in the back room of a private home in a black neighborhood. A group of ABLF members was there, all of them hostile, regarding me as the outsider I was.

The group leader called the meeting to order, and told the members I had fought in Vietnam and had come to teach them how to fight.

"Shit," drawled one, "this honky don't look like he can kick my ass!"

I glanced at the protester. He was one of the toughs. I had anticipated such a reception.

"Stand up," I told the protester. He frowned because I had challenged him in front of his friends.

It was time for a sample of combat training.

The black jumped away from the group to the rear of the room where there was no furniture.

I followed him, watching to see if he was reaching for a knife. I moved at him suddenly, as if to strike, and he dodged, instinctively swinging a fist at me. I caught his arm and in one motion threw him over my shoulder, smashing him hard enough on the floor to bounce his body. I kept control of his arm and kicked him swiftly in the side, but only with enough force to let him know it could have been worse.

As he lay stunned, I twisted his hand back, bending his wrist painfully.

"Does it hurt?" I asked him.

"Y-yes!" he gasped.

"Tell them it works," I said.

"Yeah!" he exclaimed. "Yeah!"

The Alabama Black Liberation Front wanted to learn how to make bombs, break into buildings, how to convert commercial rifles to full automatic fire, and how to organize guerilla teams for attacking the police or military. The rank and file membership didn't want firearms or hand-to-hand combat training. It offended their pride. They thought they knew it all. This was fine with me, since it reduced what I needed to show them.

We used the basement of a Baptist church for some of the classes, others were held in homes. I made a lesson plan, gathered some training aids, and commenced with the project. At first the sessions were popular, but after several weeks attendance was low. It took time and patience to learn, and most of the "revolutionaries" were not willing to make the effort.

I learned about ABLF activities from my students. The Communist Party wanted the ABLF to copy an aspect of the national Black Panthers by giving free meals to elderly people in the black communities and sponsoring free lunches for black school children. This was a tremendous public relations ploy, but it required money. The ABLF took the Party-plotted lunch program and went to the streets to find a way to pay for it.

When they were turned down frequently for donations by black businessmen and discovered white-owned businesses would hardly contribute at all, extortion began. Teams of threatening Liberation Front members made visits to a few reluctant black businesses and if sufficient charity was not forthcoming, they used terror tactics to get the money.

Shop windows were smashed. Customers were threatened. Storerooms were burglarized and, in some cases, employees or owners beaten. Word to other businesses to cooperate got around fast.

Blacks opposed to the ABLF were afraid to speak out, and citizens avoided gangs of ABLF members on the streets.

The free lunch program failed, but the collection of money continued. The Alabama Black Liberation Front preyed on their own kind, legitimizing their thievery with a smokescreen of revolution.

Some clarification is necessary to understand the situation from this point on. Only a small clique within the actual ABLF was loyal to the YWLL or Party—those the Party leadership had installed. Those puppets were chosen for their ability to be managed, not their brains.

The actual membership of the ABLF was a casual thing. Faces came and went and false names were common. There were few genuine members but lots of visitors, friends, and hangers-on. The ABLF gave its Party advisors many organizational headaches, being at best an unreliable gang and at worse a loose coalition of potential lawbreakers.

Party types will go to any length to avoid violating the law. It gives the government too good an excuse to come down hard on them. A safe distance was maintained between the Marxists managers and the rowdy, violent elements of the ABLF-inspired groups.

The Party had deniability. Crimes were committed not by ABLF officers or members, in the Party line, but by others.

A leader of the ABLF group I had been training asked me to take several of the members and break into a grocery store one night.

It was a loyalty test, and I knew it.

I could visualize myself in jail in some minor town like Brighton or Powderly for breaking and entering, and then trying to explain the circumstances to the local police. Fortunately, the burglary went off well because we discovered a way to pull the entire door jamb out of the wall.

The ABLF carried out quickly salable items like cigarettes and beer. They were not stealing food to give to the poor.

I didn't put the incident in my FBI report.

More break-ins followed. I accompanied them as advisor, showing how to recon the area first and post security, which reduced the chances of encountering late-night witnesses or police patrols.

Direct strikes against individuals were becoming more common as well. The ABLF had first been content to take care of that matter unassisted, but as they felt more severe tactics were necessary, they pressed me into service.

There had been a recent split inside the ABLF even the Party could not resolve. The disaffected members left the group and attempted to establish their own Liberation Front, something the Party did not want.

The ABLF decided to execute the defectors.

The first shooting in which the ABLF forced my involvement was the ambush of the drunk. Officially, the incident never happened, and in court I will plead the fifth about it. I had hoped the brutality of the attempted murder would cool the decision to make war, but the next day those stunned, scared assassins were bragging, embellishing their roles in the shooting.

Having to assist or advise in the ambushes did not present me with a moral problem. The ABLF could just as easily turn against me, and they knew where I lived, worked, and spent my spare time. To keep them fooled and survive, I had to keep my cover. If they were indeed successful in killing each other off, it dropped the odds in my favor.

I had not owned a personal weapon since leaving the military. I hadn't felt I really needed one, but the situation with the ABLF was changing that. I chose a large-frame .22-caliber revolver with a long barrel, adjustable sights, and hand-fitting target grips. I wanted the caliber because the .22 was an easily obtainable cartridge. In the high-velocity Long Rifle .22 ammunition, it was a man-killer and did not recoil, making it easy to place all shots fired on target.

The cylinder held eight cartridges, as many as most .22 automatics, but being a revolver, it would fire without malfunctioning as fast as I could pull the trigger. There was no safety to slow down response time, and the double-action mechanism made cocking the pistol unnecessary before firing. With the long barrel, I did not lose muzzle velocity, and in practice, the target grips, sights, and heavy, stable frame made it easy to hit with the pistol as if it were a rifle for fifty meters or more.

The .22 is often disregarded as a killing caliber, but is in fact the most favored of close-range assassins. I was not buying a .44 Magnum to impress my friends. I was buying a practical weapon for actual use in life-or-death confrontations.

The ABLF was armed with a variety of sporting rifles, shotguns, and pistols of every caliber. I tried to gather the members for drills on quick reloading, clearing malfunctions, and combat firing techniques—if for no other reason than to improve my chances of living through a firefight with them on my side—but they would not attend. All they wanted to do was shoot.

The next incident was a raid (which I cannot legally claim), on a group of ex-ABLF at their headquarters house. They had been collecting protection money meant for the real Liberation Front, and that was a killing offense.

I told the men going on the raid that we needed to know the floorplan of the house, how many enemy would be in it at the time of the raid, and what they had as armament. All this was important to me because I would be present during the assault.

The ABLF raid leader told me none of that mattered. He wanted to simply take his people and as many weapons as possible and go in shooting. Then he wanted to burn the house down as we left. I began making plans to stay *outside* the house. It was going to be hell inside, with a half dozen black revolutionaries running through the rooms shooting and screaming.

They had several quart-sized wine bottles prepared for the

raid, filled with gasoline and tightly capped, with rag fuses taped to the necks.

We drove to the target house late on a weekend night. Some of the raiders had been drinking earlier, and I was expecting one of them to accidentally shoot through the windshield.

We parked several houses away from the target and walked quietly to the vacant lot next door. I sent half the men to the back door and half to the front, including the raid leader. They were excited now, and didn't notice I assigned myself to the backyard.

I checked my pistol for the last time and knelt in the brush and garbage of the vacant lot, watching the back door of the house.

With a crash, the raiders pushed open the front door and went in shooting, the back-door team only a second behind them.

The inside of the house sounded like a disaster in a fireworks factory. Window glass shattered. I heard bullets tearing through the woodwork and out into space.

It didn't last long. Commercial weapons don't have large ammunition capacities, and the raiders were too busy to reload.

A man jumped out of a window on the side of the house facing me. He had a shotgun in his hands. I didn't know whose side he was on, and he was running in my direction.

It was dark, but he saw me. He was about ten meters away when he lifted his weapon, stopped, and shot at me. The blast from his shotgun was too high, and I fired six times at his center mass. The man dropped to the grass.

I dashed to him. He was facedown and not moving. I grabbed his shotgun. It was a cheap single-shot model. I flung it away.

The ABLF then came pouring out of the back door. They were too bunched for me to count them. "Burn it!" I heard the raid leader cry.

The heavy wine bottles smashed against the wooden sides of the house. Most of the rag fuses failed to stay lit, going out as the bottles were thrown, but all it took was one. The roar of ignition and brilliant glare of the flames was spellbinding as the gasoline spattered from the basement to the roof.

I reloaded in the orange light of the fire, putting my empty cartridge cases in my pocket, and rolled over the man who had come out shooting at me. He was still breathing.

I didn't recognize him, so he wasn't one of ours, but I could tell he had been shot even before he jumped from the window. Bloody rips from shotgun pellets covered his face and arms. I felt sick inside.

In the heat and light of the fire, with shadows of the raiders dancing across me, I felt a sense of displacement. For a moment, Vietnam was not ten thousand miles away. It was with me, with the body lying in the grass and in the napalm glare of the fire.

I wanted to go to Muggavin and quit.

We had to withdraw. I took a last look at the house, the entire rear wall engulfed in fire, the flames reaching above the roof and illuminating the houses nearby, and I ran away with the blacks.

Miraculously, only one of our own raiders had been shot, and it was not serious. A bullet had nicked one of his fingers.

The house burned down. In it was one dead man, I later heard. Outside was the only other confirmed casualty, the man in the grass. The wounded had apparently escaped. I estimated there had been at least four people in the house at the time of the raid, but by the time the tale had been retold, the raiders claimed to have killed at least ten.

After the raid, not much happened. Police inquiries in the black neighborhoods struck some fear in the right breasts, and ABLF combat operations were suspended until further notice.

In my next meeting with Muggavin, I told him I thought I was finished. I wasn't where I could gather much genuine intelligence about Party operations, and working with the ABLF was making me crazy. Muggavin understood, but tried to convince me to stay.

Then Muggavin gave me a piece of heartstopping news. He told me there was an undercover police agent in the YWLL who, not knowing who I really was, was reporting on me. Muggavin described the man to me, and I recognized him. Muggavin said he was probably working for the Jefferson County Sheriff's Department. I asked what I should do about him. Muggavin replied I could do anything I had to, but added if I could avoid getting the agent hurt, to try to spare him.

As I watched Muggavin drive away, I was worried. If Muggavin was willing to sacrifice that man to me, it stood to reason he would sacrifice me to someone else. But I had no choice. If the agent was passing information about me to the police, they might arrest me. The police did not know I was working for the FBI, but even so, if they had enough evidence to prove I was taking part in these murderous ABLF battles, they would jail me for as long as they could.

I had already lived a parallel to the situation. It was like volunteering for a long range patrol. The enemy would kill you if they saw you, but so might your own side, mistaking you for the enemy because you looked so much like him, moving through the jungle.

At the next YWLL meeting, I took one of the leaders aside and talked to him about the Liberation Front. I told him how they refused to take orders or training and how they were going to compromise themselves and possibly the Party. Of course, none of this was news to him, but I didn't want to go straight into my real reason for the discussion.

After I finished listening to him explain to me how "their disadvantaged upbringing and emerging black pride was hampering them in taking the necessary steps for their liberation," and we were talking very conspiratorially, I brought up the subject of security.

I told the leader I suspected the new man who had been attending our open meetings of being a government plant, on the basis of his actions.

The communist listened, and I thought I could tell that he also had reservations. The truth was, the suspected agent was fairly clumsy in his role, alternating between overzealousness and withdrawal. He dressed badly for his part, his appearance a bit on the sterile side rather than simply seeming to be neatness. Leftists usually exposed their resentment of capitalism by artfully underdressing, assuming the appearance of the workworn proletariat. I could also tell by the undercover agent's expressions that the things he heard in the meetings sometimes disagreed with him so strongly it showed.

The leader promised to set the Security Committee to investigating him. I knew the agent was doomed then. The Security Committee was made up of the most hardcore of the controlling members, and they knew how to investigate and expose an agent, which could result in the man getting a visit from the ABLF.

I didn't want him hurt, I just wanted him out of the way. Whatever happened, I never saw him again.

Knives were the most common weapons owned by the Alabama Black Liberation Front. Knives were cheap, concealable, and didn't have to be reloaded. I saw a way to use this to my advantage, and created knife-fighting classes to get better attendance out of the ranks.

A knife fight is a vicious, bloody thing. It is far more personal than a gun battle.

I was by no means a professional knife fighter. I had only read about it, and learned a few tricks from friends. In fact, I was learning from the ABLF.

The majority of the blacks I knew liked to carry switchblades or large folding pocketknives, and threaten with them. They had learned their knife fighting from watching dramatic knife tactics in movies or on television. The serious knife fighters, the killers, often carried two knives apiece, and didn't show a blade until they attacked.

One night, just as a weekly training class was going to begin, one of my students came in cut. He had been in a knife fight on the way to the meeting. He said two men had challenged him on a nearby street corner, and when he became involved in what he thought was going to be a fistfight, one of them had suddenly knifed him across his forearm and ripped open his jacket. The cut across his forearm was not serious, but I bandaged it. The class wanted to immediately go back and get the offenders. It would be practical application of the training.

There were six of us. We walked to the corner where the attack had occurred. It was an unlit street intersection with a barbecue café on one side. The rest of the houses were private homes.

We figured the attackers were inside the barbecue café, and sent one man to look. He came back a few minutes later and confirmed that two men resembling the description given by our wounded comrade were inside.

The café had no telephone. The blacks with me favored the direct approach, so the six of us went in the front door. I had my air force survival knife in a belt sheath. The rest of my gang had pocket knives.

The two blacks who had cut our man were eating barbecue

sandwiches at a table in the small dining room. There were no other customers. When we walked in, the two street fighters took one glance at us and knew why we were there.

They stood, hands slowly reaching inside their pants pockets, eyes narrowing as we approached.

"You cut my friend!" one of my men said as he drew his knife. "Now I'm gonna cut you!"

The two street fighters tried to run past us for the front door. Thinking quickly, one of my men hit one with a chair, knocking him to the floor, and the other found himself trapped in a corner.

I went for the cornered fighter, crouched low, my knife in my right hand, my left hand forward as a block.

It was not a logical move. It was the heat of the moment. I should have left the cutting to the blacks. As I closed in with the street fighter, my men were tangling with the downed attacker, shouting and bumping into each other as they maneuvered for position.

My black opponent showed his knife, holding it out at me, rotating his wrist, scribing circles in the air with the point of his blade. I kicked a chair out of my way and kept moving forward, stabbing at his face with boxerlike jabs to intimidate him. It was working, backing him to the wall.

The man suddenly ducked and charged me. I grabbed his knife arm with my free hand, turned him, and cut him across his chest and throat with a powerful slash. Blood sprayed onto the wall, but the fighter did not go down. He twisted away from me and ran into the free-for-all in the middle of the restaurant floor.

I spun and tried to determine who was who in the tangle. Sharp knife blades were flashing in the mob, and the combatants were grunting and swearing, white teeth and eyes strikingly prominent on their black faces.

My opponent was hurt, arms flailing, knives stabbing into him. The other street fighter was trying to reach the door, two of my men chasing him, plunging their blades into his back.

Both street fighters were quickly down and their knives kicked away from them. Three of my blacks were cut, one limping from a deep stab in his thigh. The others had gashes in their hands and arms. It would take stitches to treat the cuts.

On the floor, the two former antagonists were still, their clothes slashed to ribbons, spreading pools of crimson running in the cracks in the floor, my men tracking the blood out to the street.

The restaurant owner was old and wore a dirty cook's apron. He had watched it all without a word. I took a last look at him as we left. I had seen old Vietnamese men with the same expression on their faces.

On Veteran's Day, 11 November 1970, I went as a Young Worker's Liberation League speaker to an organized protest in a suburban Birmingham park. I wore a camouflage combat uniform and jungle boots, with a belt and pistol around my waist. The pistol was a stage-prop .45 automatic. I had it strictly for theatrics.

A band set up their instruments. The protest was to consist of rock and roll music and speeches from representatives of different leftist groups.

I talked to the crowd about the illegal war waged by the United States against Vietnam, of the cruelty of the war against the Vietnamese people, and called for the United States to get out of Vietnam. I had memorized the speech.

The teenagers in the park applauded, and I was followed by representatives for women's liberation, racial equality, and the usual anticapitalism rhetoric.

Before the Alabama Black Liberation Front, it had simply been crime. Now it was *revolution*. There were more knifings, shootings, and beatings. I was becoming accustomed to the blacks preying on each other.

I managed to keep my reports going to Muggavin, carefully eliminating the violence from them. I was getting deeper into the Party. I was now allowed to attend meetings where long-range plans for future protests and actions were concocted. I was even slated for cadre school in Chicago, a step up the ladder.

I learned how the Communist Party was funneling money and assistance to striking workers in hospital or sanitation jobs in north Alabama, strikes that were largely provoked and organized by the Party, often without the knowledge of the union members.

A notable incident that would seriously affect me occurred when several of the ABLF went to occupy a house rented by an old black woman. The sheriff's department was coming to serve eviction papers against the woman, and the Party saw an opportunity to get publicity.

Arrogant, armed, and accustomed to violence, the ABLF resisted the sheriff's men, threatening to fire on them if they did not leave the woman alone. The police surrounded the house and, after a siege, managed to storm it and arrest the ABLF members. After the blacks were jailed, the Party organized a fund-raising campaign in the black neighborhoods to help the imprisoned revolutionaries.

I attended meetings where the legal defense for the arrested members was discussed and reported to Muggavin on what the defense attorney might say in court while the trial was underway. With my information informally passed to the prosecution, the defense was outmaneuvered.

I should not have done it. People in the Party realized there had been an internal compromise and, in a special meeting, announced to us there was a security problem.

When I heard that, I knew to expect trouble.

The leader said changes would be made in the meeting schedules, in who would attend and why, and security checks would begin for all the members of the Young Worker's Liberation League.

The first thing that happened was I was denied access to most of the ABLF meetings, except when I was specifically giving a training class. My latest project was to attempt to organize the ABLF into militarylike neighborhood "defense groups," so they could protect themselves from attack by the police or military. The Party had frequently told them there would be a day when white soldiers would invade the black neighborhoods to kill, loot, and rape in an effort to wipe out the black race the way the Nazis had tried to eliminate the Jews.

Jim Vines, the friend I had made in 1968 when he helped me while I was on the run, had returned from air police duty with the air force, discharged due to an injury. I worked Jim into the YWLL with Muggavin's knowledge, because at some point I was sure I would need some backup. Jim was mustached and urbane and open to a little intrigue.

The party tightened up security steadily, organizing the YWLL into cells of three, with no overlapping of committee responsibility. Luckily, Jim Vines was in a different cell from me, which at least gave me information about another group, but what he had to tell me was disheartening. He said every member of the YWLL was under suspicion, and each of us was being carefully investigated.

I drove home one day and realized something was wrong when I saw my front door standing open. When I entered the house, I found my mother had been beaten, my locked office broken into, and my desk searched.

With a cold compress held against her temple, my mother described to me how two black men had entered the house without warning and demanded to see me. Learning I was gone, they began ransacking the place. When my mother had tried to stop them, they knocked her down.

By chance, Jim Vines had arrived at that time, parking in the backyard, and the blacks ran when they heard his car. Jim guarded the house with his shotgun and called the police while his wife helped my mother to bed.

Jim went home after the police had taken a statement from my mother. I had come home only a few moments after the police left.

The ABLF had found nothing incriminating in my study, because there had been nothing there. I kept no copies of my reports, anticipating a search one day. I told my cell about the break-in but acted as if it had been a robbery attempt. They took my news with sufficient concern, but I felt a distance from them.

My life was now in danger, and the ABLF was not above striking at my family. I had to begin to disengage without seeming to be doing it and quickly increase security measures for myself, my family, and my house.

Next my car was stolen.

I awoke one morning and was dressing to go to work when I looked out the window and saw my VW was missing. I found it a block away. Whoever had taken the car had broken the driver's window, unlocked the door, and pushed the car from my house. No attempt had been made to start the car, but the glove box, trunk, and under the backseat had been searched.

In a telephone call from one of the Alabama Black Liberation Front members, I was told there was going to be a security meeting at my house that night and I was ordered to be there. A "security meeting" meant an intense questioning, which would probably degenerate into a fight. This was it. The ABLF was coming for the confrontation.

I called Muggavin and told him what was going to happen. He said for me to call the police and get a tactical squad there to surround the house. I made the call and gave the information to the police, asking them to call Muggavin for verification. I then went home to move out my family.

Hours passed. I waited inside, wondering what was happening. I went outside in the freezing weather and walked around the house and into the backyard, ignoring the shivering police who waited in the shadows holding their ice-cold shotguns and pistols.

Finally the commander of the police tactical team knocked on my front door. The Alabama Black Liberation Front was late. The police, exposed to the weather, did not want to stay any longer. I stood talking with the commander and his men in my front yard. They were dressed in heavy blue nylon parkas, shotguns slung on their shoulders.

At that moment, a carload of ABLF members turned the corner and stopped near my house.

"Here they come," I said. The police officers looked frantically at each other, not knowing what to do.

I waved at the ABLF and left the group of police. I walked to the road to meet the car. The faces of the blacks were a lot like the police, eyes wide and jaws slack.

"What's happening?" one of the blacks asked.

The police watched, trying to appear as inconspicuous as possible standing there with their weapons.

"There's been some trouble here," I lied. "The cops are after a guy who broke into a house on the next block. They're searching all over the place."

"Oh," said the black.

"Why don't you guys come on in?" I asked.

"No, no, we can't stay. We have to get to a meeting," said the driver.

I said good night to the revolutionaries as if everything were all right, and they drove slowly away. The police left soon after, thoroughly embarrassed. I was angry at their inability to endure the cold. They were soft. Under other circumstances, we might have all been killed.

Once back in the house, I decided I would have to confront the Party myself, on my own terms. Neither the FBI nor the police were capable of protecting me constantly. I had volunteered for this. It was my responsibility.

The ABLF had a scheduled meeting at a church in a black community near Bessemer. I called Jim Vines and told him I was going to the meeting to resign, and I needed some help. He drove to my house with his short riot shotgun.

I explained my plan to Jim as I arranged my pistol on a strap inside the right sleeve of my field jacket. With a shrugging motion, I could drop the pistol out of the baggy sleeve right into my hand.

We drove in my VW to the church. The ABLF knew I was probably coming, and had a sentry outside. When I parked the VW, he ran into the basement of the church.

Jim pumped a shell into his shotgun, opened his door and stepped out, keeping the gun from sight. I got out of the car and looked back at Jim. He nodded, signaling he was ready.

They started coming out of the church slowly, hands in their coat pockets. There was a white member of the YWLL with them, one of the cadre that conducted indoctrination classes. I didn't talk to the white man. I went straight to the black leader, an ABLF officer I had trained many times. He stood stiffly, his men behind them.

They understood force. It was what I had for them.

"You fucked up," I told the black, using the favorite ABLF obscenity. "When you let weasels like him tell you to go after me." I pointed to the white communist.

The black knew I was ready to fight, and I had all of my attention on him. He knew I would kill him first.

The group of revolutionaries stepped forward to maneuver around me, but stopped in their tracks when Vines raised his shotgun over the roof of the car.

"We're going to settle this right now," I said, "just us." I prepared to let the pistol drop.

The white communist was not a fighter. He worked in a hospital, inciting discontent among the black employees there. Tonight he was scared.

"I—I didn't have anything—" the white stammered.

"Shut up," I ordered. He abruptly quit talking.

"You're all a bunch of fuck-ups," I said. "You put the heat on me and you should have known better. I trained you. Now I'm gonna show you what I didn't teach you." The long-repressed anger burned in my stomach like hot coals. I was ready and willing to kill as many of them as I could.

The black started to take his hand out of his jacket pocket. I dropped the pistol from out of my sleeve to my hand and swept it up into his face in one motion.

The knife he had been going to pull fell out of his hand. I wanted to kill him. I took all the slack out of the trigger.

"Move again! Just do it, you son of a bitch!" I said.

He stood transfixed, staring into the muzzle of the pistol. He had not even seen where it came from.

"We ain't gonna make no trouble," he said softly.

"If I ever see any of your people *anywhere,* they're dead. Do you understand?" I said.

"Yes, yes, I do," he answered.

I looked at the white. He was pale, as if he might faint. "The same goes for you and your goddamned Party." He managed to nod weakly; I don't believe he could speak.

Jim had the riot shotgun tight into his shoulder, aiming down the barrel at the group of ABLF as if he were on a firing range. I backed slowly to the car, sat in the driver's seat, and started the engine. "Get in," I said to Jim, and we drove quickly away.

I was through with the Party and the Alabama Black Liberation Front. Maybe with more experience, I could have handled it better. Maybe I should have kept a lower profile and gone on deeper into the Party. But it was not maybe. It was done.

I wrote a resignation to Muggavin a few days later. I had held up under the stress and the tension of a penetration of the Communist Party for almost a year. I apologized for my mistake and told him I hoped I had done nothing to harm any other operations.

All I wanted to do after delivering my letter to the FBI was to be left alone. I was fed up with the entire affair. I had a job as a commercial artist. I could try to live like other people and forget about Vietnam, prison, and covert operations.

Eventually I found an outlet for myself.

I became a racer.

CHAPTER FOUR
Racer

With a screaming whine like the jet turbine of a helicopter gunship, the Porsche braked. The driver was hopping out of the seat harness, throwing belts loose, while the next driver was squeezing past him to get behind the wheel.

Out front was the grandstand straight of Daytona. The brightly colored cars that flashed by had the purpose and menace of fighter aircraft, skimming along the asphalt, helmeted pilots avoiding catastrophe by fractions of a second.

I dashed my notes down and added more oil as our desperate crew checked the tires. The engine couldn't last.

Peter Gregg, the International Motor Sports Association National Champion of the United States, stood behind me, his arms folded and face grim, his Nomex driving suit wrinkled and sweaty. He had two team cars in this race—the oil-burning Porsche 99 being serviced, and Porsche 59 out on the track, somewhere back in the field after an engine change. I was on his team.

The jacks dropped 99 to the pavement. It was a machine of scoops and slots, wings, airdams, and love-hate lines, glistening white, with the red and blue stripes of Brumos Racing down its center.

Crewmen danced out of the way. The Porsche launched itself back into the battle.

I looked at my watch. We had been racing over nineteen hours. The crew had dull faces and no one joked. This was my last race. I was already making plans to join a growing war in the Middle East.

My eyes burned from fatigue. I rubbed them, remembering the first time I had put a wrench to an engine.

After leaving the army, I had bought a Volkswagen sedan.

Having been satisfied with my friend George's, I taught myself mechanics by servicing it and began experimenting with ways to improve its performance. I had an interest in sports cars, and while my VW was not a racer, it was a start. I experimented by adding parts to make it handle better, go faster, and stop quicker —and surprised myself by building a car that was far more potent than I had anticipated. It was good old-fashioned hot rodding.

This led to bigger things.

Even as I was passing myself off to the Communist Party as a revolution-advocating radical, in my spare time I was reading engine and chassis manuals, absorbing an education in racing and competition-bred automobiles. The logical extension of a VW was a Porsche.

I couldn't afford a Porsche at the time, but my desire was pushing me toward something more sleek than a VW sedan, so in 1972 I bought a new bright red VW Karmann Ghia. After applying all the mechanical engine and suspension tricks to the Ghia that had proven so potent on my VW sedan, I had a genuine Q-ship—a car that seemed to be of modest origin but was actually fast enough to challenge acknowledged sports cars.

I entered my Ghia in slalom events, a type of racing where agility and acceleration of the car and skill of the driver were more important than top speed. Making the Ghia beat the quicker cars took all of my mechanical ability, like a highly tuned, dual-carbureted engine and racing brakes, plus my best possible driving. I was quickly recognized as a threat to the "real" sports cars in my class, so they moved me to more difficult classes where they thought my Ghia and I would be beaten.

Even though I was then in competition against actual race cars and race-prepared street cars, I still won. I took my class championship for two years straight.

Asphalt Combat

I bought my first Porsche during that time, a dark-green vintage 1963 model 356B. When a friend wrecked it (with me in the passenger seat) by sliding off a country road into a stand of very sturdy trees, I bought a more advanced Porsche 912.

I first entered the 912 in closed-track Porsche Club of America events, and got a taste of the type of racing where speed *and* cornering was paramount. Most of the other cars entered were powerful six-cylinder Porsche 911 models. I had to surpass the ones I could by literally outbraving the drivers, going into the turns faster, braking later, and coming out quicker than they dared.

I also tried rallying, and ran the brutal "special stage" rallies where rugged stretches of dirt road had to be run at high speeds. I never won, only doing a lot of damage to my car, since crashing and bouncing over mud puddles and ditches was common. Though I was no success at rallying, I did learn one valuable lesson. I had a fatal flaw for a racing driver.

I was *too* aggressive.

I knew that to win, you had to finish the race, but I was willing to sacrifice the car, becoming involved in individual struggles with other racers. The realization of this shortcoming made me reconsider. I was treating racing like combat.

Members of the Sports Car Club of America (SCCA) had begun to ask me for assistance in preparing their cars, and I made a decision that was largely spurred by my quitting the FBI. I felt burned out on undercover work, false friendships, odd hours, and daily tension. My initial successes with VW's and Porsches showed me there was opportunity in the repair and preparation of them. I decided to make sports and racing cars a profession.

In 1974 I quit my job as a commercial artist and with Jim Vines, my old shotgun backup, opened my own shop. I was soon in the daily business of repairing VW's and Porsches, with my own staff of mechanics.

Showroom Stock

While attending an SCCA race, I met a driver who impressed me. His name was Jim Roberts, an ex-U.S. army officer and a dentist who specialized in periodontal-disease treatment in Birmingham. Roberts raced a white Opel 1900 Ascona sedan with a roll bar inside it, in a new Sports Car Club of America class called Showroom Stock.

Not allowed high-performance modifications, two things

were at once apparent in Showroom Stock: the ability of the car itself and the skill of the driver.

Jim Roberts was clearly superior to his competitors. Soon the two of us had an arrangement. Because Roberts was such a winning driver, he would drive. Because I could prepare winning engines and suspensions, I would maintain the car, making it as fast and sturdy as possible within the rules.

In 1974, our first year together, we recorded nine wins and six second-place finishes out of seventeen starts in our class, finishing second overall in the Southeastern United States Division.

In 1975 we logged sixteen wins out of nineteen starts and won the divisional championship, so capable was our car-and-driver combination. If the car would stay together, Roberts would win.

Between our races—which were still on a club and therefore amateur basis—I had begun to volunteer myself to professional teams in order to learn. I helped with the high performance full-race-prepared Porsche 911's.

I closed my private shop in 1975 and took a job with Bavarian Motor Works (BMW) of North America, relocating to Mobile, Alabama, on the Gulf of Mexico. Roberts moved up to faster racing classes. At BMW, I met Jim Crawford, a master mechanic. Crawford had many years in the business and taught me a great deal. We became good friends, and after he left Mobile to go to work in Jacksonville, Florida, so did I.

Our employer was none other than the championship United States International Motor Sports Association (IMSA) racer, Peter Gregg. Gregg was the owner of Brumos Racing and Peter H. Gregg Mercedes-BMW-Porsche. Both admirers and detractors alike called him "Peter Perfect." Gregg raced and, like Dr. Jim Roberts, he won.

Gregg had come up through the ranks as a slalom racer, SCCA road course amateur competitor, then professional racer. He had raced virtually all of the competition cars Porsche had built, including the incredible 917. Gregg was then running the new turbocharged 930 series Porsche. This was the top of professional sports car racing in the United States. It was a long step from modifying my VW sedan. I should have been satisfied, but I wasn't.

Racing had been fine, a consuming distraction, and all the

sweeter for my having been successful in it. But it was still not the challenge combat or undercover operations had been.

While I was living in Jacksonville, I applied to Bell Helicopter in Iran, feeling the need to get back into action. Turmoil and revolution were beginning to seethe there. Bell sent me the paperwork to apply.

It wasn't a decision I would have trouble explaining to racing drivers like Jim Roberts or Peter Gregg. They drove because they felt the same thing, but their way of expressing it was at high speed. Racing, for them, was life. For me, it had been a temporary substitute for warfare.

I was scheduled for one more race, the upcoming Daytona 24-Hour. Our armament for this race would be our own Brumos car, a single-turbo model, and a new twin-turbo 935-77 from Germany. Peter Gregg would drive both cars, with co-driver team support from Tione Hezemans, a German, Brad Frisselle, an American, Rolf Stommelen, another German, and Claude Ballot-Lena, a Frenchman. My friend Jim Crawford and I would be in the pit crew.

The twenty-four hours of Daytona was the biggest and most important sports car event in the United States.

It was a special race for me, being my last, and I badly wanted a victory.

February 1978: Daytona

The start of a "24-hours" is deceptively like that of any other race, but the enormity of the undertaking is such that only well-prepared professionals and overzealous amateurs attempt it.

The band in front of the grandstand played the theme from *Star Wars,* the majorettes twirled their batons, and the cars were gridded, with much color and anticipation.

At 4:30 P.M., the race began. The starter snapped the green flag at the end of the pace lap. At first there was a track full of cars, all racing as if it would be over in an hour. The Brumos team's Porsches were doing it too. Peter was in his own car, number 59, Rolf Stommelen in the 935-77. The 935-77 was painted in the red, white, and blue Brumos colors and bore number 99.

5:30 P.M.: Ninety-nine came in. The crew changed tires and Tione Hezemans replaced Stommelen. Things were moving now, and as 99 accelerated out, 59 was coming in for fuel and a windshield cleaning. The pit routine was underway.

6:35 P.M.: Ninety-nine made it in for the driver change. Mike Colucci, Peter Gregg's new chief mechanic, leapt over the wall from the pit road, shouting "*Oil! Oil!*" One of the mechanics quickly added two liters to the tank.

Ninety-nine zoomed back into the race. We had just seen the very beginning of the car's oil problem but didn't know it yet.

7:00 P.M.: Fifty-nine came in for an unscheduled pit stop. Extreme vibration was making the car impossible to drive, so the crew checked the suspension, pulling and jerking at the parts. Everything was tight. Both front tires were removed and examined. A wheel weight was gone. New tires were fitted and 59 went out again. Precious minutes were lost, but it could have been worse.

At the time of the pit stop the signals chief notified us 99 was in first place and 59 in second.

It was cold and getting colder. The excitement of the start had faded and the realization that this would be a long one was settling in.

The night became a series of pit stops and driver changes. Brad Frisselle swapped out with Peter for his turn at 8:47 P.M.

The crew was changing tires on 59 when the unusual occurred. Jim Crawford ran to his appointed tire and slapped his impact-gun socket on the big center hubnut to spin it off. He pressed the trigger and the gun *failed.* Another mechanic finished his tire and dashed to the unchanged wheel, spun the hubnut off the axle with a good tool, and 59 was gone as soon as the tire was changed. Crawford was astounded. Impact guns fail very rarely.

Ninety-nine was still first and building a lead. Fifty-nine was still second. Brumos was out front and going strong at 9:00 P.M.

Very little of the race could be seen from the pits. All we could do was endure the cold and wait between pit stops.

9:36 P.M.: The car pitted beside us came wailing in for a stop right across our front, locked his brakes, slid, and just missed coming through our pit wall. That woke us all up.

The pit stops were about an hour apart for our cars. Fifty-nine was running like a train, but 99 was taking more oil with each stop. "I think we have a turbo going sour," a mechanic said. "It's sucking the oil right into the motor."

He was right. The smoke visible when 99 was on trailing throttle testified to that.

10:59 P.M.: Fifty-nine got its first brake pads.

When the oil level in 99 got low, the pressure gauge showed it when braking, a signal to get the car in and tank up again. A twin-turbo Porsche was a thirsty car for fuel, but 99 was having to stop just to have its oil topped off.

The lower headlamps on 99 were sandblasted almost opaque. Hezemans was driving by the two bug-eyed lights mounted on the deck lid. The windscreens were pitting as well, making them hard to see through.

Midnight came. Everybody was tired. Any normal race would have been over by now, but this blasted thing just kept on.

1:12 A.M.: Fifty-nine went by the signal crew shelter slowly, flashing his lights. "He's doing twenty-five mph and bouncing up and down!" the signal pit radioed us.

We made four spare tires ready. It took a long time for Ballot-Lena to limp around to us. The car popped up on its built-in air jacks.

Something more than a tire was wrong with 59. The engine was turned off. Colucci was up in the left rear wheel well, shaking the brake disc. He told the mechanics what tools to get. A floor jack lifted 59 high and jack stands were braced under it. The trouble seemed to be in the diagonal suspension arm or the axle half-shaft.

Toolbox trays slammed open and shut. Three men were working, taking the entire left suspension off the rear of the car. The spare part was brought up, an axle, diagonal arm, and brake cooling duct all built together.

1:32 A.M.: Peter Gregg came to the pits to see the problem. He asked a few questions, knowing the lead 59 had built up over third place would absorb most of the time it would take to fix the car, making a catch-up drive easier.

1:42 A.M.: The new suspension was nearly installed when 99 came in, stopping just short of bunting 59 off its jackstands. Peter Gregg got into 99 after Stommelen was out. The front brake pads on 99 were changed, the first time for that car, and Jim Crawford had another heart-stopping experience.

They were putting the wheels back on 99, and Crawford stuck his new impact gun on the hubnut and all it did was give a little burp. "Air!" he yelled, but his voice was lost in the roar of passing cars. The rest of the crew was wiping glass, fueling and oiling, finishing their jobs.

"Air! Air! *AIR!*" he bellowed, making himself heard.

The mistake was corrected by a man who saw the line had been uncoupled. Crawford got the air and tightened the nut, amazed at his bad luck. Peter Gregg then rocketed out of the pits in the twin turbo, with all his wheels on tight.

Fifty-nine had left just a moment before 99, the suspension fixed, but 59's second place had dropped to fourth.

The air lines were rerolled and the tools put back in the boxes. It was windy and very cold in the pit.

Peter was turning the fastest laps yet in 99, the timers told us. The lead from 99's first to the second-place car was sixteen laps, and Peter was increasing it.

3:00 A.M.: This was the worst. The hours from three till dawn always seem to be the coldest, the darkest, and the most tiring. The awesome length of the race was apparent as fatigue slowed reactions and some of the crew tried to catch cat naps.

Fifty-nine finally regained second place, a tribute to the driving of Ballot-Lena and Brad Frisselle. Our crew felt better all around.

Ninety-nine's oil consumption was so high now it seemed to be living on borrowed time. Anything could happen.

4:25 A.M.: Ninety-nine came in for brake pads again and got full service as Stommelen changed out with Hezemans. The windscreen was badly cracked. The white paint on the airdam was chipped and gouged from sand and rocks. The entire back of the car was sooted black from the oily exhaust.

The airdam on 59 was cracked and a piece was missing. It didn't seem to hurt the handling so we decided not to take the ten minutes to replace it.

The sun would be up soon. We were all looking for it, on the chance it might warm up our frigid pit.

Fifteen hours of racing were over.

8:20 A.M.: It was full daylight now and the clouds were clearing when the right rear axle broke on 59 and Ballot-Lena nursed the car back to the pits. Both engine oil lines were severed by the flailing axle, ruining the engine.

The spare engine and transmission with axles were quickly manhandled out to the pit road by our crew. Fifty-nine was propped up on jackstands and the fiber glass tail section removed. Oil was all over the asphalt. By 9:00 A.M. the old engine was on the ground.

Jim Crawford was one of the engine changers, and he was rolling in the oil and tools under the car, working as fast as he could. Fifty-nine's lead would help some, but this quirk of fate was going to hurt very badly. It was a wrench race now. The new engine was being bolted in.

10:17 A.M.: Fifty-nine was back in the race. The announcer told the crowd it took one hour and forty-five minutes to complete the engine change.

The signal chief, on the radio, yelled to us over the din, "He's coming back in; he's not going very fast!"

10:29 A.M.: Ballot-Lena pitted. He pointed to the tach and wiggled his fingers like the engine might be missing at a certain rpm. We added water to the turbocharger's intercooler radiator. The deck lid was down and 59 was back out at 10:32 A.M. That fixed it.

10:55 A.M.: Hezemans in. Ninety-nine was emitting huge clouds of smoke as it revved. The drivers exchanged and 99 headed back into the fray. "The engine is sick," Hezemans said, "but we have only hours now. You never know."

Throughout the night the race had looked endless, and lost time didn't seem to matter much, but in the light of day, and with 4:30 P.M. in sight, we felt we were racing again.

11:30 A.M.: Ninety-nine was leading by more than thirty laps.

The routine was back. The cars went around, pitted on schedule, got tires, gas, oil, and clean windshields, and went right back out. We were told 59 was making up time fast.

1:07 P.M.: Twenty-one hours down, three to go. Peter was out in 59, going hard. It was that last effort.

Jim Crawford was exhausted. He had cleaned up some from the oily mess he was in earlier, but he still had dirt around his eyes and it made him look terribly old.

2:19 P.M.: Ballot-Lena replaced Peter in 59. We figured that 59 would probably get no higher than fifth place. If that were so, it would not be from lack of effort.

There was some tension about the finish, but our exhaustion took the edge off. Most people just wanted it to end now.

The field seemed sparse. Only thirty-two cars were left of the original sixty-seven.

The sun was shining and it was actually getting warm. Fans and spectators were out in force now, and the Brumos pit became a hot spot for picture takers and autograph seekers.

Ninety-nine's lead was equivalent to about an hour. If the engine blew before three thirty, it was all over. Meanwhile, Johnny Rutherford, our closest competition, was blasting away in his own Porsche 935, smelling a win. He cut down six laps on 99 in no time.

At 3:23 P.M., it happened. The signal crew called our pits with an electrifying message. Ninety-nine was slowing down and could be stopping. A new surge of life energized our worked-out crew. Four tires were set up and the fuel hose was ready as 99 hobbled in.

It was a flat tire. The air jacks boosted 99 up and the change was made rapidly. Ninety-nine went out, but the driver decided not to overstress the car. The rear suspension did not feel right to him. Caution is the word for a twenty-four-hour race. Take it slow, don't blow it, remain running later, and later, and . . .

Although it was much warmer now, most of our crew were still wearing jackets, too dulled to realize we could take them off.

4:00 P.M.: Half an hour to go. We were going to make it.

4:10 P.M.: Ninety-nine was called in. Hezemans would drive it over the finish line. The front of the car was hastily cleaned off and a prominent Brumos Porsche decal applied over the battered fiber glass for the victory photograph.

At 4:30 P.M., 99 howled to the first-place finish, the checkered flag waving for us in the afternoon sun. Brad Frisselle, in 59, crossed shortly after for a ninth-place finish.

All I could do was smile.

CHAPTER FIVE
Saudi Arabia

On the road below us, big black shapes rumbled by, with the jerks and mindlessness so peculiar to tanks. This was it. We had been in ambush in North Yemen since nightfall.

The flares burst in the sky over the road, brilliant white. I recognized Russian T-62's, the first time I had ever seen them except in photographs.

I took direct aim at a tank and squeezed the rubber-covered firing lever of the LAW.

November 1978: Kansas City

Bell Helicopter was pulling out of Iran since the Shah's hold there was sinking by the day. I had received a letter from them several weeks before, explaining the delay, informing me they were not hiring anyone for Iran for at least six months. They were obviously waiting to see how the revolution was going to end.

It had seemed a stroke of luck in the summer that I had met a man who said he was currently working in the Middle East. He suggested I call Saudia, the government airline of Saudi Arabia, which had an office in Kansas City.

I telephoned Saudia, told them of my situation with Bell, and they mailed me employment information and an application. I sent the completed application back and was pleased to promptly get airline tickets to go to Kansas City for an interview and physical.

Virtually all of the applicants with my group were pilots, air crew, or aircraft mechanics. I was feeling out of place. My only commercial experience in which I thought they would have an interest was automotive. The interviewer in fact told me Saudia had many staff cars that needed maintenance, an innocent-enough job. It was at least a start.

Soon after returning home to Jacksonville, Florida, I received notice that I was hired, and a packet of tickets and traveling documents arrived. I thought I was very lucky, since other applicants I had talked to said they had waited months. I had December to prepare to leave. My reporting date was just after the New Year, in Jeddah, Saudi Arabia.

3 January 1979: London

I had an overnight stay near Heathrow Airport at the Heathrow Holiday Inn, and sat in my hotel room reading the London *Times*. The next day would see me on to Jeddah. I was expecting to send for my wife and son within a month, as soon as I was settled.

My room phone rang, and a soft-spoken man with a British accent asked me if I was the "F. Camper" on the Saudia list. I thought the caller was connected to the airlines in some way, so when he asked me to come down to the hotel bar, I accepted. I was expecting a briefing or talk before I arrived in Jeddah, and I had a lot of questions.

The bar was dim, with recorded music playing in the background. Barmaids in sexy parodies of old English skirts and bodices carried trays of drinks as they weaved around the tables and booths. As my eyes were adjusting to the dark, I saw a lone man in a corner booth stand and smile, offering his hand as I approached him.

"You must be Frank," he said. "My name is John Davis." I shook his hand and he sat opposite me in the booth. He seemed no older than myself, and had blond hair and a gentle face.

The barmaid stopped at our table. "My friend is not much of a drinker," Davis said to her, which surprised me. "How about just a white wine?" I nodded, and the barmaid left.

"How did you know that?" I asked.

"Reading your dossier," he said. "You drink only socially,

you don't smoke, and you were with the Special Operations Group in Vietnam, attached to the 5th Special Forces. Am I right?"

"Yes," I managed to say, slightly shocked. The SOG code and notation about the 5th Group were with my 201 File, but I'd never told Saudia about it.

"You also did an admirable job with the FBI a few years ago," Davis said, still smiling.

"Are you with Saudia?" I asked as my wine arrived.

"No," he told me. "I represent an interest in the Middle East. I'd like to talk to you about a possible agreement between my people and yourself."

"I already have a job waiting," I said, wary now.

"That is precisely the point," Davis said. "I should tell you we obtained your name from Bell. You were going to work on weapons systems for them. I take it you have no aversions to military duties?"

"No."

"How do you feel about working for Israeli interests?"

"In Saudi Arabia?" I asked.

"Would you describe yourself as pro-Arab?"

"No, I don't think so," I said.

"Then you're only going to work for them for the money."

"That's blunt, but true," I said.

"Israel is a small country," Davis said. "To survive, she must work at it very hard. That means being realistic and being flexible."

"You don't have to go into that," I said, sensing a God-and-country talk coming on. "If you have a deal, let's hear it."

"Yes," Davis said, "you would be pragmatic, wouldn't you? Most of you Vietnam chaps are. My offer is a simple one. We need people in places where they can pick up information."

"People who aren't Jewish," I guessed.

"Absolutely. You're on your way to Jeddah now. This is the time to make up your mind."

"Who exactly would I be working for?"

"Israel."

"The Mossad?" I asked.

"Technically."

"What if I say no?"

"Then we part friends."

"Why me?"

"Your background."

"Do you have identification?" I asked.

Davis pulled his wallet from his inside sport-coat pocket, opened it, and in a window case was a card that named him, in English, as a member of the Israeli Embassy staff in London. It had his photo and a military rank shown.

"We want reliable people in the right locations. You'll just tell us what's happening in your area," he said.

"The pay?" I asked.

"It depends. No productivity, no pay. There are other advantages. There could be a future in this for you."

"What if I get caught?"

"Don't get caught."

"Do you coordinate this through the U.S. Embassy, or whoever, to let them know?" I asked.

"There is a hitch there," Davis said. "The Yanks are a bit sticky about their chaps working for us. I wouldn't tell them if I were you."

I took my first drink of wine. Davis was so cool, so assured.

"Then how do I handle this with my people?" I asked.

"You stay away from them, especially the military. Don't even go to the U.S. Embassy if you can help it. The last thing you'd want to be accused of by your own side is spying against them."

"When I get to Jeddah, who do I report to?"

"Someone will contact you. He'll be British. A popular sport on the Red Sea is diving. He'll ask you to go diving. You tell him you have a bad ear and can't take the pressure of a deep dive."

"Then?"

"He'll know what to do."

"Sign and countersign."

"Quite," Davis said. "It's all really a low-key type of affair. Save your questions. When your contact has found you, ask him."

"But what if I don't get placed where I can do any good?" I asked.

"Oh, I think you'll find the opportunities in the Middle East to be prolific these days," Davis said, glancing at his watch. "I really must be going," he said. "Please don't get up."

He stood, adjusted his sport coat, and offered his hand to

me. I shook it. "A last tip," he said with a boyish grin. "Do be careful. The Arabs are such ghastly drivers."

With that little joke tossed off, he was gone.

I drank my wine, thinking over the whole situation. The "chance" encounter with the man who had all the answers in Jacksonville made sense now. Somehow, the Mossad was monitoring Bell Helicopter's personnel lists and was picking up some intelligence assets from the Iranian crisis.

A stranger gives me a phone number, and I get a job.

On the way back up to my room, it made a convoluted sense. The worst that could come of it would be a couple of years at good pay under the Saudis. I could keep the Israelis happy with minor bits of information, stay out of trouble, and make money off of them too.

Once back in bed, I reopened my copy of the London *Times*. The newspaper detailed the fighting in Ethiopia and Uganda, and probable war in Yemen, a region on Saudi Arabia's southern border now broken into north and south halves. Northern Yemen was aligned with the other Arabic sheikdoms that were spotted around Saudi Arabia's edges, but Southern Yemen went by the name of People's Democratic Republic, and had Soviet and East German advisors and Cuban combat troops to enforce the title.

If you counted the Arab-Israeli wars and quickly collapsing Iran to the north of Saudi Arabia, I would be working on a sandy, oil-rich political island surrounded by strife.

Surely there was some opportunity in that.

5 January: Jeddah

I drank a last cup of breakfast tea in the Taj Palace's hotel restaurant and left to begin my in-processing, with only vague ideas of where to go. At first, I was lost in Jeddah. It was a large and complex port city on the Red Sea, and my first impressions were of crowding, garbage, new construction, and mazes of un-marked streets. There seemed to be about twice as many cars and trucks as the city could hold, parked, wrecked, or racing past me.

The mix of nationalities was fascinating. Everywhere there were Koreans, French, Ethiopians, Germans, Egyptians, Americans, Sudanis, Yemenis, and that was just a start. Genuine Saudis were almost rare, lost in the mass of foreign engineers, technicians, and specialists.

Mercedes limousines pushed through the traffic jams, around overloaded dump trucks and Japanese pickups carrying mournful, kneeling camels as cargo. Shrouded women weaved through the traffic and in and out of the rows of open-air shops that sold spices, gold, and silks. Arabic music vibrated from stalls stacked with new radios, stereos, and televisions. The heat and dust lay over it all, rotting the butchered goats hanging from market hooks and fermenting the garbage mounds in the alleys, slowing the clouds of green flies that covered them.

On the west side of the city, past the edge of the jumble of mud-brick hovels and steel-and-glass office buildings, were the glinting, turquoise waters of the Red Sea. An armada of tankers, freighters, and cargo ships was anchored out to the horizon.

On the east side of Jeddah was the shimmering tan and brown expanse of desert that kept going until it vanished in the haze.

The Saudia offices I needed were scattered widely in the city with no apparent consolidation, most of them with no signs. I eventually found one of the personnel offices and began to have my folder full of forms stamped and signed.

The clerks were young, white-robed Saudis with checked red-and-white *ghutra* headdresses. They drank hot tea constantly from small cups and seemed very self-important, rejecting paperwork on a whim, sending many of the new men back to a previous clerk in another office or even across town to another building. I was no luckier than anyone else, getting my first taste of Arabic-inspired frustration at doing the same thing many times over to achieve a single result, until I gave my file to one supervisor who had his desk in a side office.

"Why do you not have your military records with you?" he asked.

"I wasn't told to bring them," I said.

"What is your military experience?"

"Intelligence and reconnaissance in Vietnam," I said, "and training combat soldiers in the United States."

"If you have training experience, I need your file. What is your assignment?" he asked.

"I'll be with ground equipment, I think," I said.

"Go back to your hotel and stay," he ordered. "Arrange to get your military documents. Return here as soon as you do."

I thanked him and left and immediately called my wife in the United States from the hotel to tell her to find my records and mail them. I stayed on in the Taj Palace Hotel for exactly one month, working in the ground equipment section of the airport as I waited. I discovered I was not on the housing list, therefore ineligible to move out of the hotel. For some reason I was sidelined. It made me worry.

When I did receive my military records, I went back to the personnel office. There were several British workmen ahead of me. I didn't know any by name, but they grunted hello as I sat down. No one had tried to contact me yet. Was one of these my man?

"What's happening?" I asked.

"They want some bleedin' mercenaries, that's what," said one.

"I had my belly full of that in Aden," said another, "and I'm not going to war with a *raghead* as my section leader!"

"What about you?" a Brit asked me. "Do you have a military background?"

"Yeah," I said, "I was in Vietnam."

"Bloody cockup, that one, I'll bet," said the man, and I nodded sincere agreement.

The office door opened and an Englishman came out. "You're next, mate," he said to one of his friends, who stood and went in. A deluge of questions burst from the others.

"Quite simple," he explained. "It's the muddle brewing down in Yemen. Seems they're short on expatriate types to keep their chaps in line. They need some instructors, some noncoms."

"Who does?" I asked.

"Who do you think?" the standing Brit answered, pointing toward the Saudis in the main office. "Good material like them."

"I knew it! Bleedin' *ragheads!* It's not for me. I'll pack it in first," said the Aden veteran.

Within half an hour all the Brits had gone into the office for the closed-door interview. I was the last, watching their expressions as they exited. None of them made any special eye contact with me.

I walked into the office and handed the Saudi my file. He indicated absently for me to take a seat as he opened the folder.

"Please, have some *chi,*" he said, and I poured myself a tiny cup of tea while he read.

"Do you think you would care to assist us in a military capacity?" he asked bluntly.

"What sort of job would I do?"

"You have technical experience with weapons, engines, vehicles. We need all of these services now, because of the emergency in Yemen," he said.

"Yes, I am interested," I said. "What are the arrangements?"

"I will give you the necessary passes. You will get the rest of the information from air force Major Abdul Aziz. He makes the assignments. I only secure the agreement."

"Okay," I said. "What do I do now?"

The Saudi removed several pass forms from his desk drawer and stamped them, asking me for passport photos to be attached to them. "Take these to Sindi outside, in the large office. He will finish the authorization. Now you must sign this," he said, pushing another form toward me, printed in Arabic.

"What is it?" I asked.

"Confidential statement. Your participation involving the security of the kingdom is secret. It is to agree to say nothing."

I signed. It was now the first week of February.

---

25 February 1979: Major Aziz

The Arabs had given the term "hurry up and wait" new depth. All my attempts to get an appointment with Major Aziz had been delayed. I was turning wrenches in the meantime, getting staff cars repaired in spite of my Arabic mechanics. I had managed to get out of the hotel and into an apartment with two American aircraft mechanics, but I was still not on the housing list because, I suspected, of having gotten involved in the military project.

On 24 February, things started happening. The Soviet-backed People's Democratic Republic of Southern Yemen launched attacks against a series of North Yemen border towns. There were about a thousand Soviet "advisors," almost as many Cubans, and about a hundred East German internal security agents in the South Yemen army, armed with Russian helicopter gunships, tanks, artillery, and small arms.

The Saudis were not simply alarmed. They almost went crazy with agitation, imagining North Yemen collapsing in days and a stream of Russian tanks coming up the coastal roads into the kingdom.

My appointment with Major Aziz was the first thing the morning of the twenty-fifth while disaster reports rolled in from Yemen. His office was in the air force section of the airport. An enlisted aide went for tea for us as I was beckoned to enter by the major, who was on the phone at the moment. He wore a blue uniform shirt and trousers, and his hair was military short. A full ashtray beside him indicated he smoked heavily, and a lit cigarette was in the hand he was using to wave in time to his telephone argument, which he concluded with a curt Arabic expletive and placed the receiver back on the cradle in exasperation. I handed him my papers as the enlisted man brought the tea. The major read them quickly.

"Vietnam?" asked the major, a touch of British in his accent.

"Yes, sir," I answered. My tea was very hot.

"You know the American one-one-three APC?" he asked.

"I'd need the manuals," I said.

"You know hydraulics? Fifty-caliber Browning?"

"Yes, sir," I said again.

"Excellent," he said. "We have an outstation in the desert near Yemen, for military use only. There is a unit of armored personnel carriers there. Can you begin tomorrow?"

I nodded, eager to get away from ground equipment.

"You have signed the security agreement, of course," he said. "We accept your word on cooperation, but I must warn you. If you discuss this assignment, you will be paid and on your way home in one day."

Following my instructions, I reported to flight operations the next morning, watching with interest as I was placed on a flight manifest by pass number, not name. For identification purposes I was officially still on the ground equipment roster, and my mail and pay were maintained there.

I was too new to be missed in the complex of shops, work bays, and storage areas of ground equipment, and few English-speaking people there even knew me. With the twenty-four-hour-a-day schedule at the airport, and odd off-days, my three days a week at the outstation would attract no notice, especially since my time records would be maintained for me. This elliptical arrangement was due to the U.S. Neutrality Act, which stated that no U.S. citizen could participate in an armed action against a nation not at war with the United States. I even grew a short beard to blend in with the bearded Arabs.

There were no British or Americans on my flight, a C-130 carrying several squads of Saudi soldiers dressed in brown mottle desert camouflage, carrying Steyr AUG automatic rifles. I had on a standard dark-green maintenance jumpsuit.

We flew southeast for several hours, landing once at a rough desert strip to pick up a few dusty, drawn-looking Arabs in dirty robes, each one armed with a Beretta submachine gun, then headed south to our stop near the war.

The outstation had an improved tarmac landing strip, a group of metal sheds and buildings, and a collection of tents. As I walked off the C-130 toward the headquarters shack, the heat from the strip came right through the soles of my shoes. We were in the Rub Al Khali—the great "empty quarter"—one of the worst deserts in the world.

I noticed the fuel dump was dug in and sheltered by earthworks, and armored vehicles were scattered around us in a rough perimeter, some of them covered with camouflage nets. Beyond the hull-down tanks and tracks was only rugged desert spotted by dried-out clumps of grass. A rutted road trailed out into the dunes. I saw a sandstorm on the horizon, a dusky wall of brown clouds.

The roar of the C-130 we had just come off was familiar as it steered around to align itself with the hot wind for takeoff, and I grimaced as the sand it blew lashed me. At that moment Vietnam was all I could think of in an unwelcome, stomach-souring flashback. I was surprised by my own reaction.

A small, balding Arab wearing European-style civilian clothes met me as I approached the building. "You are our new volunteer, yes?" he asked in good English. "I will take you to the living quarters. Are you American?"

"Yeah," I said, then pointed toward the sandstorm. "Looks like bad weather coming."

"It is only the *shamal.*" He laughed. "We have no rain, just nd. It even falls out of the sky."

I was quartered in a hut with three young Arabic mechanics ho slept on pallets, while I had a cot. My responsibility was to e the heavy trucks and armored personnel carriers that oper- ed from the outstation had at least basic maintenance done to em. Our shop was a high-roofed open shed with a concrete or and center grease pit.

We changed engine oil, fuel and air filters, and did chassis brication. Most of the trucks were abused and dented, the umpers crushed and the head- and taillights broken out. My elder did more work than the rest of us put together.

I was quickly learning some functional Arabic, since my ew didn't speak English.

The boxy, U.S.-made M113 armored personnel carriers were adly neglected, their track-link pins worn and loose, road wheel ubs unserviced, and engines leaking oil. The deck-mounted .50- aliber heavy machine gun on every one that came in was filled ith sand. I found some with the bolt-to-barrel headspace wrong,) maybe it was a gift from Allah that they would not fire. An nproperly assembled .50 is a bomb when you trip the trigger.

I taught my mechanics to strip and clean the fifties with the ack crews watching so they would learn too. We built a good arts-cleaning vat rigged from an oil drum to make the job easier. oon some of the troops were bringing their rifles by to clean em, and I discovered they used whatever oil was handy—usu- lly one-liter cans of motor oil—as a lubricant. When I arranged) have a case of genuine weapons' oil flown down from Jeddah, I ecame a local hero.

American citizens were supposed to register with the U.S. mbassy, but I didn't because of my anticipation of the Mossad ontact. Sometimes there were U.S. air force personnel at Jeddah irport, mostly flight crews delivering equipment to the Saudis. I tayed well out of their way, assuming even casual conversations ith them to be forbidden. To my consternation, my outstation ssignment still kept me off the housing list. Getting a house or partment was necessary before my family could be flown in, but realized as long as I worked under a security cover I could not ave a family there.

I noticed on the back of my first paycheck a deduction code for the Palestinian Relief Fund. I was contributing to the PLO. Most of the clerks in the Saudi government offices were Palestinians. There was even a PLO office in Jeddah, and the day I had driven past it in the old VW sedan I had bought for transport in town, there had been a guard in the office doorway with an AK-47 assault rifle.

There wasn't much the PLO couldn't get in Saudi Arabia, the organization's chief benefactor.

Contact

One day at the airport, as I was buying a cold can of apple juice and a scrambled egg sandwich doused with Tabasco sauce from a busy little one-man shop, a man in flight mechanic's overalls whom I took to be American or possibly British looked at me as he walked up to buy a sandwich.

"Beastly hot, isn't it?" he asked me.

"Sure is," I answered. He was British.

"It would be a nice day to be diving," he said as he took his sandwich from the Arabic cook. We walked a distance from the shop.

"I hear the diving is good in the Red Sea," I said, noticing a dead fly cooked into my egg and flicking it out.

"You haven't done any yourself?" he asked.

"No."

"It's really rather grand. We have a club here, you know. Perhaps I could invite you to go with us one day."

"I have a bad ear," I said. "I can't go too deep."

He smiled. It was a slightly superior smile, from a man who looked to me to be very common and unassuming.

"Then you must have dinner with me as a consolation," he said. "I live in the number-five block at Sharbotly camp. Can you come over?"

"Anytime," I said.

"Name's Derek," he said. "Don't shake hands with me. We're old chums."

"I'm Frank Camper," I said.

"I *know* who you are, mate," he said.

* * *

Derek lived with his wife and child, a little girl not yet school age. That he had a family with him unsettled me. It seemed such a risk.

He briefed me on how and when to meet him. He also said not to write anything down, that we would use oral debriefing until codes were necessary.

My assignment to the outstation did not please him, because it called special attention to me. "A bad thing for a new man," he said. It would be better for me to keep "my head below the parapet" for a while until I knew more of the local language and customs.

"Ishmail, the head of the ground equipment section is a chap I'd like you to get to know," Derek told me. "He's PLO. Be nice to him."

I went back to my bed that night uneasy. I had to be very careful. This was deadly business.

Late February 1979: Gold to Amin

"Special Flights" was located at the far end of the Jeddah Airport for privacy. It consisted of a few service hangars and a cluster of helicopters, private jets, and diplomatic planes. Past that was only the desert, and the tank and armored-car park. I had to go to Special Flights from time to time to meet someone or arrange to have parts or documents air-delivered.

One day, as I parked my Saudia Toyota Landcruiser beside the Special Flights fence, on an errand to locate an aircraft mechanic who also worked outstations, I saw something unusual. One of the unmarked Saudia-owned small corporate jets, usually in service to ferry sheiks and their families to Europe, was parked on the ramp and a busy group of carpenters was carrying woodworking tools and lumber aboard.

I found the man I needed, quickly concluded our business, and asked him what was happening with the carpenters.

He told me they were building wooden pallets down the aisle of the jet's passenger section so a shipment of gold bars going to Idi Amin from the King of Saudi Arabia could be loaded.

Despite the negative way the Western press presented him,

Amin was a Moslem and depicted very differently in the Middle
East, where he was regarded as simply carrying out anti-Chris
tian wars. His government in Uganda was rapidly collapsing in
early March of 1979, and the gold was to help prevent that. It
wasn't the first shipment, the mechanic told me. I drove back to
ground equipment shaking my head. Derek would be interested
in this. *Pallets* of gold bars!

March 1979: The Yemen War

The first week of March saw ceasefires hastily arranged by
Jordan and Iraq fail to stop the fighting, and South Yemen
troops and armor plowed deeper into North Yemen. Saudi Ara
bia threw in all it could to back North Yemen, calling on the
United States (and anyone else who might help) for support.

By mid-March, about three thousand Soviet and Cuban
troops had been shipped as reinforcements to South Yemen from
Ethiopia, and they were performing combat missions in helicop
ters and armored vehicles.

U.S. M60 tanks, F-5 fighter aircraft, more M113 tracks, and
antitank and antiaircraft missiles were being pumped into North
Yemen from the United States via Saudi Arabia, along with civil
ian and military technicians. It was getting hard for me to avoid
them. At times our airstrip seemed like a forward operations base
in Vietnam, loaded with crates, new vehicles, and busy people
loading and unloading big C-130 cargo planes.

The M60 tanks had been painted desert tan before delivery
to us. The painters had worked fast, with overspray on the track
links and missed spots revealing the original olive-drab finish on
the hulls. The freshly painted tanks had no markings, of course

At the outstation, the groundcrews fueled the C-130's. From
time to time, we saw Saudi-piloted F5's flying over us on their
way to combat missions against the invading South Yemenis
Some of our cargo planes returning from supply drops in North
Yemen came back with the dents and slices of antiaircraft hits in
their aluminum skins.

A unit of Saudi Special Forces moved to the outstation, liv
ing in nomadic-style tents on the other side of the airstrip. I met
their commander a few days later, a young captain who spoke

English and had trained with the British SAS and who was very interested in American LRRP and special-operations missions in Vietnam. He invited me to visit his men for some weapons practice.

I watched his platoon shooting at empty oil drums with their Beretta M12 submachine guns and took a turn on one, shooting the randomly spaced drums from ten to one hundred meters. It was the first automatic weapon I had fired since 1969, and I was pleased to discover I hadn't lost my touch.

The Special Forces troopers were friendly, and I spent many evenings with them, drinking tea and discussing desert and jungle war with the captain, who was a student of warfare. The SF troopers seemed to effect many ways of the Bedouin, their historical romantic figures, in the way some Americans have tendencies to revere cowboy gunfighters.

There was a precedent of Americans being involved in security and defense in the kingdom, so my presence at the outstation wasn't that unusual. The Vinnell Corporation, mostly Americans, had a training contract with the Saudi National Guard and schooled them in armored-car and small-unit tactics. Raytheon, the California-based aerospace corporation, ran a sizable part of the kingdom's missile defense net, and of course Lockheed supported its C-130 aircraft in the Saudi Air Force.

Mission Alert

U.S. air recon intelligence spotted a South Yemeni armored column advancing on an important airstrip in North Yemen our C-130's were using. If the strip were lost, vital supplies to the town and garrison there would be cut off. The Saudis wanted to hit that column.

The column was an independent battle group and was well led, camouflaging by day, moving at night. The Saudi F5's did not have night-bombing capability, and the armored column had radar-aimed quad 23-millimeter Soviet antiaircraft guns and probably SA-7 Strela shoulder-fired heat-seeking missiles.

The unit of Saudi Special Forces at our outstation was there just for such opportunities as this armored column. The next C-130 in brought a shipment of new M72A2 LAW's, the American disposable, light antitank rocket. I was impressed. They were really going to do it.

The Saudis had only been trained on French and British light antitank weapons. I knew the LAW, and told the SF captain so. He immediately arranged for a training session.

I explained the assets and limitations of the weapon to the quiet, intense troopers, the captain interpreting for me. The sights were complicated (even without language barriers), and it took a lot of practice for a soldier to be accurate aiming the LAW.

The selected gunners, exactly half the unit including the captain, each fired a LAW to get the feel of the weapon. There weren't enough spare tubes for more than that. Their targets were two wrecked trucks well removed from the airstrip. Some of the hits were so close to us we had to duck fragments, while other shots flew off to explode in the desert much farther away than I thought LAW rockets would go. About a third of the shots hit near the trucks, only one hundred meters from where we fired.

I told the captain that to actually damage an armored column, his platoon would have to get within fifty meters of the targets and fire volleys. There were enough LAW's to give each gunner about four each. He agreed, and gave me my biggest surprise since I had been asked to go to the outstation. He wanted to know if I would accompany the ambush. I accepted on the spot.

Mission Briefing

The map showed the road the armored column was using, along with the contour lines of a narrow pass and what seemed like a bluff close enough to the road to give us the advantage of high ground. A C-130 could fly us to within three kilometers of this site, using a short, rough strip for our dusk insertion and dawn pickup. I took two canteens, a rucksack with four LAW tubes in it, and a few candy bars, wearing my dark-green jumpsuit. I was not offered a sidearm.

The captain held the last briefing before we boarded the cargo plane. He was almost a swaggering desert warrior chieftain as he told the men to shoot only for the soft-sided fuel trucks, mobile antiaircraft artillery, and armored cars. He said he would have flares launched to illuminate the column, which would be the signal to fire.

Ambush

I lay in the dark eating a candy bar, my LAW's laid out beside me. All along the bluff the platoon was spread out in pockets of two—one gunner, one assistant. My assistant was slightly off to my left, away from where the vicious rocket back-blast would go.

At a cool, dark 0400 hours we heard the engines. The lead vehicles had on their dim blackout driving lights. My stomach contracted. The rattle of tracked vehicles became prominent. I grabbed a LAW and extended it to fire, my assistant sticking his fingers in his ears.

On the road below us, big black shapes rumbled by, with the jerks and mindlessness so peculiar to tanks. This was it.

The flares burst in the sky over the road, brilliant white. I recognized a hump-turreted Soviet T-62 tank just fifty meters away, the first time I had ever seen one except in a photograph. There were also wheeled armored cars and some trucks with frozen, shocked men on them.

I took direct aim on the T-62, forgetting the captain's order not to go for a tank, and squeezed the rubber-covered firing lever of the LAW. Most of the other gunners fired at the same instant. A broadside of LAW rockets crashed into the vehicles, rocking us with concussion as we threw away the empty tubes and armed new ones.

The T-62 I had hit was stopped like a stunned behemoth, a ball of smoke rising off it. I aimed centermass and fired again. The rocket burst in a shower of sparks and yellow-white flame against the hull.

More LAW rockets were ripping off the bluff into the column, in overlapping explosions. The glaring light of the descending flares made the vehicles seem stark and unreal, like a bad dream.

My tank was trying to crawl off the road, crabbing sideways, one track locked and one slowly turning. I aimed my third LAW at it and fired, hitting it again and causing parts to fly from the engine deck. One of the flares went out, and as I armed my last LAW, I realized some of the vehicles were burning, making orange light in the shadows.

The damn T-62 wouldn't stop, so I launched my final shot into its turret, the blast obliterating my view for an instant. Then the second flare died and the road below us was in darkness, except for the flaming hulks of a few trucks. Night blindness overwhelmed me. The image of the flares was still on my retinas.

The machine guns of the stricken convoy suddenly started booming wickedly, big bolts of tracer flashing over the bluff. My assistant grabbed me, pulling me up and running. My last glance at the T-62 was fleeting, but it looked like it was still moving, smoking like a house on fire.

The actual armor-piercing capability of the 66-millimeter LAW warhead—as compared with its advertised numbers—is a strange thing to think about while running for your life across a desert with absolutely huge 12.7-millimeter Russian heavy machine gun tracer rounds zipping past at head level.

The terrain and probably fear of another ambush luckily kept the armored cars near the road. We had a hell of a time rounding up all of our people. A few of them had tried to run the entire distance to the pickup strip, and we found them gasping and prostrate. Every man was eventually accounted for, a small miracle.

At dawn, the C-130 came in steep and fast and we scrambled aboard. The aircraft was off the ground even before the ramp door was up. We learned several hours later that some F-5's caught the stalled, disorganized armored column still in the pass and bombed the absolute hell out of it.

Laughing and slapping each other on the back, we had a beach party back at the outstation, sans ocean. The Special Forces troopers sang, danced, ate, and waved bayonets for swords.

I felt as good as they did. Let Castro send us a bill.

When I returned to Jeddah the next day on the morning C-130, I found a message at flight operations for me to report to Major Aziz as soon as possible, so I went straight to his office. He waited until I was seated and furnished with the customary tea before he began talking. Then he told me I had made a mistake.

He said I did not understand my job, that my presence in a combat zone was an error, and I was fortunate to be safe.

When I tried to explain, he only smiled and asked me to listen, not talk. He said I was now reassigned to Jeddah Airport, and asked for my air force pass. Our one-sided conversation ended with him thanking me for my help and his apology that he had to follow regulations. I was unsure of what to say, but told him I preferred a combat support job to routine maintenance.

He seemed to think over my plea, then said he would pass the word on to the right people. The meeting was over.

Depressed, I went to my apartment, took a shower, and went to Derek's that evening, telling him what had happened.

"It's just as well," he said. "It was foolish to accept a mission shooting at Russian tanks."

I was exasperated now. I had expected Derek to appreciate the raid.

"Actually, I'm relieved you're not at the outstation any longer," Derek said. "Go back to ground equipment. Be a good chap and make friends with Ishmail, your leader there. After all, you're no good to us dead, are you?"

April 1979: Ground Equipment, Staff Car Section

The work in Staff Cars was incredibly boring. I went on a straight five-day week, struggling with an endless stream of crashed, abused, and worn-out cars, jeeps, and trucks and a small horde of Arabic mechanics who were mechanical innocents at best.

I took my duty in the best attitude I could, knowing I was lucky I had not been kicked out of the kingdom as fast as they could stamp an exit visa in my passport. Meanwhile, the Yemen war faded away. I was friendly toward Ishmail.

The housing office finally put me on the list, and in June I had my family in Jeddah. The days passed routinely.

727 Crash

Of course, life at the airport wasn't all without excitement. One hot day, with a *shamal* blasting in out of the eastern desert, our visibility down to a hundred meters or less, I had a small crew out on the edge of the first airstrip trying to fix a truck.

The strip was out of service, with a deep trench dug across it to the infield landing lights. Electrical cables were being sought by a crowd of pick-and-shovel Yemeni workmen.

All the displaced dirt was piled beside the trench like a barricade almost six feet high on the airstrip. The Yemenis were toiling away in the sandstorm, the truck my men were trying to fix just a rock-throw from them.

A motorized wheelbarrow, just a tiny cableless cart powered by a lawnmower engine, chugged back and forth across the strip moving dirt, driven by a turbaned Yemeni with a weathered face.

The sandstorms hit us out of the desert, changing the normal winds, which were off the Red Sea. This reversed the direction of takeoff for the planes taking off even in the storm, pointing them east instead of west.

Normally, we had all three strips open. In the tower, a controller got his wind direction and lefts and rights mixed, putting a Tunisian Air 727 on the trenched strip. Those of us on the strip, or working beside it, did not know this, and the pilot of the 727 could not see the trench in the sandstorm.

Bent over the engine of the disabled truck, we were wondering how to get a harmonic balancer back on the crankshaft with the keyway worn wobbly, while the heat and swirling, gritty sand suffocated us. I heard the 727 coming, but thought it was on the serviceable center strip.

Suddenly right on top of us was the overwhelming scream of a jet airliner thrown desperately into reverse thrust. I looked up and saw a wing tip flash over my head, then gaped at the sight of the side of a massive Boeing 727 ramming at high speed into the earthwork barricade beside the trench.

The nose of the plane lifted as it jumped the mound, the nosewheel tires bursting, but somehow the strut stayed intact. As the main landing gear under the wings hit the dirt, both sets sheared off, exploding an avalanche of dust over us.

One quad set of main gear wheels bounced back and upward, colliding with the starboard fuselage-mounted engine, smashing it. I was on the starboard side, watching landing gear, loose tires, pieces of engine cowl, and dirt scatter.

The 727 cleared the trench and came down on the strip hard, the fuselage bending just ahead of the wings as the nose slid and the tail went up before it all slammed flat, but the speed was such that the plane was still hurtling forward down the runway on its belly, a lone spinning and vibrating tire following it in high, surrealistic skips.

It all happened so fast that I had not moved from my truck. My heart was pounding as I saw the skewing, fishtailing aircraft slide out of sight in the sandstorm, I prayed it would not burn. Yemeni workmen were scattered on the runway, little men lying prone. The aircraft had gone right over them. Some moved, some did not, their ragged clothes fluttering in the wind. We dropped our tools and ran to them.

The driver of the motorized wheelbarrow was headless. The leading edge of one wing had hit him as sharply as an ax.

The 727 slid almost all the way down the strip to Special Flights, its nosegear strut ripping a long gash in the runway. The fiber glass belly of the aircraft disintegrated, but it did its job, and the 727 did not burn.

Injuries to the passengers and crew were minor, and after the disruption, we went back to work in the *shamal*. We never found the Yemeni's head. Someone said the desert dogs got it.

On 4 November 1979, we heard the news that the U.S. Embassy in Teheran had been overrun by Islamic "students" and the staff was held hostage. Derek was sympathetic but said, "Now you know how we feel. We live with terrorism."

20 November–4 December 1979: The Battle of Mecca

We were just off the plane, standing in line for Customs inspection in Jeddah Airport. I had taken my family to London and New York for a visit, and we had returned on a late flight the night of the twentieth of November.

The news of something unusual passed down our Customs line like a shock wave. *There was shooting in Mecca.*

Mecca is about forty miles east of Jeddah, and it is the center of the Moslem faith. It is the home of the Grand Mosque, with the Holy *Ka'aba* within, where thousands of Moslems make the *Haj* each year to reaffirm their faith. An armed disturbance in Mecca seemed about as likely as firefights in the Vatican.

Over the next few days, as I went back to the greasy struggle at ground equipment between irresistible Arab mechanics and immovable broken-down cars and trucks, I gradually discovered what was happening.

Since in the Moslem calendar the century was turning from the year 1399 to 1400, the sacrosanct Grand Mosque was to be the location of a religious ceremony to commemorate the event, with King Khaled himself scheduled to be present at dawn prayers to dedicate the new century. The sprawling courtyard of the Grand Mosque was packed with Moslems who had come to witness an occasion that would be more historic than they suspected. In the crowds of thousands of pilgrims was a force of about two hundred rebels armed with Soviet weapons laboriously smuggled up from Yemen, waiting for the king and his entourage.

Saudi intelligence, the CIA, British MI6, and even the Mossad knew nothing of what was planned. It was only chance that prevented the king's assassination. He was forced to stay in Riyadh that fateful morning due to poor health, and did not make the dawn prayers, sending his representatives instead.

The rebels saw the group of minor royalty and holy men take the stage facing the robed masses in the square. They burst out of the crowd, waving weapons, and captured the dignitaries. Other rebels, positioned near the doors and gates, overpowered the unwary police guards and tried to seal off the Mosque.

There was no king present to kill, but the leaders of the revolt carried on. It was too late to stop. One of them stepped to a microphone and told the throngs of confused worshippers that he was the last prophet to come to man from Allah, and denounced the decadence of the royal family. Many astounded worshippers went down on their knees in respect. Others tried to escape, climbing over walls or getting out through secondary doors not yet closed by the rebels.

What the rebel at the microphone had said was powerful. In the Moslem religion, the last prophet was yet to come. As in the Christian religion, the coming of the last prophet was the sign of the end.

After the news reached Jeddah, no immediate action was taken, because in the first few days Mecca was in terrible disorder and no one seemed to know what to do. The rebels had shot a few police and military outside the Mosque who were foolish enough to make targets of themselves, even though there was no official siege yet and no countermeasures being taken other than observation. An unknown number of worshippers were also shot by the rebels, mostly for being in the way.

At least two hundred rebels held the Grand Mosque. Afterward, the kingdom would claim five hundred, which may have been a face-saving statement to explain why the battle lasted for as long as it did.

In Riyadh, the king met with his advisors. The Grand Mosque, center of the faith, could not be damaged, but every effort to negotiate with the rebels was met with shouted religious slogans and rifle fire.

The Saudi Arabian National Guard, Special Forces, and police encircled the Grand Mosque and waited for orders, as military and civilian casualties increased. Rebel sharpshooters up in the tall, elegant minaret towers of the Grand Mosque (the highest structures in the city) were shooting down at opportune targets. The situation was not only critical militarily, it was a religious catastrophe and a major embarrassment to the king. When several days had passed and there were no results besides dead soldiers, a desperate king issued a special dispensation to allow the army to fire on the Grand Mosque with whatever force was required.

This would be the same as the Pope giving a battery of artillery the word for a fire mission on the Vatican—during Easter holidays.

The first attempts to take the Grand Mosque were frontal assaults by Saudi soldiers covered by machine-gun fire. Intensive return gunfire broke each attack, and soldiers trapped inside the Mosque were killed by the fanatical rebels. Special Forces units also tried to storm the walls, but they too were chopped up by crossfires in the alleyways surrounding the Mosque.

In desperation, heavy machine guns and then cannon fire were directed at rebel positions in the Mosque. The Saudis were shooting their most holy shrine to pieces.

After the end of the first week of fighting, we in Jeddah were ordered to lend support. I had been expecting it, since we were so close and had much of what the besiegers needed, such as fuel, water, trucks, and other supplies.

Military convoys formed each morning on Mecca Road before daylight. Mecca Road was the only route out of Jeddah to the Grand Mosque, and it was desert all the way. I went with a group of my mechanics on a wrecker to rescue breakdowns and ferry back empty trucks. The convoys to Mecca were like races, with the Arabic drivers flying over the pavement.

The first roadblocks were at Ring Road, which surrounds Mecca. Normally, these roadblocks served to prevent infidels (any non-Moslem) from entering the Holy City. I was obviously not a Moslem, but I did have a pass, so the soldiers let me through. I was finally stopped at the last roadblock, located where the road came down out of the mountains around Mecca (giving a good view of the entire city), but it was as far as I needed to go. The empty trucks out of the city were driven up the hill to us there.

Smoke and dust were visible rising from the Mosque, the central feature of the city, and the crackle of small arms and thud of cannon fire were audible. The sun was just beginning to rise. Men leaving Mecca told us there were still bodies in the street from a week ago. The snipers in the minarets were too accurate to risk rescue attempts to recover the dead.

Mullahs began calling the faithful to dawn prayer, their voices distant and singsong, and amazingly the level of gunfire decreased and the tracers stopped arching and bouncing over the city rooftops. As soon as prayers were over, the fire increased like the volume of a radio turned up.

I learned the Saudis had managed to blow up one of their own ammo dumps by crashing a jeep into it, and an armored car assault into the Grand Mosque itself had been a disaster. The main gates had been blown down by tank guns, and the armored car unit rolled into the Mosque firing. They could not maneuver inside the building and soon became jammed. The crews abandoned the cars, running for their lives out the gates.

Once I was back in Jeddah that evening, I heard the United States and Great Britian had offered assistance in retaking the Mosque, but Saudi Arabia had refused. The king was even announcing to the world press that the "incident" in Mecca was under control, which was obviously not true.

The army tried to choke the rebels out with huge piles of

urning tires, using the smoke to cover for rushes and rescues, ut that also failed, only covering the city with a heavy, acrid loom. Water was also used by the Saudis as a weapon after they ealized many of the rebels were hiding in the ancient corridors nd vaults under the Mosque. Firehoses were dragged to the valls and pushed into openings, flooding the foundation so thoroughly that enough sand was washed out to threaten to tilt the ninarets, so the water had to be stopped. The king did not want o *literally* destroy the Mosque in order to save it.

I was at the Jeddah Airport when the French commandos rrived. The king had finally asked for help. After a second false ublic announcement that the rebels were vanquished—and a teady continuation in the fighting—royal pride took a fall. The iege was then into its second week.

The French were also barred from Mecca. Instead, they vere asked to study the situation and submit a plan, working rom a war room in Jeddah. It didn't take long to devise a solution. They advised the Saudis to get portable jackhammers onto he roofs of whatever buildings they could inside the Mosque, nd under cover of heavy machine-gun fire, cut assault holes hrough to the rooms underneath. When the holes were ready, eavily armed shock troopers would wait until prayer time something both sides had been honoring, since religion was an ssue), shoot the rooms and halls full of tear gas, and assault. It vas dirty pool, French style, and it worked.

The Saudi soldiers dropped through the holes and swept hrough the buildings, firing and throwing grenades, driving the urprised rebels down into the foundation maze of passages. The ebels had effectively used the subterranean complex as communication trenches and bunkers, allowing them to disappear down a hole and pop up elsewhere. Jars of nomadic "survival rations," ig clay pots of dates mixed with water, were found stockpiled in he halls. The rebels even had a hospital and command post in he vast basement.

It took stubborn, brutal, room-to-room fighting to defeat the ebels. In the end, an exhausted rebel military leader and a badly vounded religious leader surrendered their remaining force of bout seventy men and a number of women and children. Some f the rebels had taken their families in with them to load weapns and care for the wounded. The revolt—and much of the enerable Grand Mosque itself—was shattered.

Interrogation of the prisoners revealed that they were Islamic fundamentalists sympathetic to Iran. None of the rebels was executed in Jeddah, which was too open to the Western press. The Saudis were sensitive to criticism of beheadings. Instead the prisoners were doled out to prestigious mosques in other parts of the kingdom for public beheading.

The rebel religious leader (his wounded arm amputated) was killed in Mecca outside the Mosque he had failed to take, but his legend was not lost on the people. Those who believed he was the last prophet, as he'd claimed, said it was not an arm the king's doctors had cut off. It was an angel's wing.

In a show of Islamic charity, the king declared the wives and children of the executed rebels innocent of the crimes of their men. They were paid cash allotments and released. Meanwhile, work crews went into the Mosque to patch and repair its centuries-old minarets, walls, and chambers.

Life went back to normal. I made a report to Derek, who was somewhat amused by the entire affair.

25 April 1980: Desert One

The BBC was the first to broadcast the news, even before the U.S. news services, that the U.S. Delta Force raid to rescue the American hostages in Teheran had failed disastrously in the Iranian desert. I had to take some condescending remarks from Derek on this. He seemed to like having an American to chastise.

30 April 1980: The SAS

I arrived in Heathrow Airport with my family on the first day of a European vacation, just in time to hear on the radio that a group of "terrorists" had taken over the Iranian Embassy in Kensington. When we arrived, our hotel turned out to be almost directly behind the besieged embassy.

The "terrorists" were anti-Khomeni, pro-U.S. Iranians, who took the embassy in protest of the bloody actions of the Islamic revolution in Iran. The Khomeni gang in Iran was holding the American Embassy staff in terror. Now a desperate group of

anians opposing Khomeni was striking back with the same tac-
cs, but in London.

Under British law, they were considered terrorists.

I stayed in London for the week of the siege, watching it
nfold on my doorstep. The British handled the affair smoothly,
ockading the streets, keeping order, not allowing a media cir-
us. Finally, under the pressure, one of the protesters in the be-
eged embassy cracked and shot an embassy official when
homeni and the Iranian Revolutionary Council did not meet
ne protesters' demands of releasing religious and political prison-
s in Iran.

On 5 May 1980, the SAS stormed the embassy and quickly
illed the desperate anti-Khomeni Iranians, who were poorly
rmed and hoping the Western world would rally to them.

The *why* of the incident was quickly forgotten in the *how* of
ne SAS assault, which was very professional. I hated the entire
ffair.

Our vacation took us out the next day to Germany and then
rreece. On 12 May we were back in Jeddah, and I had made up
ny mind it was time to leave Saudi Arabia.

I had developed opinions over the year and a half I had been
n the Middle East. Of course, I had come to Saudi Arabia with
ome preconceptions of the "Mideast Conflict," being basically
ympathetic to Israel. As with almost any set of preconceptions,
owever, I was wrong. Looking at a problem up close is always
ifferent from having the luxury of the clean, distant view.

I developed the opinion that the Arabs and Israelis had spun
heir religious wars out of control long ago—and I am measuring
n the hundreds of years—for any outsiders to enter it and make
ense of the situation. I saw issues I thought both sides were
vrong about, but I had the dispassionate eye of a visitor.

My final opinion was that whoever was the strongest should
ontrol Palestine/Israel. So far, that looked like the Israelis.

Sometimes I talked politics with Derek, and I found him
nore moderate than I would have expected, but I was too neutral
o suit him. We never really got along. As a result, I never drew a
hekel of pay. Derek insisted (perhaps rightly) that so far I had
roduced nothing worthy of an expense on Israel's behalf.

5 June 1980: Idi Amin

I stood in the sparse shade of a tree on Corniche Road across from the king's palace, watching the speeding convoy of motorcyclists and limousines brake to turn onto a side street. Amin was in the largest limo, a black stretch-chassis Cadillac, and I studied his jowly profile and gaudy uniform as the car slowed. The big murderous dictator had escaped Uganda before it fell.

Amin and his entourage of wives, children, and servants were now living in Jeddah after traveling through other countries that would not grant him residence, the most notable being Libya. The Amin clan was fortified in a hotel near the Jeddah Palace, financed even now by Saudi gold.

21 June 1980: The PLO

Ishmail, the chief foreman of ground equipment at the airport, was a PLO recruitment officer. As I was busy getting my pay, paperwork, and tickets ready to leave, he invited me to his house. It was exactly what I had been working toward. My cultivation of Ishmail—a tall, friendly man—had been slow but steady. Perhaps he could sense I had no antagonism for his people.

Ironically, the very goal Derek had set me toward I was achieving, but I no longer wanted to be part of the game. The option to pull out of a job I didn't like was the primary reason wanted to work on my own.

"You're quitting?" Derek asked when I told him.

"I've been here long enough," I said.

"You Americans! You think you can stroll in and out at whim! We can't do that! We're fighting for our lives!"

"You told me my information was worthless," I said.

"Yes, *now!*" Derek said. "But for God's sake, man, give it time!"

"This isn't the right place for me," I said. I didn't want to say I didn't care. That wasn't true. Actually, I cared too much. One day I was liable to take sides.

"What are you going to do now?" he asked.

"Central America, I guess. It's closer to home."

Derek only shook his head. "All right. I'm sorry to lose you. could have sent you to Israel for training."

I shook his hand as I left. Now I only had one more turndown to do if Ishmail made me the same offer.

During my visit with Ishmail, he expressed regret I was leaving and tactfully asked me if I would consider staying and working with his people, the Palestine Liberation Organization. I tactfully declined, explaining I was on my way home and had other plans, but he insisted. He said he could arrange for me to work out of London doing organizational work, not combat.

"We get help from the United States," he said. "Our rifle grenades were made there. If the United States didn't want us to buy them, we couldn't."

"But the tactics you use," I protested. "A PLO team captured a school in Israel and held the children hostage. A lot of those kids got killed." I was talking about the Ma'alot incident in 1974.

"We are fighting to get back our whole country," he said. "It precious to us. Their children were precious to them. They have to share our pain."

He spent an hour showing me photographs and telling me of Israeli injustices in Palestine, asking me to reconsider, upping the ante to his supreme inducement. He said I could meet and be hired directly by Yassar Arafat.

When I graciously but firmly turned him down, leaving honor in my refusal, he took it well. I left his home with some PLO literature and Ishmail's wishes for my safe return to the United States.

On 22 June my family and I were on connecting flights from Jeddah, back to London and then New York.

CHAPTER SIX
Merc School

As our passports were stamped and my family's luggag
waved through Customs, I had made up my mind what I wante
to do next. I was now thirty-four, and ready to commit all th
way to my chosen profession—paramilitary and covert opera
tions as a freelancer.

Staying in the Mideast would have required taking sides.
wanted to work with more independence than that.

In Mexico, not long after settling into Birmingham, Ala
bama, I decided on my tactics while taking a vacation to th
mystic ruins of the pyramids of the sun and moon near Mexic
City, and the eerie, ancient Mayan city of Palenque near Guate
mala, far into the jungle. Those were good places to think.

In 1980 I knew of no private schools of instruction in th
United States for people who wanted to work overseas in a mili
tary capacity—a long way to say mercenaries. There was Cobra
in Powder Springs, Georgia, run by the experienced and compe
tent Mitch WerBell, but that was really a bodyguard/executive
security course. Those who needed to learn how to deal wit
foreign troops and weapons, with little or no support and unreli
able supply, had nowhere to go.

My idea had really begun in 1969, while I was chasing thos
miserable, half-frozen Ranger students up and down the nort
Georgia mountains. I could create *my own* training school. Ther
was a need for it, but I didn't want to copy what I felt were rigi
military mistakes I had seen at Ranger School.

Ranger students were great at absorbing punishment, but i

my opinion the course had been slack on developing personal initiative, an absolute must in combat. I didn't want to create a scaled-down Ranger School.

The one military school that had impressed me was the 5th Group Recondo (Reconnaissance-Commando) School that operated in Nha Trang from 1967 to 1970. I had become an LRRP before the school was in operation, but I had taken the short course the Special Forces was exporting to LRRP units in 1966. By 1967 several of our platoon had gone on to the formalized course.

I still had an original Recondo school course schedule, consisting of two weeks of patrolling and enemy weapons, followed by a real one-week combat patrol. I figured two weeks, handled right, could teach a lot, especially if it ran twenty-four hours a day. I began to plan a Recondo-type course for a mixture of ex-military and untrained civilians, and I knew just what to call it. Let the army have its Ranger School.

Now there was the Mercenary School.

I conceived the course as a combination of basic field combat and survival on the commando team level, with much emphasis on tactics, international weapons, and surprises to disrupt straight-line, book-solution thinking. The entire two weeks would be spent in the field, regardless of weather, and issue chow would be mostly Third World-type rations—raw and unprepared beans, rice, and vegetables. I had seen too many soldiers complain bitterly about canned rations, but Merc School students would know better. They would cook over slow-to-build and easy-to-spot campfires, and canned food would seem like a gift from God to them.

My students would have to endure direct live fire under conditions designed to make them think they were in danger. Most hand-to-hand combat would be full contact, for realism. The booby traps would also be real, with just enough explosive in them to stun. Students would carry police-model spray cans of CS tear gas to use on each other, and team leaders would have CS grenades and powerful but nonlethal concussion grenades to use in ambushes.

To show the students they were not invisible, invincible, or John Wayne, cadre snipers would use scope-sighted .22-caliber pellet rifles to keep patrols honest.

Getting captured on Escape and Evasion would be serious,

bringing genuine deprivation and torture, the best incentive not to get caught.

To graduate, a student would have to pass every phase of the course, especially the critical compass-run overnight patrols, the improvised rappeling, and the weapons-knowledge tests.

Over the next six years, only two out of every ten students who started the course would graduate.

The Bunker

I placed ads in the paramilitary magazines and set out to locate enough Soviet, American, and European military weapons to outfit a light platoon, making it necessary for me to obtain federal firearms licenses for both semiautomatic and full automatic weapons as well as sound suppressors. For safety, new students on patrol would be armed with replica weapons that matched the actual piece in size and weight but would not fire. All shooting would be done under controlled conditions.

I needed a headquarters and storage place for the school's weapons and equipment, so in January of 1981 I opened The Bunker, near Birmingham, in the little town of Dolomite. It was a squat, flat-roofed, thick-walled building with slit windows, located inside a barbed-wire-topped, chainlink-fenced yard. I painted the building in dark patterns of black, green, and brown to look the part.

The Merc School had a home.

The Crystal River Incident

Society wasn't ready for Merc School. The first class was briefly arrested in March of 1981 by a local sheriff as we emerged from the Florida swamps after a week of training. He thought we were foreign commandos sent to attack a nuclear power plant in his county.

The area I chose for the first class was a place I knew well, Crystal River, near the small towns of Inverness and Wildwood, almost on the gulf. It was the exact area George Larkins and I had E&E'd past a small army of searchers in January of 1968.

I allowed the class to be arrested in order to keep us legal. Fading back into the jungle and leaving the local-yokel sheriff behind would have been easy.

The arrest made international headlines because initially the press also thought we were going after the nuke plant accepting the sheriffs' first statements. It took a day to straighten out the misunderstanding, and, and with embarrassment for everybody, we were released.

One of the men in the first class was Robert Lisenby, who had combat experience in Vietnam. He had written to me and asked to help instruct, and I had accepted. He was going to turn into an entire operation by himself just a month later, in the Cuban section of Miami named Little Havana.

The Mercenary Association

At the end of the second class held in northeastern Alabama in the rugged Little River Canyon, in June 1981, the Alabama Board of Education was waiting for me back in Birmingham. Their man was Jim Reid, an ex-Special Forces officer and certified hero of special operations in Southeast Asia (in addition to other feats, he had knocked out a Russian-made PT-76 tank single-handed). Reid was understanding, but insisted that I either apply for a state private-school license or close down.

In the ordeal with the Board of Education, Reid became entangled in the licensing fight *on my side*. In the end, the license was denied by Reid's boss.

Outlawed by the state of Alabama, I formed the Mercenary Association, making the students members and the school a function of the association. This solved the legal problem. I also arranged for a regular training site in a remote forest thirty miles west of Birmingham near the Warrior River.

By the end of our first year, we'd accomplished four classes and the kinks had been worked out of the program. We even had our own unit patch I had designed and a motto, "Live to Spend It," originated by ex-marine and Vietnam veteran Sandy Debski. The insignia was a green-and-black V-shaped combat patch, with the word "Recondo" at the top in an arch, and a jagged lightning bolt striking downward off it. The graduate students called it the Black Lightning patch and wore it with pride.

My son Barret had taken the June class—Operation Bama Canyon—and graduated at age fifteen, making me very proud of him.

A Primitive Course

With the exception of modern firearms, I had designed Merc School to be a savage, regressive course, appealing to and developing the natural warrior in those who had it.

Humankind had existed in various forms for a few million years, probably resembling what we would now recognize as people in only the last 300,000 years. As close as a thousand years ago we were still fighting with spears and clubs, but in the past four hundred years, technology had accelerated past us, with no time for taming the human animal. To me, that was exploitable.

I wanted to reach into my students and draw the savage warrior to the surface, then put modern weapons in the hands of the union of instinct and intellect. My goal was to make fierce *and* smart soldiers, and not apologize for it.

I was constantly looking for ways to improve the course, to eliminate slack, to increase realism, and as I found them, the changes were put into effect on the spot.

Basically, the first week was all combat and the second week escape and evasion. Combat week began with seventy-two hours of running through live automatic-weapons fire, saturation at unexpected times with choking CS gas, surprise attacks with concussion grenades, all-night chases through the woods without boots, and savage man-to-man fights with lightly padded clubs.

Most of the quitters did it in that time.

Mixed into those first days and on through the rest of the week was weapons practice, constant day-and-night patrolling, and hand-to-hand combat, all on a dawn-to-dawn schedule. To eat or sleep, the students had to make their own time.

For spice, the training teams battled each other in kickfights on slack rope bridges high over shallow streams, carried each other on exhausting stretcher races, and often a lone student was stripped and sent running for his life with the entire class on his heels. Once he was caught, he was gassed and beaten and then dragged back for a "prisoner handling" class.

Escape and Evasion would begin by surprise, the students expecting it any time other than when it began. They scattered to the field without all of their clothing, equipment, or food to avoid being shot or captured in the first few moments of shock.

Cross country runs were always made with packs and weapons, and the students sang spirited Merc School cadence songs. Here's a sample:

Castro, Castro, did you know?
Those men in the jungle are Recondo!
Prowl through the jungle night and day!
Kill everything that gets in our way!
Hey Recondo! Hey! Hey! Recondo!

Recondo, Recondo, where you been?
Over the border and I'm going again!
What you gonna do when you get back?
Gonna pack my gear for the next contract!
Hey Recondo! Hey! Hey! Recondo!

Hunted and confused, the students didn't know if E&E would last one day or seven, so every dawn and dusk they had to creep close enough to base camp to see if the recall flag was up, bringing them in range of the pellet-rifle snipers, ambushes, and search teams. A .22 pellet can hit you hard at twenty meters. A bruise in a vital spot could fail you.

If captured, a student was stripped, tied to a tree, and randomly gassed and beaten. If he could manage an escape, he would not fail the course, but escaping usually meant spending the remaining days and nights on the run, nude, with no food.

When the recall flag did go up, the students were taken to rock-face rappel, then back to The Bunker for weapons and equipment cleaning, testing, and follow-up classes on booby traps, map and compass, and first aid.

As I had planned, the Merc School carried on in all kinds of weather, the courses beginning in March and continuing through November each year. Sessions began to get names like Operation Poncho, Heatwave, and Frozen Rifle.

Through snowstorms, ice, tornadoes, floods, and sizzling heat, the weather never stopped the school, not once.

The Death Merchants

By the end of 1981, something had evolved outside the program. It was an unofficial, all-volunteer, shadowy group of Merc Association alumni who stalked new students during training and did savage things to the strays they caught. They called themselves Death Merchants, a melodramatic name in daytime but one to be taken very seriously in the dead of night in the field.

The Death Merchants kept their identities secret from the new students, so no one would ever know who they were. They obeyed no rule, did not work with the schedule, and struck when they wished. It added another dimension to the training, making students and instructors alike unsafe.

Medic!

Injuries at Merc School were common. The medic was always busy with broken fingers, arms, legs, noses, and dislocations, freely applying splints and slings. Gashed flesh, ripped by knives or bayonets or burst open by a blow from a club or rifle butt, was sutured in the field. Field surgery was common to extract projectiles from the dreaded pellet rifle or fragments from booby traps.

Evacuation from the field had to be a matter of life or death, and there was never a death, thanks to well-enforced safety rules with firearms. Few men, however, made it to graduation unscarred.

Weapons

In a normal combat course, we taught from a variety of U.S. AR-15 and M16's, CAR-15's, .30-caliber M1 carbines, and the .45 M1911A1 pistol. Soviet weaponry included the AKM

AK-47, SKS carbine, Tokorev pistol, and RPG-7 rocket grenade launcher.

There was also training with the FN-LAR, HK-G3, Browning Hi-Power pistol, bolt action rifles, pump shotguns, and submachine guns such as the Uzi, Ingram, HK-MP5, and British Sterling. From time to time we'd bring in Thompsons, MP-40's, M3 "Grease Guns," or exotics like factory-silenced Sterling-Patchetts.

We used sound suppressors on the M16's, many of the SMG's, and on some pistols. The tiny Beretta Jetfire and full-size Colt Woodsman being well suited to the task.

Many firearm and ammunition myths were refuted, such as that .45's "knock" people down (they don't) or that Russian ammo would fire in U.S. weapons but not vice versa (it won't). There was every condition in the field to make the best firearm fail, from the expected extremes of weather and dirt to the abuses and imaginative mishandling by the students. Some of the conclusions I reached in observing our weapons performance were surprises, and some were not.

The veteran Browning Hi-Power pistol was still the overall best, in my opinion, of the .45 Colts, now 9-millimeter Berettas, and 7.62-millimeter Tokorevs.

The Kalashnikov AK-47's and AKM's were indeed the most reliable assault rifles, if not the most handy, and the civilian Ruger Mini-14 in .223 proved the operational equal of many far more expensive combat rifles of that caliber.

Uzis were rugged and reliable but could still jam, and we used both the original issue full-auto version and the civilian models.

The British Sterling SMG was the most accurate of the open bolts, and the closed HKMP5 was a great urban gun but not a good field weapon, being somewhat dirt sensitive.

Sterling's Patchett, the silenced version of the standard Sterling, was marginally quieter than the super-trick suppressed MP5SD.

No pump or gas-operated shotguns—from basic 870's to space age SPAS dual-actions—ever survived a complete school; once they got dirty they could not be cleaned.

Ingram M10 .45 or 9-millimeters were primo room-clearing or raid tools, but the little brother M11 in .380 ACP was a specialty piece seeming to fit no purpose but assassination or ultra-close-range commando duty, where the subsonic quiet of the .380 bullets coming out of its suppressor at about twenty per second could be used to advantage.

The M11 was my personal favorite. It was not much larger than a .45 automatic, but with that buzz-saw rate of fire it took a lot of skill to handle it properly. It was a small, brutal weapon, easily concealed under a jacket in its special shoulder holster, a crossbody harness balanced out on the opposite side with two spare thirty-two-round magazines.

I used the M11 as my carry weapon many times in place of a pistol, when it was out of its "operational kit"—a Kevlae reinforced zipcase that held suppressor, extra magazines, accessories, and doubled as a bulletproof vest if desired. All packed and zippered, the "hit kit" looked like a small black overnight bag.

The Mercenary Association, International

Most of the students coming to join and train with the association were from the United States, but an increasing number in each course were foreign. Most were from military or police units, like French Commandos or ex-Legion troops, French Army, Dutch Commandos, the German, Canadian, British, and Spanish armies, Mexican, Japanese, Brazilian, and Panamanian police and counterterror units, and reservists from Ireland, Hong Kong, the Philippines, and the Sudan. By 1985 I could count graduates in twenty different countries and attendance by men from no less than another ten.

Of course, I had many current U.S. military and police in attendance at all times, proving the association filled a need.

In addition to the graduates with combat as their military professions, many association members were turning up in foreign combat zones as early as the end of our first year. One or more two-week sessions in the Alabama woods improved their odds on survival.

Official Notice

It did not take a number of domestic and foreign government agencies long to realize a side effect of the Mercenary Association was as an intelligence-gathering asset.

Domestic law enforcement and intelligence agencies wanted to know if I was training criminals or members of radical or violent groups. Foreign agencies wanted to know who was coming to their respective countries and, sometimes, from *other* countries. For that matter, so did U.S. intelligence.

Many of these intelligence agencies also realized the association was a good place from which to recruit, and each class increased the pool of qualified graduates.

I left the hiring as a matter between the graduate and the "employer," but I made the decisions on what governments or agencies to cooperate with. I respected the privacy of our membership and the identity of our graduates, but I would not protect criminals or terrorists.

Through its members, the Mercenary Association was deeply involved in coups, wars, and rescues. It gave the association a flavor no mere training school could have had.

Special Mention

Hard training produces character, and the ordeal of graduating a Merc School qualification course brought out the best in many a member.

A few worth mentioning were people like El Toro, a Mexican karate expert who could (and frequently did) wipe out a whole team of gringos . . . the Swamp Turkey, who originally went in only to take pictures and reverted to a barefoot, mud-covered, slinking, hit-and-run trooper . . . Chuck Pekor, a sky-diving, unarmed combat specialist who taught actor Robert Duvall how to knife fight at Merc School with a vicious Tanto blade . . . Charlie Morgan, our armorer, an absolute master of automatic weapons and proud wearer of a captured Soviet hammer-and-sickle belt buckle . . . Slug, the heavyweight teenager with a thousand-meter stare who took two years to graduate but won a rare special Mercenary Association citation for bravery in a real shoot-me, shoot-you standoff . . . Crazy Gerald, the tall, handsome black who parachuted and shot Ingrams perfectly, but was on the eccentric side . . . Everett, who kept going for days with a completely separated shoulder and would not quit . . . and Captain Zack, who created a new definition of devious.

Hundreds of men and a few women came through Merc School from 1981 to 1986. I wish I could give them all the credit they deserve. There just isn't room.

Vietnam, Alabama

Some Vietnam combat veterans suffered during our training, having flashbacks or uncontrollable fits of sorrow. I sat, well removed from the class, with a sobbing veteran more than once. I understood their problem very well, having done my time in the Ia Drang, the Pleiku Plateau, Kontum, and Cambodia, on LRRP recons.

In my most private thoughts, I wondered how much of Vietnam I had invested in Merc School. Sometimes, in a frightening way, it seemed to me I was reaching out to ghosts, trying to compensate for the loss of friends who had made mistakes in combat and died for the sin. I didn't know if I could make up for the ghosts with the earnest, live students I was teaching, but I tried, I really tried.

Graduation

Two weeks after arrival, a small group from the original class would gather in the private meeting room of a Birmingham restaurant, faces and hands clean but showing fresh welts and scars, camouflaged fatigues washed, and left shoulders adorned with hastily pinned or sewn-on Recondo patches. They would eat, drink, and laugh.

Each man would be given his diploma of graduation with honor, citing "Demonstration of personal ability, stamina, and courage during combat mercenary training under hazardous and adverse conditions."

Then the association toast, the old Legion standard, would be given:

"Viva la mort!"

"Viva la guerre!"

"Viva la sacre mercenaire!"

And with a shout, it would all be over.

CHAPTER SEVEN
Little Havana

As I tumbled out of the car door, I saw the police with their M16's, aiming at me. My Ingram submachine gun was still under the seat.

Moving fast, the SWAT teams rushed at us from behind parked cars. Lisenby was on the other side of our Chevrolet, raising his hands.

The bomb I had been carrying on my lap was wired to be electronically detonated. I realized one of the police radio transmissions could easily blow it, and it was powerful enough to destroy the car and all of us near it.

---

11 April 1981: Dolomite, Alabama

The phone rang about 10:00 P.M., Saturday night, and immediately I recognized Robert Lisenby's voice.

"Hey, I'm in Miami," he said. "Do you want some work?"

"What's going on?" I asked.

"Just fly on down. How quick can you get here?"

"I don't know," I said. "What's the deal?"

"We've got a paying job. You don't mind working against Cubans, do you?"

"No," I said, deciding quickly what to say. "Let me call the airlines and find out what flights are available. Give me your number; I'll call you back."

Lisenby read off the area code and phone number of a Holiday Inn in Miami. I next called the Birmingham airport and learned I could catch a flight to Miami within the hour. I called

Lisenby back and gave him the flight number and arrival time. He said he would be waiting for me at the gate.

Getting my clothes stuffed inside my nylon travel bag took a few minutes, and then I dialed the telephone number of the Birmingham office of the FBI. The night-duty officer answered, and I asked him to locate an agent I had talked with about Lisenby. The duty officer tried but told me there was no answer at the man's home. I had little time, and left the message for the agent to call me back as soon as possible.

I waited for the return call as long as I could. If I was late, it might make Lisenby suspicious, so I left for the airport. As I was going through the security station before entering the boarding gate, I saw a local policeman on duty there and had an idea.

I approached the policeman, and was mildly surprised to discover his name was one I wouldn't forget quickly—John Kennedy, the same as the assassinated President. I gave Officer Kennedy a note, explaining who I was and where I was going, with the telephone number of the Miami area Holiday Inn on it. I asked him to relay it to the FBI, then have my plane radioed so I could be informed if the message had been received and understood. Kennedy didn't know me but agreed to do what I asked.

In flight to Miami, I leaned back in my seat and thought about Lisenby. After our arrest near the nuclear power plant just a month ago, he had confessed he had contacted me for the purpose of recruitment into his political organization, a private group that called themselves the American Rifle and Pistol Association (ARPA). They were headed by a medical doctor with political aspirations, and their beliefs seemed to be extremely right wing.

I had recently been given a tour of the doctor's extensive country estate, a long recruitment talk, and a thorough questioning about my own racial and political feelings. I gave them neutral answers.

It turned out that the doctor wanted me to join his organization so I could be his training officer. When they finally asked me if I was interested, I told them I did not join groups, but said I would keep it under consideration.

I did not personally like their racial and political ideas, and I didn't like the recruitment attempt they had made to snare me, which included Lisenby coming to Merc School.

After the tour of the doctor's property, I contacted the FBI and seriously discussed Lisenby and his ARPA group. With no specific operation planned, however, I had no employment agreement, so the matter had been left alone.

Lisenby's call had come so unexpectedly and at such a late hour, there was no chance for coordination between the FBI and myself.

The flight attendant walked down the aisle to my seat and bent down so she could speak to me and not be overheard by the other passengers. "I have a message from the pilot," she said. "Your arrangements have been made." I nodded and thanked her, and she walked away.

With her message as a reinforcement, I was able to relax a bit more, thinking I was not operating alone.

Grinning, Lisenby met me just as I was coming off the plane. I gave him a smile and handshake I did not mean, but made it look good.

It was after midnight as we walked out to the airport parking lot, to his bright-red Chevrolet Citation rental car.

Miami was still awake even this late, the streets crowded with traffic, the sidewalks teeming with the after-dark crowd. Most of them were black or Spanish, dressed in colorful clothes, drinking, walking, singing, blocking the walkways in groups or sitting on parked cars.

It was a dangerous city, America's Casablanca, and the sale of cocaine in quantities large and small, and the frequent shedding of blood by those involved, was among its prime activities.

Cocaine was the reason Lisenby was there.

He described his assignment to me in our room in the Holiday Inn.

"I've got to take out a drug dealer down here," he said. "The guy paying the bill for this is another dealer. They have a kind of war going on between each other. This guy I'm going to hit has done some bad things and made his friends mad. They have to make an example out of him."

"Is he Cuban?" I asked.

"Yeah. All of them are. Ain't it funny, them using us gringo mercenaries? Last night I bombed a pleasure boat. I totaled it too. Man, I was scared. You should have been here, I sure could have used you. The boat was the first part of this job. My partner was supposed to show up but he didn't. I need a backup man, that's why I called you."

"What happened with the boat?" I asked.

"I used two charges," Lisenby said. "The first one was a small charge, to draw the owner out to the boat. The second was a big one, a high-explosive incendiary. They were timed a couple of minutes apart. You should have seen that thing go off! I used a gallon of thickened paint remover with a charge tied to it. Just like napalm! But the guy was smart, he stayed in his house. I went back this morning and checked it out. The boat is a total loss, it's gutted from end to end."

Lisenby was talking fast, his eyes almost gleaming. He was excited with his assignment, and he wanted me to be as well.

"What have we got to work with?" I asked.

Lisenby pointed to a large cardboard box in the corner. I knelt over it and looked at aluminum-foil packets of explosive-grade ammonium nitrate, bottles of mixer, electrical blasting caps, military flares, concussion bombs, and a .45-caliber Ingram M10 submachine gun with a sound suppressor and extra magazines of ammunition.

There was a lot of potential death in that box. I examined the packets of ammonium, reading over the directions.

"That ought to do it, right?" Lisenby asked.

12 April: Miami Recon

We rose early that Sunday morning and went down to the restaurant for breakfast. Lisenby told me the dealer he was being paid to hit had a place of business in the section of Miami called "Little Havana" because it was almost completely Cuban. Even the advertising signs were in Spanish, not only on the storefronts but on the billboards as well.

We had agreed that I would be paid half of the $5,000 fee he was charging his drug dealer in exchange for my assistance. I was surprised Lisenby simply assumed I would be willing to go along with him, and considered this was one way he could test my willingness to commit crimes—and possibly blackmail me into complying with his group.

After we ate, he drove us to the target. It was a barber shop at an intersection in Little Havana. Lisenby explained that the shop was a front for drug deals.

The barber shop itself was long and narrow, with a glass front. A single concrete-block wall separated it from the next shop in the row, which sold statues of the Virgin Mary, crucifixes, reproductions of the painting of the Last Supper, and many other icons important to the Catholic religion. Directly across the street was a small café, with stools and chairs outdoors so the patrons could enjoy the Miami sun while they had coffee or a traditional Cuban meal.

"Our man will be in the barber shop," Lisenby said as we parked near the intersection. I watched the shop. Since it was Sunday, it was closed. It was a good day to do the reconnaissance.

"How do we get him?" I asked.

"Well, I've been thinking about that," Lisenby said. "I have two ideas that might work. One, we wait for him to come out and nail him with the Ingram, or maybe we follow him home in the traffic and do it on the road. You can drive, right?"

The question wasn't if I could simply drive a car. He was asking if I could handle trick or stunt driving, for which I had won so many trophies with my Ghia.

"Sure," I said.

"Well, no problem. You drive, get us right up on the left of his car, kind of blindside him, and I'll put a whole magazine from the Ingram right in the back of his head.

"The second way is to get him with a bomb. I really like that idea better, because it's less risk to us. I've got the stuff to make a hell of a charge. We can take off the whole front of his building," Lisenby said.

"But what about the people out on the street?" I asked.

"It's their fault for being there," he said.

We spent that Sunday morning driving around Little Havana, determining where the best exit and approach streets were, where to park the car if we decided to shoot him or bomb him, and generally taking a complete look at the area.

We took a long drive outside town to a field, and I watched while Lisenby test-fired one magazine from the Ingram into the dirt. The weapon functioned flawlessly, the sound suppressor dampening the muzzle blast down to only a fraction of what it would be unsuppressed.

He also drove me past the destroyed boat, so I could see the damage myself. He was right. The boat, a big, expensive day cruiser, was burned and shattered.

Driving back to the hotel, I wondered if the FBI had brought the room under surveillance yet, and if they would know we were moving for "security reasons," as Lisenby put it.

It didn't take long to get our belongings and leave. Lisenby took us a few blocks away to another hotel, and we checked in. We watched television, ate dinner, and talked about the possible variations of shootings or bombings we might encounter. Lisenby gave me $200 for escape-and-evasion money in case we were separated, and I pocketed it. I had spent my own money to get there, and with no prior agreement from the FBI to pay, it was possible I wouldn't even get expenses out of this affair.

13 April: The Bomb

After breakfast, we packed and left, checking out of the hotel.

It was now Monday morning. Lisenby had decided to abandon the idea of trying to shoot the drug dealer. He wanted to bomb him. He drove us to a shopping center and began to search through the stores for the items he would need to complete the bomb.

He bought electrical wire, 9-volt radio batteries, insulated plastic tape, sacks of nails, nuts, bolts, and screws, work gloves, and small tools at a hardware store. In the household accessories section of a department store, he bought a mechanical sixty-minute cooking timer, a plastic shoebox, and a deep aluminum cake pan.

Once he had everything, we drove to the outskirts of town, checked into a cheap hotel, and carried all of our equipment inside. Lisenby spread out the explosives and other components on the bed, and we put on our gloves to prevent leaving fingerprints.

Lisenby mixed the white ammonium nitrate powder and clear liquid activator together inside the cake pan. The explosive itself was now ready.

Inside it, he placed two blasting caps wired together because ammonium nitrate required a good boost for positive detonation. I prepared the timer, so I would know how to disarm it if necessary, wiring a 9-volt battery into a circuit designed to be completed when the timer counted down to zero, causing the battery to fire the blasting caps. I tested it carefully to insure it was safe to handle with the battery connected, the blasting caps wired into the circuit, and the timer operating.

"How long after you mix this stuff do you have before it's no good any more?" I asked about the ammonium nitrate.

"I don't know," Lisenby said. "I've always blown it just after mixing it, but I'm sure it'll hold for a day."

He set the cake pan full of hardening ammonium nitrate into the plastic shoebox and taped the timer beside it, the unattached wires from the timer dangling outside the box. Lisenby then embedded the nails, nuts, bolts, and screws into the ammonium nitrate in a thick layer. Those were the projectiles the bomb would throw. They made it heavy. He then taped over the metal hardware to insure it would stay in place.

Once the wires were spliced from the timer to the blasting caps and the battery contacts connected, the bomb would be ready, needing only the dial of the timer to be set to the desired delay.

"Okay, we're through," Lisenby said, studying the bomb while I gathered the tools and tape. He told me to wait while he went to talk with his employer, leaving me alone in the hotel room.

I lay on the bed looking at the bomb and wondered about the FBI. Were they watching this hotel now? Had they been behind us today while we were shopping? I assumed they were going to wait for the last minute and move in to arrest Lisenby when he actually was placing the bomb.

The telephone was there beside my bed. I considered using it, to call the local Miami FBI office to make sure they were aware of what was happening, but I didn't know if Lisenby might somehow be able to tell if I made any calls. Perhaps he wasn't really going to meet the employer. Perhaps this was a test to see what I would do.

I did not touch the phone.

We made sure there was nothing left in the room and, leaving the key on the desk, locked the door behind us. Lisenby had returned with a shopping bag in which to carry the bomb.

He handed the bomb to me, the lid loose on the shoebox. "When we park near the barber shop, you change to the driver's seat and take the Ingram. I'll arm the bomb, time it for five minutes, and walk to the shop," he said.

"What if you have trouble?" I asked.

"I've got my pistol," he said, revealing a snub-nose .38 Special he carried in a belt holster under his light jacket. "But if I come running like hell back to this car, shoot any goddamn Cubans chasing me."

Lisenby parked the Chevrolet on the street we had chosen as the most direct escape route, and we swapped seats. He waited until he knew I was ready, then reached inside the sack to arm the bomb. I pulled the Ingram out from under the driver's seat, screwed the sound suppressor to it, and inserted a loaded magazine.

I heard Lisenby twisting the timer dial, and he looked quickly at me.

"It's armed," he said.

I could do nothing but nod in agreement.

He opened his door and stepped out, carrying the shopping bag in one hand. In five minutes, it would explode. I expected the FBI and local police to come charging in now, once they saw him on the way to the target with a package. Five minutes was not enough time.

I was also worried about hostile Cubans. I was parked on a side street in Little Havana, on a bombing mission inside *their* territory.

There was sparse traffic on my street and no people at all. I sat and waited, counting off the minutes on my Porsche racing watch, the sweep second hand moving toward detonation with no compassion. When the bomb exploded, it would sweep the main street with bricks and glass fragments, hitting the shoppers and restaurant diners across the way like the blast of a claymore mine.

The little religious shop next door to the barber shop would go with it, and the girls in there selling their plastic madonnas would die with the drug dealer.

Where was the FBI?

Suddenly I saw Lisenby coming back, walking fast and *still carrying the sack*. His face was pale. He made it to the car, shoved the package into my hands, and said, "Disarm it quick."

I dropped the Ingram, reached inside the bag, opened the lid of the shoebox, and felt for the wires that connected to the battery. There had to be less than two minutes left on the clock, if the thing was working accurately.

After finding the right wire, I pulled the connector cap off the battery and was able to take a breath again.

"What happened?" I asked.

"The door was locked! They locked the damn door! I don't believe it!" Lisenby said. "Let's get the hell out of here."

I drove us away. "Let's call them," I said. "Maybe they just went out for a minute."

"No, hell, no. . . . I can't do this twice in one day. Let's go to a hotel."

"How about the Holiday Inn again?" I suggested. "That ought to be okay."

"Yeah, sure," Lisenby said.

Once we were checked back into the Brickell Avenue Holiday Inn, Lisenby told me to leave the bomb in the car. "I don't want that son of a bitch in my room," he said. All we took out of the car were our clothes and the weapons. Even the box of flares and concussion grenades stayed in the trunk.

Lisenby was upset. He had told his employer the target was going to be dead that afternoon. I was upset because the FBI had failed to stop Lisenby. I wondered if they were willing to let Lisenby murder the man, even at the risk of harming civilians in the area, but I couldn't believe that. There had to be something wrong. I was beginning to suspect I was alone in Miami.

"We'll get him in the morning," Lisenby said.

We stayed in the room, the time passing very slowly for both of us. I wanted to somehow get out and find a way to alert the FBI. Lisenby wanted to figure a way to make the hit with no problem.

I tried to talk him out of completing the job, arguing he was doing it too cheaply and the drug dealer would own him after the killing. Lisenby countered by saying he had already accepted too much money and could not back out.

Using a different approach, I told him we should leave Miami and come back in a few days with more sophisticated equipment, like remote-signal detonators, so we could blow the bomb from a distance. Lisenby also turned down that idea.

He was in no mood to watch television. The pressure was on both of us.

After the sun went down, I made a move to try and get out of the room.

"You want a Coke?" I asked.

"Yeah," Lisenby agreed, and I opened the room door. He was lying on the bed, paying no attention to me. I closed the door and went out on the open walkway.

We were on the second floor. In direct sight just under us was a Coke machine and a pay telephone on the wall beside it.

I went down the stairs, my eyes on the phone. It could be easily seen from the room. I dropped my coins in the machine, bought two bottled drinks and, acting on a feeling, never even looked directly at the phone.

Drinks in hand, I turned and went back up the stairs and tried the room door knob. It was locked, so I knocked.

There was a noise from my left and I looked aside. Lisenby stepped out of a shadowed inset in the wall. He was holding his .38 Special revolver and wearing no shoes.

"What are you doing out here?" I asked.

"Watching you," he said, and I realized he had followed me out, then from his hidden position on the second-floor walkway tracked me with the pistol all the way down to the drink machine.

If I had picked up the phone, he might have killed me.

I acted as if I didn't understand and handed him one of the Cokes. He unlocked the room door and we went back inside.

Lisenby was a drinker. I reasoned that in his nervous state, if he had something alcoholic, he might get drunk, or at least less careful.

"Some bourbon sure would go good with this," I said, sipping my Coke.

"Yeah," Lisenby said, "I could use it. Did you see a liquor store around here?"

"No, but that's no problem. All we have to do is get a cab driver to go buy some for us," I said.

"Hell, we ought to get some girls too," he said.

We sat on our beds and drank the Cokes, talking about women, and finally I got Lisenby to laugh. I suggested that he go down and find a cab driver, but Lisenby said no. He told me to do it.

He lay back on the bed, watching the television now, and I left the room again. I went out to the front of the hotel where a cab was parked and gave the driver a $20 tip, asking if he knew where I could get a bottle and a couple of whores. He told me it was no problem and he would be right back and drove away.

I went inside the office, looking quickly around. Only the night clerk was there. "Where are the telephones?" I asked.

He pointed to a side door. "Right around that corner," he said.

I saw the bank of pay phones in an alcove, found the telephone number of the Miami FBI office in the phone book, and called it.

"This is Frank Camper," I said. "Where the hell is my backup? I'm at the Brickell Avenue Holiday Inn."

"*Who?*" asked the duty agent.

"Camper! I've been down here since Saturday night! The guy I'm with is on a bombing mission."

"A bomb?" asked the agent.

A sick feeling moved from my stomach up to my throat. There really was something wrong. No wonder Lisenby had almost planted the bomb.

"Listen carefully to me," I said. "I coordinated with the Birmingham office of the FBI Saturday night. They know I'm here. I am with a man who is going to bomb a barber shop in Little Havana at the intersection of 8th Street and 8th Avenue."

"Yes," said the agent, "go on."

"We are in the Brickell Avenue Holiday Inn, room 227. There are two of us. I have a beard, the other guy does not. When you move in, *don't* shoot the guy with the beard, understand? We have a red 1981 Chevrolet Citation. It's parked in the lot outside. We're leaving to hit the target tomorrow morning."

"Yes, I understand," the agent said.

"I have to go now," I said. "I can't stay on the phone long."

"I have the information," said the agent.

I placed the receiver back on the cradle, looked carefully out into the lobby before I came out of the alcove, then hurried to the room.

Lisenby opened the door.

"Got it on the way," I said, giving him a grin. "The cab will be back in a few minutes, and you'll have to go down and pay him."

"Fine, fine," Lisenby said, seemingly more relaxed.

We watched television for a short time, until we heard an automobile horn blow from the parking lot. "I think that's him," I said.

Lisenby left the room. I made sure he was gone, then I went to the Ingram, made sure that it had a loaded magazine in it, and moved it to where I alone knew it was and could reach it quickly.

Lisenby opened the door, laughing with the two black prostitutes following him. They were both young girls, dressed in seductive clothing, their faces made up with cosmetics to appear older. One of them carried a large bottle of whiskey.

The girls and Lisenby were jovial, joking with each other as they found glasses into which to pour their liquor. They drank heavily, and I accepted a glass but didn't drink much, which none of them noticed. I was expecting a knock on the door at any minute. I stayed near the Ingram, trying to act as giddy and playful as my roommates.

One of the girls attached herself to me, and I took her aside while Lisenby and his girl spilled liquor on the rug and wrestled with each other in an undressing game.

"What's wrong, you don't like me?" my prostitute asked.

"No, you're fine," I said. "I'm just tired. It's my friend who needs to unwind. Is that okay?"

"Yeah, sure," said the girl. "I guess I don't have to get my hair messed up."

Two hours later Lisenby was drunk and asleep. The girls were gone, financed for a cab ride home with a fistful of money Lisenby had insisted they take. He had drunk most of the bottle.

I was on my bed, very awake.

The FBI knew for sure where we were now, but so far nothing had happened. I was forced to my original assumption, that they would strike as we were moving in toward the target, but I couldn't be sure.

Each noise alerted me. Lisenby snored.

That was how we passed the night.

14 April: Ambush

Lisenby awoke just after 7:00 A.M. with a reasonably clear head. I asked him questions about the girls, and he remembered enough to answer some of them.

We packed our bags. Lisenby called his wife to tell her he would be home that night, and we went down to breakfast. We both had cold cereal and coffee, talking about general subjects while we were among the customers in the restaurant.

When we walked out to the car, Lisenby placed our travel bags in the trunk, then unlocked the doors for us. He drove.

I kept expecting the FBI, wondering when and where, looking around, but I had to do it carefully and not make Lisenby suspicious. He was very calm, placing his pistol beside him on the seat and making sure I had the bomb in my lap, ready to arm.

The Ingram was again under the seat. I had retrieved it from my hiding place earlier, explaining to Lisenby I had moved it to prevent the girls from seeing it.

We drove away from the Holiday Inn, and after a few turns were on "Calle Ocho," Southwest 8th Street, which led directly to the barber shop.

Lisenby was explaining to me we would do it exactly the same way as we had tried before, when he looked into his rear-view mirror.

"Hey, what's this?" he exclaimed.

A car was trying to squeeze us out of traffic, and Lisenby had to steer us to the sidewalk. "Crazy son of a bitch," he said.

Then I saw the police cars. There were several of them behind us, all moving fast, cutting through the traffic as we were forced off the street by the unmarked car, the Chevrolet bumping as our front tires hit the curb.

Lisenby braked, looking around frantically. There were police cars ahead and behind us, and men dressed in dark-blue uniforms were standing up from the low rooftops, aiming M16 rifles at us.

Police officers rushed our car, pistols drawn and ready. Lisenby looked at me, his mouth partially open. Then the police were banging on our car, yelling for us to get out.

I opened my door and was jerked from my seat, slammed against the side of the car, and my legs kicked apart. Someone grabbed my arms, twisted them behind me, and I felt the hard shackle of handcuffs being locked on my wrists.

On the other side, Lisenby was getting the same treatment. Radios were squawking, police-car roof lights were flashing, and there was still the tramp of men's feet moving into position.

I was walked to a nearby police car, then pushed inside it onto the backseat. I was alone in the car with all the doors locked.

Then a realization struck me. The police radios might detonate the bomb accidentally, because the wires leading to the blasting caps could act as antennas and transmit enough energy to the caps to make them explode.

I called to one of the nearby police officers who came to me, kneeling beside a partially opened window.

"Tell your people to cut off the radios," I told him. "There are electrical blasting caps in that bomb." He knew exactly what I meant and rushed away.

I heard voices shouting for the radios to be turned off, and in a moment the street was silent.

Many of the officers quickly took cover as they learned the Chevrolet had a bomb in it. My car was behind the Chevrolet and I could see it clearly. I knew the potential of the bomb and decided I was in danger if it exploded.

Then I saw Lisenby again. A plainclothes police officer had him by the collar and was pushing him toward the Chevrolet.

The officer forced Lisenby to his knees and stuck his head inside the Chevrolet on the passenger side. I could hear him demanding Lisenby to disarm the bomb.

The officer was holding Lisenby. If the bomb exploded, it would kill them both.

Lisenby told the officer what to do to make sure the bomb was safe, and I watched him do it.

A television news video crew came up to my car and began taping me through the window as Lisenby was led away from the Chevrolet.

In a moment two police officers got into my car and we drove to the Dade County jail. I could tell by their talk they thought I was as guilty as Lisenby. That meant the officers on the street who had made the arrest also did not know who I was. I could have been shot down if Lisenby tried to resist.

The police officers took me in through the back of the building, and I was turned over to plainclothes agents. As I was being led down a hallway, I saw Lisenby waiting in a side room. An officer brought him from the room and into the hall with me.

He seemed resigned. I did not speak to him.

We were led toward another video news crew, who also taped us as we walked handcuffed through the halls. After that, Lisenby was taken away again, and I was guided upstairs to an office, uncuffed, and offered a chair and a cup of coffee. A senior Miami SIS (Special Investigation Section) officer, wearing street clothes but with his badge pinned to his sportshirt, reached out and shook my hand.

"Thank you," he said. "That was a very brave thing you did. If Lisenby had blown that bomb, he would have killed a lot of innocent people."

At 7:30 P.M., after ten hours of answering all the questions needed by the Miami police and making a statement to the Dade County District Attorney, I was at the Miami Airport boarding a jet back to Birmingham.

Robert Lisenby stayed in jail.

NEWS ITEM: 15 April 1981, The Miami Herald
COMMANDO INSTRUCTORS SEIZED AGAIN
(by Patrick Riordan & Al Messerschmidt, Herald staff writers)

  Two free-lance commando instructors were arrested Tuesday morning as they drove through the streets of Little Havana, carrying a deadly bomb on the floor by the front seat.

  The men, Joseph Franklin Camper, 34, of Dolomite, Alabama, and Robert Lisenby, 30, a firearms dealer from Troy, North Carolina, were charged with possession of the bomb and a MAC-10 machine gun.

  The same two men were arrested less than a month ago near the Crystal River Nuclear Plant in Citrus County, where they were running a training camp for would-be soldiers of fortune.

  Miami police said Tuesday the car was a rolling arsenal, with a .45-caliber machine gun, a .38-caliber revolver, and a pipe bomb and hand grenades in the trunk.

  But their most fearsome weapon was a plastic-explosive bomb in a cake pan studded with makeshift shrapnel.

  "This kind of mechanism is intended to kill or maim people," Miami Police Chief Kenneth Harms said.

"Based on our information," Harms said, "I believe that it was their intention to detonate [the bomb] sometime around midmorning, at a time and place where people would be present, which would result in probable loss of life and serious injury to anyone present."

15 April: The Cover

The FBI had acted only to turn the case over to the Miami police, and it had been handled by them. No one explained to me why the FBI had failed to follow up on the message I had sent them after leaving Alabama.

My actions were to be considered secret, since it would expose me to retaliation by Cuban drug dealers, and the Miami police promised not to reveal my cover.

July 1981: The Cover, Blown

I received a telephone call from the Miami police. It was one of the special investigation section officers who had handled Lisenby.

"Frank, I have some bad news," he said. "The FBI has released your name as the source of information against Lisenby."

"What?" I asked. *"Why?"*

"I don't know. Lisenby's defense attorney has the information now. We did the best we could to cover for you. I think this is an unnecessary and stupid move on the Bureau's part."

The FBI's disclosure of my part in stopping Lisenby was incredible. It exposed me to counterattack by the Cubans.

As soon as reporters in Miami and Birmingham got the news, my phone began to ring again.

I was furious with the FBI. I called their office in Birmingham and demanded an explanation but was given nothing. They didn't want to talk to me.

Robert Lisenby pleaded guilty to reduced charges of violating the federal firearms laws. I was not called to testify against him. I had been exposed needlessly.

An unusual incident I can only categorize as attempted retaliation happened a month later. I was driving back to The Bunker one night, coming from a movie. A car passed me but deliberately stayed just ahead.

As I slowed to turn into The Bunker's back gate, the lead car braked, forcing me to stop halfway through my turn. Something was wrong. I drew my M11.

The passenger side door of the blocking car opened and two black men rolled out onto the road. They appeared to be fighting. The driver remained at the wheel. It had to be a setup. I was supposed to believe what I saw and try to break up the fight, and then they would jump me.

Instead, I came out with the M11. Even in the dark the men recognized my weapon, and M11's are small and square and do not resemble pistols. The car sped away, abandoning the two men. One ran, I pinned the other against the Bunker fence. He was terrified.

"Next time, you're all dead," I told him, and let him sprint away into the night. I wanted his employers to know I would fight fire with fire.

CHAPTER EIGHT
El Salvador

The soldier was going to hit me in the face with the butt of a carbine.

I reached out and grabbed the muzzle of his weapon as he was unslinging it from his shoulder, momentarily stopping him.

I knocked his feet out from under him with a sweep of my right leg. He fell, trying to keep the carbine, but I jerked it away from him, still holding it by the barrel.

The other guards shouted at me, their carbines in their hands. I had about half a second to make a decision. I could try to explain and apologize and get killed, I could stand and fight and get killed, or I could run and maybe survive.

I ran, throwing the carbine away from the guard, who had landed flat on his ass, a very shocked expression on his face.

My only escape route was away from the guards and down the hill toward a stand of trees.

The guards opened fire.

The cracks of the carbines were sharp and loud in the morning air. The shots were going somewhere past me, into the trees.

I ducked behind the first tree I thought would stop a carbine bullet, and looked up the hill. The bastards were coming after me.

Now my whole mission was compromised.

Things had been happening fast since I stepped off the plane two days ago, one of those situations where days and nights blend and all sense of time is lost.

My original idea was to go to El Salvador, using the cover of a journalist, and make contact with the Salvadoran Marxist rebels, gain their confidence, and be invited to their field camps. Once there, I could evaluate their capabilities, intentions, and resources.

It was a reconnaissance operation, but I would be carrying a camera instead of a rifle and the enemy would be personally escorting me. As always, success was a gamble. It was a long shot.

The whole trip was on speculation. If I came back with usable information, it would help me establish myself with a certain senator whose committee needed intelligence on communist-backed guerrillas in Central America. If I came back with nothing, I lost out all the way around. Call it freelance spying.

After the long taxi ride through the countryside from the airport, I checked into the El Presidente Hotel, left my travel bag in the room, and took another taxi downtown so I could begin to make my connection.

I went to the Estado Mayor, the central Salvadoran military headquarters downtown, and visited briefly, asking for a letter from the government to prove that I was in the country as a journalist. Afterward, I took my taxi to the U.S. Embassy and had a discussion with a U.S. Naval Intelligence officer who gave me details of his knowledge of the guerrillas.

Leaving the embassy, I went to the Camino Real Hotel, where various news offices were headquartered, and began my operation.

It was necessary for me to obtain a "Salvadoran Press Corps Association" identity card and establish myself as a left-wing journalist to make my cover. I discovered that was not difficult, as most of the newspeople living in the Camino Real were political liberals, if not leftists themselves. They viewed Salvador as the Vietnam of the 1980s.

I told them of my affiliation with the Palestinians and dropped hints about my days in the antiwar movement in the 1960s. After a few cups of coffee, I was one of the gang, looking down out of the hotel windows at the soldiers in the streets, criticizing U.S. presence in El Salvador, and being given tips on whom to see and where to go in town to meet the rebels.

El Salvador was ripe with the type of violence people in war zones learn to exist with, accepting sudden death the way people in more peaceful places accept the possibility they might have an accident.

I was walking along a city street on my way to the café

where I hoped to be introduced to a rebel organizer, when a small car made a U-turn out of the traffic on my side of the street about twenty-five meters ahead. I saw the car's front tires bump the curb as the driver realized he had not turned sharply enough. The driver stopped, shifted into reverse gear, and backed the car away from the curb.

Soldiers with rifles came running from a sandbag bunker on the street corner, yelling at the car, which was inside a white-painted "off-limits" zone alongside the curb. The off-limits area prevented car bombs from being parked near the military installation on the other side of the wall from the sidewalk.

The driver saw the soldiers and panicked, clashing the gears and racing the engine of his car. The soldiers were aiming their German Heckler-Koch G3 rifles at him. The man opened his car door, raised one hand, and surrendered.

They fired.

The combined thunder of their high-powered 7.62-millimeter NATO assault rifles was deafening. The glass in the car burst, and paint chips flew as the bullets punched oblong holes in the sheet metal. The driver, hit many times before he could fall, tumbled out of the driver's seat to the pavement, his feet still in the car.

The soldiers changed magazines, then slowly walked to the car, weapons pointed at the corpse. The engine still idled. One of the soldiers reached inside over the body of the driver and switched it off.

I moved past the scene. The driver's blood ran down the street gutter. I did not look back. I couldn't afford any trouble. That had been on my first day.

Now I was running for my life down a narrow residential street in San Salvador City, past school children walking home. The shooting at me had stopped, presumably because of the children, but the soldiers were still coming. I knew they would be radioing to other strong points ahead because there were sandbagged forts at most street intersections.

I changed directions and sprinted down an alley, saw a wire fence and climbed over it into a junkyard of old tractors and road construction machinery. The rusting vehicles were overgrown by clusters of high yellow grass.

The soldiers knew I was unarmed, so they were very brave in

*the chase. I knelt behind a tractor, trying to catch my breath and
plan my next move.*

Shortly after the car incident on my first day in San Salvador
City, I had found the café and my rebel contact. In the course of
our discussion, I convinced him I was in sympathy with the guerrillas. He said he could make the arrangements for me to visit a
camp in the mountains, then told me to go back to my hotel and
wait for his telephone call.

The guerrillas were always eager to manipulate the Western
press to help their cause, and they accepted me only to use for
their own ends. This time the situation would be reversed.

I waited that night in my hotel room, inspected my small
Olympus XA-2 camera and film, and decided what to wear. I
chose my khaki bush jacket, black trousers, and a sturdy pair of
canvas ankle boots with heavy-lugged rubber soles.

The call came the morning of November 11, instructing me
to return to the café and wait in the back room on the alley. I put
my camera and film in my bush-jacket pockets and went for
breakfast, thinking I would eat at a street café or restaurant
rather than in the hotel. Anticipating the day ahead, I left the
hotel and walked down the hill.

There was a small crowd standing on a street corner in the
row of private homes that lined the street. As I approached the
crowd, I wondered why they were staring into one of the walled
homes.

There were several police officers and soldiers in the house. I
heard the people in the crowd talking, and understood enough
Spanish to learn there had been a double murder. A Death Squad
had come during the night looking for a young man who lived
there. They had found him. His body was still lying in the doorway of the house, the main attraction for the crowd. He had been
chopped dozens of times with machetes, his blood congealed on
the floor tiles under him.

His teenage sister had been unfortunate enough to be in the
house when the attack came. She had apparently run, trying to
escape through the garden, but the assassins had caught her and
she was killed also. Her own blood trailed from inside the house
where they had begun to hack at her to where she lay, butchered
in the garden, facedown in the flowers.

Death was a daily companion in El Salvador. It was not a

distant threat, not a remote possibility. It was there, each hour on the hour, and such corpses were the byproduct.

I did not stop for breakfast, but instead went directly to the café and was allowed entrance to the back room where a curtain covered the doorway to the alley. An old Volkswagen sedan driven by a teenage boy came for me, and we drove out of the city through the army roadblocks into the countryside. On the long road that went to the airport, the boy steered us off a dirt trail and skillfully maneuvered the VW like a jeep over the ruts and rocks. He spoke no English, and I didn't want to let him know I understood some Spanish so we couldn't talk extensively, but he seemed to be friendly. In the afternoon, we stopped at a little village. The boy told me to wait.

I sat on a wooden bench until a rebel guard in civilian clothes came out of one of the thatched-roof adobe houses and searched me. He took my camera, then motioned for me to follow him into the house.

Sitting at the table inside, I was given coffee and wondered what was going to happen next. I heard people talking outside the house, as the door opened behind me.

"You are American?"

I looked up from the table into the face of a thin woman wearing a green army shirt and a homemade skirt. Behind her was a hawk-faced man carrying a bolt-action 98k Mauser.

"Yes. I'm here to do a story," I said.

"We have had that explained to us," she said. "I speak English and will escort you."

"The guard out on the road took my camera," I said. "Can I get it back?" No photos, no faces.

"There will be time for that later. Your camera will be safe," she said as she sat on the bench across from me. Her rifleman propped the 98k against the wall, folded his arms, and assumed a patient pose.

"Do you live here in the village?" I asked.

"We have a camp in the forest," she said. "I will take you there if you wish to go."

We ate tortillas and drank strong coffee at the table as the sun went down behind the volcanic mountains outside. The night was cool, and it would be cold before dawn. They were apparently hoping that after dark I wouldn't know where I was going.

At the end of the meal we thanked the owner of the house

for the food and walked into the jungle, the man with the Mauser following a well-traveled footpath ahead of us. The woman walked behind me, clearly comfortable outdoors.

The path led to a fork that crossed a stream. "The river is that way," the woman said, pointing into the trees where the stream flowed.

We walked steadily alongside the stream, the trail wide and clear. Both the man and woman made very little noise as they walked, unconcerned with the darkness. Stars were shining by the time we saw the guerrilla campfires flickering through the trees.

The sentry challenged our approach, was satisfied when he heard familiar voices. We filed past him toward what seemed to be tents camouflaged in the foliage. With the campfires burning and rebels moving around and talking, I knew we were in what they had to consider a very secure area. I had carefully counted pace and changes of direction from the house.

There were men and women in the camp. I could see a few FN FAL and G3 rifles near the fires, each weapon carefully laid on protecting canvas or hung from a tree branch off the ground.

"This is our people, our army," the woman said to me.

"Do you have any Cubans with you?" I asked.

"No," she said. "Sometimes there are officers from Nicaragua that come to visit, but the Cubans do not come here."

"But you accept help from the communists," I said.

"The government accepts help from the United States," she said. "When you are in trouble you take help where you can find it."

Water was boiling for coffee over one of the campfires. As the pot became low on water someone would refill it from a small bucket they carried back and forth to the stream.

We sat around the fire and I was given a plastic cup of coffee liberally laced with milk and sugar. My eyes had adjusted to the light and I could see more of the area. What I had thought to be tents were actually canvas tarps over bunkers. A U.S. M60 machine gun was clearly visible in one behind me.

I told the woman my readers were interested in how the guerrilla lived. She said it was a hard life because to become a guerrilla, you had to give up your home and family to go into the field.

"It will be worth it," she said, "because when the government is destroyed and Salvador belongs to the people, we can all go home and live with our families again."

"Do you feel the United States is against the people of Salvador?" I asked.

She paused before she answered, as if considering her response, since I was from America.

"I am sorry to say we believe this. It is the facts," she said.

Her honesty made me want to explain our position to her, but I was there to get information, not attempt diplomacy. "I'm sorry," I said, "if it seems that way to you. The people of the United States don't understand all of the aspects of the war here."

"In Nicaragua the people fought for their land and now they have it," she pointed out. "That is what we are doing now."

"What about your weapons? Where do they come from?" I asked.

"Some are a gift from the people of Nicaragua. They no longer need them. We have the FN rifle, the Uzi submachine gun, and the government rifles, the G3's. We take them from the army."

"What about ammunition? Hand grenades?"

"We use ammunition taken from the government, and we have boxes of it from Nicaragua as well. The same with hand grenades, except we don't have enough." She reached inside a sack beside a bedroll and produced a U.S. M26 fragmentation grenade to show me.

"You do have Soviet weapons? Do you have AK-47's?"

"No, not here. Our people prefer the FN because it will shoot the same ammunition as the army G3."

"Have you been trained with the AK-47?"

"No. I have seen them. Some of the people from the west of the country have them, those units over the Lempa River."

I looked around at the camp. "Are you afraid the government will find you here?"

"They do not come very far off the road," she said, "and if they do, we know about it long before they arrive. If they make a large attack somewhere, we take our weapons and equipment and leave."

"But rebel camps have been surprised before," I said.

"Those near roads or those caught where the army has surrounded them. It has not been many. The people are on our side and tell us if the army is coming."

"What do you think about the army? Are the soldiers any good?" I asked.

"They are brave. They are Salvadorans. What you must understand is they would not fight for the army if they understood the reasons we make war on the government. When we can speak to them, make them see, they come over to us."

"Can I ask you about your tactics? Do you patrol certain areas?"

"We do not have to patrol to get information," she said. "It comes from the people. They walk past the soldiers, see how many of them there are in a position, what weapons they have. We do not send our patrols unless we have to search for something or we are looking for army units in the forest."

"Does the army use small recon patrols to try and find your camps?"

"Sometimes they do. These patrols are trained by the *Tropas Especiale* from the United States. Some of them have been captured by our people."

"How long do you believe it will be before you win the war?" I asked.

"I don't know, but the people of Salvador are very strong now. We control the roads and villages. The army only controls the cities and the highways. They cannot come into the forest or deep into the countryside."

"What would the government have to do to make peace with the rebels?" I asked.

"The army must stop killing the people," she said.

"What about the United States?" I asked.

"They must stop providing weapons for Duarte to use against the people of Salvador. He is a murderer."

"Do you believe Nicaragua is a model for the Salvadoran people to copy?" I asked, to get the depth of her Marxist orientation.

"The people of Nicaragua have taken control of their nation. Somoza was as terrible as Duarte," she said.

"All right, now—" I said, but she raised her hand.

"It is late," she said. "You must leave early in the morning. We have a blanket for you to sleep with."

"My camera?"

"The guard will give it to you in the village. We have put fuel in the car that brought you here, and your driver will be ready to take you back." She left the fire and walked away, telling one of the men nearby to bring my blanket.

I took the offered blanket and spread it over my body, using a sandbag for a pillow. One by one the fires were banked and movement was slowly reduced to the changes of the guard.

It was easy for me to compare El Salvador to Vietnam, Angola, or Rhodesia, all recent spots where the "people" had fought to overcome a government, only to discover themselves under harsh new masters, the romance of revolution as dead as their economies.

We were up with the sun the morning of the twelfth, and I walked back to the village with a group of rebels. The VW and driver were waiting there. I listened to many casual conversations.

My camera was returned to me, and I checked to make sure it had not been damaged. The guerrillas who had accompanied me from the camp were making coffee and visiting with friends. They waved good-bye to me.

The driver drove me back to San Salvador City on a different route, confirming my suspicion he had been trying to confuse me before, but the harsh fact was that the enemy camp was only sixty kilometers from San Salvador.

I went back to the El Presidente Hotel, took a shower, and made my notes about the size, activity, location, type of unit, and time of my recon, with details about the weapons and interview. Then I decided to take a walk outside and see the city.

The report seemed to be a good one. I had intel on a new offensive, and the probable location of Radio *Venceremas*, the mobile rebel propaganda transmitter. I had overheard a lot. They thought I wouldn't understand.

After leaving the hotel, I strolled down the hill and noticed a squad of local soldiers in U.S. helmets and green uniforms, all guarding what seemed to be a private residence.

I slipped my Olympus out of my pocket and walked to the nearest guard. I rationalized that any interest I could show to the local military would reinforce my cover as a journalist.

"¿Permiso?" I asked in Spanish, and showed the guard my camera and press card. That was when he started to jerk the

carbine off his shoulder to buttstroke me. There was no explanation. I had seen the driver shot and killed on the street downtown. I knew the guard would kill me if I didn't stop him.

The soldiers were climbing over the fence into the junkyard.
I could hear them spreading out and poking into the grass with
their carbines.

I was well concealed in the grass, leaning against a tractor
and wishing I had a weapon. The rustling of the grass became
louder as the soldiers searched.

One of them walked by me. I held absolutely still. Then
another passed. I chanced a look around the tractor and saw a
young Salvadoran soldier pushing through the high grass, following the path made by the first two men.

This was my chance.

I crept near the path, keeping my head well below the top of
the grass. The soldier had to think himself safe. He was watching
the man in front of him, not looking down or to his sides. When
he came even with me, I quickly stood up and grabbed him by his
head, twisting it brutally to take him down. I hit him so fast he
dropped his carbine. I forced him to the ground, my knee on his
back, grabbed his throat with the fingers of my right hand, and
crushed his larynx as I pushed his face into the grass, muffling his
choking. When I knew he was unconscious, I picked up his carbine and took the three ammunition magazines in his pouch.

The carbine had its safety off and the fire selector on full
automatic. I left it that way.

The other soldiers had stopped, looking back my way, wondering what had happened to their last man. One of them called
out for him.

It was now or never. A moment before they realized anything was wrong, I sprayed the entire carbine magazine in a
sweep across the junkyard, the bullets glancing off the road machinery and kicking up dirt and grass. The soldiers dropped, and
I dashed across an obstacle course of steel wheels, engine blocks,
and heaped, cleated vehicle tracks.

They were yelling, trying to establish each other's positions
and situation. One of them saw me and began to fire before I
reached the tin shacks near the fence, the bullets clanging loudly
into the sheet metal. I crouched, chanced changing magazines,
and fired back near the bobbing heads in the grass. If I could get

over the fence, I would be in a ghetto maze of shanties and alleys, and my chances for survival would increase greatly.

The soldiers were not as brave now. To shoot at me they had to raise up out of the grass, and I had made that too dangerous. With a tool shack as cover, I clawed up the wire fence and dropped awkwardly down the other side without losing the carbine.

Running through the alley with a carbine in my hand, I felt conspicuous as hell. I was sweating and breathing fast from the exertion. People watched me out of their tiny huts, each one walled off from the others with cane fences. The place stank of pig shit, garbage, and rancid cooking grease.

I didn't think I could get to the U.S. Embassy. It was possible the soldiers had identified me and figured out I was staying in the El Presidente Hotel, and there were Salvadoran army guards outside the embassy.

I began to walk, keeping the carbine down against my leg so it wasn't as visible. I controlled my breathing, gathering my thoughts. I knew I couldn't walk around the streets of San Salvador with a carbine in my hand, but I didn't trust my situation enough yet to abandon it. I didn't really want to kill a Salvadoran soldier. I wasn't even sure I hadn't killed one already.

Then I had an idea. If I went to the Camino Real and the liberal newspeople, they would accept without question my story that the government was after me.

My trek through the ghetto alleys was going well, the soldiers lost far behind. I walked until I saw a street ahead, then dropped the carbine and magazines behind a fence.

Looking carefully out from the alley, I saw only traffic and shops. Salvadorans were going about their business, paying me no attention. There was even a grocery market across the street. I was thirsty. I casually walked into the market and bought a carton of orange juice, watching the streets for patrols through the window as I drank it. I then hailed a taxi and rode to the Camino Real, going past many soldiers in the streets, but they did not stop me.

Upstairs in the hotel, I met one of the American journalists who knew me. I told him about the incident with the soldiers near my hotel and he said he had heard about it before I arrived. The army had sent out a general alert for roadblocks to be on the lookout for a bearded American wearing a tan military jacket.

I told him I needed to have someone go to my room in the El Presidente and recover my clothes and notes, because I had evidence of atrocities committed by the army. The journalist was more than willing to help me since it involved an antigovernment action.

The journalist took my room key, sent one of his assistants to the El Presidente for my things, and loaned me a room for the night in the Camino Real that belonged to a reporter who had gone on assignment.

Soon I had my belongings back, including the notes of the rebels' camp. I stayed up late with a crowd of journalists, swapping war stories and making friends with them. One of the reporters offered to take me to the airport early in the morning so I could get out of the country.

We drove to the airport at dawn, the valleys still dark under the volcanic mountains, pale sunlight only beginning to brighten the sky.

In the airport parking lot, I said good-bye to the journalist and went in to the ticket desk. The first available plane out was going to Belize. I bought a ticket for it. The agent filled out my ticket, paying no special attention to my name. I took the ticket and walked to the next station to pay the exit tax and watched the airport guards out of the corner of my eye.

The plane was boarding. I went to passport control. They were rushing to get the last few passengers through, and I fell into the line. There was one agent inspecting and stamping the passports and an assistant checking a book beside him, which would contain any passport numbers they wanted to stop.

The security man with his book was talking on the telephone as I had my passport stamped. I walked out to the plane with the other passengers, went up the stairway and into the aircraft. The door of the plane closed and the engines started. I was going to make it.

We taxied down the runway, accelerated, and lifted off. I was out of El Salvador.

CHAPTER NINE
Belize

We had been in the air for a few minutes when a stewardess spoke to me.

"Are you Señor Camper?" she asked.

"Yes," I said, puzzled.

"We have a radio call about you from El Salvador airport. They say we have to return you there, but we are out of their airspace now and the pilot says we cannot go back. We will be landing in Belize City soon, and you can contact the Salvadorans from there," she said.

"Of course," I said. "Did they say why?"

"No, señor, I'm sorry," she replied with a smile.

I knew what had happened.

Someone at the airport had caught my name on the flight manifest or at the passport control, but a few minutes too late.

I drank a cup of tea as we flew to Belize, lounging in my seat, feeling extremely relieved.

Visiting Belize had not been part of my original plan. My report needed to be turned in as soon as possible, with a copy going back to Salvadoran intelligence. Belize would be a delay and a complication, forcing me to maintain my cover until I could leave.

I processed through Belizian passport control, telling them I was a journalist come to interview the British garrison there.

Belize, formerly British Honduras, was what we called dirt-poor in the United States, and looked it. Belize City was a slum, a decaying ghetto by the sea. The natives were black, not Spanish, and spoke English with a strong British accent, being descendents of colonial slaves.

Now the official presence of the mother country was all but gone. Belize had its independence, and only a few units of the British army stayed behind to keep the country from being swallowed by Guatemala, which claimed Belize was originally a part of its land. The situation was serious enough for Central American maps to show a dotted borderline between Belize and Guatemala, with the legend "Border in Dispute. Reclaimed by Guatemala." Belize airport had British Harrier jet fighters, ground-to-air missile batteries, and infantry stationed nearby, all to repulse a Guatemalan attack.

I checked into a cheap waterfront hotel in Belize City, stowed my bag, and took a taxi to the British military headquarters, which was a rambling jungle camp. I reported to the gate guardhouse and was told by a corporal to wait until an officer came for me. I stood outside the guardhouse, watching the soldiers walking the dirt streets of the camp.

"Yes? May we help you?" asked a clean-shaven officer wearing captain's pips on his jacket epaulets. He had approached from a walkway behind me.

"I'd like to get permission from your command to do a story here in Belize," I said.

"What news agency do you represent?" he asked.

"I'm freelance," I said, giving him my name.

"Follow me, please," said the captain. He walked on a stone path toward a long, white, tin-roofed building. A large iguana watched us from a washed-out hollow under the path.

"Wait here, please," said the captain, and indicated for me to take a seat in a scattered group of wicker chairs outside the building. I waited, resting in the chair, planning what I was going to do after I had this formality arranged.

Finally, a middle-aged, balding man in civilian clothes came to meet me. He took a seat beside me and broke a wry smile. "So, you're Frank Camper," he said.

I nodded.

"I read a message from El Salvador concerning you not an hour ago. I wondered when you'd be dropping in to see us," said the man.

"A message?" I asked, faking ignorance.

"You must allow me to introduce myself," he said. "I am

with an intelligence branch. I often meet with foreigners traveling through Belize. In fact, in this case, I must say it is mandatory."

"I didn't mean to cause any trouble," I said. "I only wanted to get permission to do my story."

"Journalist? Is that what you're using? Pretty thin cover, that. Why were you shooting at those chaps in San Salvador City?"

"They shot at me first," I said.

"And you were out with the terrorists there?" he asked.

"Doing interviews," I said.

"Of course you were," the man said and smiled.

"Am I in trouble in Belize?" I asked.

"Oh, no, even though you seem to have made a good number of enemies in El Salvador. I'm running some checks on you now. If the results are favorable, and I'm sure they will be, I'd like to offer you a small job."

That statement surprised me. "Thank you," I said.

"I'd also like to invite you to stay and eat with us," the man said. "The noon meal will be served soon."

I accepted and was shown by an orderly to the officer's mess, which was in two open-sided tents. I was seated at a table with the junior officers and served on china by black Belizian natives wearing white jackets. The ranking officers sat in the next tent. The arrangements were nothing like I had seen in the American army and I thought the situation interesting, if not outright theatrical. I had come to the right place at the right time.

The young officers and I talked. They told me of their patrols along the Guatemalan border and discussed the condition of the Belizian army, a force armed mainly with clubs in the garrison and good intentions in the field.

After we had eaten, the plates were cleared away by the orderlies and we were served coffee and tea. Everything was done precisely and with ceremony. When the meal was finished, I rejoined the intelligence agent and we went to an office.

"As you are no doubt aware," he said, "Guatemala poses the worst threat we have. They maintain heavily armed patrols on the border and rarely pass up a chance to harass our lads. If it weren't for the defenses we have here, Guatemala would have moved in right after Belize was granted independence."

"What can I help you with?" I asked.

"Our intelligence indicates there may be a coup in Guatemala either before or after the elections in March," said the man. "A radical change of government there might adversely affect us here."

"I think I understand," I said.

"Would you be willing to take a trip into Guatemala in the event of a coup and help us size up the new government?"

That sounded reasonable. I told the agent I agreed. He said my contact was to be through the Belizian consulate, which had been moved out of the British Embassy in New Orleans to its own office in Washington, D.C.

I left the camp and went back to my hotel, thinking how fortunate I was to have escaped El Salvador and been hired by the British, all in the same day.

I went out in Belize that night to find a restaurant. I had seen better alleys than some of the main streets, and all of the buildings seemed to be falling apart. The black citizens were poor, almost destitute.

The police station had no glass in its windows, only slatted shutters, and a single Land Rover on duty. The black policemen carried ax handles.

I ate a meal of Chinese noodles and wine in a tiny restaurant and walked back to my hotel, carrying a local newspaper under my arm. I was going in the side door when a group of blacks approached me from the alley.

"How about money for a drink, man?" one of them said to me.

"I'm broke," I said, and they moved to cut me off from my doorway.

"The hell you say, man. You're a Yank. How about some money for a drink?" the tough demanded. He had three friends. They were all barefoot and wore undershirts and baggy trousers.

I tried to squeeze past the man blocking the doorway. He would not move. They wanted a handout, or they planned to rob me.

"Look," I said, throwing up my hands in mock appeasement, "I'm really sorry, but—" and I kicked the leader in the groin.

He doubled over, a knife he had been concealing falling to the ground. I punched the man beside him with a straight karate blow to the stomach and threw myself into the man blocking the door, slamming him against the door frame.

The last man ran away.

The leader was rolling around clutching his balls, the man with the dented solar plexus was on his hands and knees retching, and the door guard had suddenly lost his nerve. He tried to run, but I caught him by his dirty shirt, spun him around, kicked his feet out from under him, then stomped on his back when he fell, hearing his ribs crack.

I climbed the stairs after that, anger quickening my breath, and lay down on my bed to read my paper. I was not surprised a few minutes later when there was a knock on my door. I opened it to find a black Belizian policeman standing there.

"I am here to apologize to you for the hooligans in the street, sir," he said. "We get a fair low class of folk down on the street. Are you all right?"

I was shocked. I had expected to be arrested. Suddenly Belize didn't seem as bad. "It's all right," I said. "There was no harm done."

"Thank you, sir," said the policeman. "I'm leaving a man on the corner to watch this place. We don't like our guests to be bothered. Have a good night, sir."

I closed the door and went back to bed, a touch overwhelmed by culture shock. The policeman was nothing like most of his U.S. counterparts.

I flew back to Miami the next day, then on to Birmingham.

I wrote my report on what I learned from the Salvadoran guerrillas and submitted it to my Senate contact.

Once back at home, operating the Merc Association and running my gun shop at The Bunker, something happened that changed the routine of what domestic life I had.

Her name was Lee Ann Faulk. She was a petite, green-eyed blonde who took a firearms course at Merc School, and I fell in love with her. At thirty-six, I was twelve years her senior. We were from two entirely different generations. For her, can openers were something electric, rock and roll began with Crosby, Stills, and Nash, and Coca-Cola was a breakfast drink.

As an excuse, I could recount a marriage of underlying tension since 1968. I had never forgiven Mavis, but I'd never divorced her either. I also had never had an affair and didn't know how to handle one. I confronted Mavis with Lee and barely survived the explosion.

I kept them separate after that, struggling to resolve a double-edged situation—to keep a wife I at heart didn't trust, or take a chance on a brash young blonde. At least I had a truce of sorts worked out with Mavis, but Lee and I were having a hard time just finding common ground.

Her friends even joked about a parody of Lee and me, comparing us to a romance between Hot Lips and Colonel Flagg on M*A*S*H, a union not even the writers of that comedy had dared.

Lee was a moral crisis with me, but I loved her, and all it took to ease my conscience was remembering how coldly Mavis had once put me out. In time, Lee and I overcame our age and social differences, but staying with me was to expose her to an extreme threat from our own government, as I will tell in the last chapter of this book.

Romance, however, was secondary to my work.

The coup in Guatemala occurred the last day in March 1982, exactly as the British predicted. I missed the actual beginning of the coup because I was held over in Mexico City coordinating with intelligence agents, but I arrived in plenty of time to do my job.

CHAPTER TEN
Guatemala

I hit the agent so hard with the .45 I thought I felt his skull give. He dropped beside his unconscious partner. I had only minutes left to escape.

The .45 was still pointed at the men, my hand shaking with rage, really operating on its own now. My finger closed over the trigger.

"Please don't kill them!" Isabella cried.

---

8 April 1983: Guatemala City

My assignment in Guatemala was to photograph defenses around the presidential palace, identify private aircraft at the airport, take a recon trip into the countryside to estimate damage done by the rebels, and see, if possible, how the Guatemalan army was handling the war since the coup. My fragmentary reports and photos would be compared to those from other agents, both freelance and professional, to piece together an overall intelligence picture. It was an old way of crosschecking, and it always worked.

Rios Montt had taken control of the government in the brief but violent coup, which was a little over a week old when I arrived at the airport near Guatemala City. The city was a dangerous place so soon after the coup in which President Garcia was put down. Security was tight and foreigners were closely watched. If I was caught spying against the new Guatemalan government, I could be killed or imprisoned.

10 April 1983: El Quiche Province

The rebels were burning the Indians' crops just a few hundred meters up the mountainside from me; the thick white smoke from the farms swallowed the sun.

El Quiche province was northwest of Guatemala City and in a combat zone. The road up from the city was an asphalt ribbon of agony, lined with burned houses, abandoned businesses, and the remains of ambushed buses.

That morning, just before the army arrested me, I was in a rented Honda Civic on my way into El Quiche, being driven in by a local agent. His name was Sebastian and he was contracted to British Intelligence. The Brits had known when I was arriving in Guatemala City and had sent Sebastian to contact me at the hotel. He was Belizian (carrying false Nicaraguan papers) and he talked in the island dialect, sounding exactly like the character Quarrel in Ian Fleming's *Doctor No*.

"We can't go through de roadblock wi' you, mon," he had told me in Guatemala City. "No, you look too much army. Got to get us a cover, look like a tourist." Sebastian drove us to a friend's house and picked up the cover, a young prostitute. She was no older than sixteen, and that was stretching it—fourteen would have been more reasonable. Sebastian said to get into the backseat with her and put my arm around her shoulder when we met the roadblock.

Sebastian told me her situation. She was from El Salvador, and her family was dead. She had been promised a restaurant job in Guatemala City, but after being smuggled across the border ("through a back door," as Sebastian put it), she discovered she had been brought in to be a prostitute, and then it was too late.

Bus service was being restored into El Quiche province now. It had been curtailed for months after the classic guerrilla war experience of having a few busloads of paying passengers robbed, harassed, and made to stand aside as the bus was torched. Of course, one bus and its passengers had been burned together. Pure terrorism in the name of social justice for Guatemala.

Soldiers manned roadblocks into the province, turning away those who did not have a legitimate need to make the hazardous trip into the mountains. Sebastian slowed the Honda when he saw the roadblock ahead. Outgoing traffic from Guatemala City was being allowed to trickle away one vehicle at a time into the war zone.

We waited our turn until the soldiers came to us. They were armed with Israeli Galil assault rifles and wore Israeli helmets, but their camouflage fatigues and jungle boots were made in the Far East, coming from the same suppliers who had sold to Third World countries since the U.S. war in Vietnam.

I was ordered out of the car while an experienced search team opened the hood and trunk of the Honda, looking under its seats and chassis. The teenage whore produced worn identification from a blue jean pocket, but the soldiers ignored her. Sebastian stepped aside while the troops spread-eagled me against the car. My wallet, passport, and little XA-2 camera were taken from my bush jacket pockets. The muzzle of a Galil was kept an inch from the side of my head as a noncom told me I was under arrest and asked what I was doing on the way into El Quiche.

I understood the problem. I was not being taken for a spy. They thought I was a reporter, but that could be just as bad. Reporters met with trouble in Guatemala. Beatings of their people, arrests, and denial to disputed parts of the country had caused the big news agencies to close local offices in disgust and try to run stringers in and out of the city when something was happening.

Sebastian started talking to the soldiers in Spanish faster than I could follow. The young whore leaned against the Honda and watched, not concerned about me but relieved she had passed inspection. I was suddenly surprised when my passport, wallet, and camera were handed back—especially the camera. Sebastian was all smiles, shaking hands with the soldiers as he pushed me into the car.

"How did you do that?" I asked as he slipped the Honda into gear and drove around the roadblock.

"I know dem," he said, "but you plenty lucky. Dey see your camera, think it's a toy, like a tourist camera. If you had a big fine camera, dey would have broke it up. I have seen dem do it."

My Olympus XA-2 35mm was small and pocketable—the very reason I carried it—and had fooled less sophisticated people before, but it was not short on quality.

"Up here we got to go fast," Sebastian said. "Give 'em the least shot at us." He was almost racing the Honda, taking it through the mountain curves tight and rapid.

He hammered out a narration of each destroyed home, each flattened place of business. El Quiche province was a model of the communist guerrillas' effort to wreck the economy of the country. The crops lay untended now, dying by the row. The Indians had fled from the fields, going where the danger was less, but safe places were running out in Guatemala.

Villages just off the road were abandoned, emblazoned with rebel propaganda graffiti ("Political power comes from the nozzle of a spray paint can," to paraphrase Mao), and even the road itself bore warnings and slogans in red paint.

"Dey come up here and kill de people," Sebastian said. "Dey make dem run. Back in de villages, everybody gone."

In spots the edges had been blown off the road where rebel mining parties had dug under the asphalt and planted charges. Big trees had been dropped across the road from the high embankments and dragged out of the way by early-morning road-opening patrols from the army.

When we came to a spot where sheet tin was laying bent and pierced by the roadside, Sebastian pointed up the hill. "It came from de church. If you want to go up dere, you got to be *so* careful. The rebels, dey leave booby traps." He parked the Honda in a concealed spot behind the trees and I could see the agitation in his eyes as I climbed out of the backseat. The whore seemed scared too.

"We don't want to stay around dis part of the world long," he said. "Not too long."

I nodded and ran up the hillside, noticing bits of concrete blocks scattered among the roots and grass. It was steep enough for me to have to grab from tree to tree near the top, where I saw the source of the debris.

Like a small Alamo, in a clearing overlooking the road and the panorama of the mountains beyond was a church and what was left of the village it once served. The church was a ruin of hollow concrete-block walls and the skeleton of a tin roof. It was never designed to be a fort.

Bullets had punched out rows of holes in the crumbling concrete. Explosions had blown out the front door and made gaps in the walls large enough to walk through.

Then I saw the booby traps.

They hadn't even tried to hide them. The rebels wanted people to keep away. It was all part of the terror. Exposed trip wires and obvious mines were randomly placed from the cracked walls of the church to the village.

As I ducked into the church through a breach in the wall, I was thinking only of the booby traps I couldn't see, the one that would keep me from spending the profits from this recon. Looking over the broken rim of the church, I saw the smoke from the fires that were consuming the Indians' corn crops. Sebastian had pointed them out to me as we'd driven up the twisting mountain road, but they were far away then. Now they were just up the hill from where I stood.

I left the church, stepping over the shattered cross blown down from over the front door, and walked into the village. I found scorched adobe walls, glassless windows, and empty rooms.

There had been a fire in the plaza, fed by household furnishings and other ejecta, and as I stood at the edge of the ashes, I slowly recognized shapes under the charred wood and rusting, twisted metal oddments.

People had been burned there.

I could see the mounds of heads, shoulders, and the rigid thrust of arms and legs. The features had been burned away. I counted at least four different adult corpses in the pyre. I photographed it all with my Olympus.

Sebastian would be getting very agitated by now. I had been away too long, and he was where an alert army road patrol could find him.

As I carefully walked through the booby traps back past the church and down the hill, I strained my eyes watching the shadows under the trees, anticipating the suggestion of movement that would mean I was not alone. A face-to-face encounter with the rebels now would be either very interesting if they decided to take me in, or fatal if they chose to shoot.

Sebastian was out of the car and waiting for me, his nerves almost twitching through his skin. We had the long drive back, hopefully without interference from either side, and after what seemed like forever, we made it.

It was early afternoon. I felt as if a week had passed.

2:00 P.M., 10 April: Isabella

I needed help badly during this recon, but I didn't expect to get it from the beautiful girl who was waiting for me when Sebastian left me at the hotel. She was my main contact on this trip, someone who could escort me around town, translate, and who understood what I had to do. Her name was Isabella, and, like Sebastian, she was a spy. What would look more natural than a man and woman together, strolling tourist-oriented Guatemala City?

I had to visit the presidential palace downtown and inspect its security. This meant looking for obvious methods of protection like guards and gun bunkers, but also for increases in security, such as new bunkers or firing positions on nearby street corners.

That part of the mission was risky. Taking photos of the palace was forbidden if they focused on details of the security, so cameras were way up on the guards' list of suspicious items. I had little choice in how to go about my photography . . . getting in there and doing it was the only way.

Naturally I used Isabella as a model, photographing over her shoulder as we mingled in the Easter crowds that thronged the plaza before the palace, keeping the viewfinder on doors, windows, and antennas as we traversed the entire four sides around the palace. It was an old trick. Later, with some amusement, I saw it used in the movie *Dogs of War*.

I timed the changing of the guards and counted their positions on the balconies that looked down on the streets, noting their armament and alertness. Isabella was very professional, posing and smiling at the right times, acting innocent, but keeping her eyes open for any sign of danger.

It took several lip-biting walks around the palace to get all the photos, each time having to leave the Easter festivities in the plaza and the cover of the crowd.

On a street near the palace was a funeral parlor. I watched what I realized was a funeral in progress. Right in the middle of Easter, a casket was being loaded into a hearse. Isabella listened to the grieving family and told me it was their son, and he had been killed for political reasons.

Before Montt, under Garcia, political killings were frequent. I saw now it continued, but to what extent I did not know.

Our palace assignment over, Isabella and I took a taxi to the airport, where I was supposed to get identification numbers of the private planes parked there. The Guatemalan army was already under an alert to watch out for a countercoup launched by Garcia's people, and it did not make my job any easier.

Isabella told the taxi driver to take us on a certain route through the city so I could see some of the war and coup damage there. We drove slowly past a tall, modern skyscraper with most of the glass blown off its front by a truck bomb. The lower floors were heaped in collapse to the street.

It had been a bank building, she explained, bombed long before the actual coup by rebels because it belonged to the Garcia family. The chassis of the small Japanese pickup truck used to carry the explosives was embedded in the street.

On other streets, there were more buildings bombed or burned, the empty windows covered over with plywood or canvas. Each one was an isolated selected target. Some of the sites were guarded by soldiers with submachine guns, who eyed us suspiciously as we rode by. When I had seen enough and photographed what I could, we left the city and went on to the airport road.

The airport was practically abandoned. Most of the outside doors were locked and guarded. Easter holiday had something to do with it, but not all. Certain areas of the airport were blocked to civilians, but I could still see the private planes from the glass-walled lounge facing the airstrip. I took as many photos of the planes as I could whenever the roving guards weren't around, but I knew that was not going to be good enough. I had no telephoto capability. I asked Isabella to show me how to get down to the ramp so I could get better shots.

She led me to a stairwell that served as an entry and exit for the airport employees, motioning for me to wait while she talked to someone below. I waited in the stairwell and watched the feet of the jungle-booted guards as they paced the lounge hall above me. Finally, Isabella called me and I hurried through the open doorway to the landing below. Isabella's accomplice, a man dressed in cook's whites, nodded to us as he emptied garbage into cardboard boxes by the restaurant dumbwaiter.

Just beyond were the rows of private aircraft. I walked down the line, photographing registration numbers, not wasting a moment. Isabella stood back by the building, watching the door. I realized anyone in the lounge who looked down steeply enough out of the windows would see me. What did Murphy say? *Anything that can go wrong will go wrong and usually at the worst possible moment.*

I was at the far end of the line of aircraft when Isabella squealed a warning. I ran the fifty meters to where she had been standing, watching her disappear up the staircase, her high-heeled shoes clattering.

I caught her quickly, bounding the steps two at a time. She said something about a guard and kept running.

I would have headed for the same door we came down from but Isabella passed it completely, going another floor higher. She hit the upper landing and in that instant of transition, one of her ankles turned.

She went down before I caught her and stifled a scream of pain. Her ankle was badly twisted, already turning blue, and the red weal from a hard impact directly on the knee of the same leg indicated double trouble.

Her breath came in muffled gasps. I held her to keep her from thrashing while I listened for sounds of pursuit.

There were none. Had it been a false alarm? Too late now.

She was forced to lie and tremble in pain, fist in her mouth to keep from crying out. Just on the other side of the door, helmeted guards made their rounds, unaware of us . . . I hoped.

The problem was going to be getting her out of the terminal without attracting attention. In a few minutes, when she'd recovered enough, I pulled her up. There were tears in her eyes from the agony of standing, but she brushed the dirt off her knee and, with me supporting her, managed a semblance of a normal walk.

We went slowly through the terminal, close together like sweethearts, faces betraying nothing. Most of the interior stairwells were barricaded. Even the elevators were guarded. We were two levels too high, looking down to the main deck, and just when walking any distance was critical, we had to keep moving until we found an unblocked stairway.

Isabella had to rest by the time we had gone down one level, trying to appear nonchalant as she sat on a bench and massaged her knee. When we finally reached the lowest floor, I saw all of the exit doors had been tied shut with wire through the handles and were under guard.

In sweet Spanish, Isabella asked a young guard blocking our way to please open his door. The boy smiled and unwrapped the wire holding the double door, explaining to us he was not supposed to do this and we should be in another place in order to leave the building. We left with polite apologies—but we did leave.

I had to get Isabella back to her house. Her ankle was rapidly becoming unusable, and the loss of her assistance was going to crimp my operation. I had no other contact like her, and when I helped her through the gate to her house, I knew I had lost a brave operative.

Her pay, and the pay to her superior, had been made, but she had asked a favor of me. She wanted her quetzales (Guatemala's unreliable currency) converted to American dollars. I agreed to do it, and told her to call me at my hotel at 2000 hours that evening.

Isabella did not call me at the hotel. I took the rented Honda and drove back to her house. It was closed and locked, with no lights showing. I didn't have the time to find out what had happened to her, but I knew if she had been arrested, I might not be far away from the same treatment.

Trouble also arrived for me that night in Guatemala. When I returned to my hotel, my door was locked and my own key would not open it. I had to go down to the desk to get the manager, who came up with me and opened the door with his key. He smiled and apologized, saying there must have been a mistake.

Looking over my room, I discovered my luggage had been carefully but thoroughly searched. Now I had to be cautious. Someone was on to me.

Sebastian met me for breakfast the morning of the third day, and I explained the events of the night to him. He told me, not surprisingly, that the assistant manager of the hotel was actually part of the security police, something like the U.S. FBI. The fact that the man was fishing for clues meant he didn't yet have anything concrete on me, but it was a very bad sign. It was time to leave.

11 April: The Airport

I had Sebastian drive me to the airport and said good-bye to him there. He had many missions behind him, his most recent infiltrating into Nicaragua and blowing a safe to recover special documents.

I had to change my tickets to conform to my new plans. I was standing at the counter with my travel bag beside my feet, the clerk writing me a new ticket to Miami, when I looked across the halls and lounges of the airport building and blinked in surprise.

Isabella was sitting in one of the rows of chairs, watching me. Her expression was strained and fearful.

A feeling of dread began to grow in my stomach. Something very bad was in the making. I slowly scanned the rest of the travelers in the airport. Which of them were agents?

The clerk handed me the ticket and told me my exit gate and flight time. I had a half hour yet.

Isabella was glancing toward a gift shop, as if indicating I should go there. I picked up my travel bag and walked to the shop, looking at curios and trinkets. She followed me in, using a rack of postcards in the shop to shield herself from observation.

"The police are here to arrest you," she said.

"Where are they?" I asked.

"In the lounge. There are two of them," she said.

"Did they catch you?" I asked.

"Yes, last night."

"What did you tell them about me?"

"Nothing but that you were taking pictures."

"Is there a way out of here?" I asked.

"No. They have you blocked. They have sent for more men," she said.

"They have to know you're talking to me now," I said.

"They think I am asking you to go to lunch. They want to arrest you in private, because you are an American," she said.

My thoughts raced. I wasn't armed. My flight was waiting now, if I could get to it.

"Isabella, I have an idea," I said, "but we have to do it quickly, before the reinforcements arrive."

"What?" she asked, nervously peering past the postcards at the waiting travelers in the airport.

"We'll go out together to the restaurant upstairs where your friends work. I need to get the police to follow me," I said. "When we get inside the restaurant, I'll take care of them."

We walked out of the gift shop side by side, faking smiles and conversation. I saw two men in sport clothes rise from their seats to follow us, a discreet few moments apart.

I was getting angry, temper pulsing in my veins. I felt my senses sharpening, my muscles contracting. I would strike first, with as much power and speed as I could manage.

The little restaurant was semiprivate, around a corner and shielded from the hall by a glass door. I opened the door for Isabella, using the opportunity to spot the two dark Guatemalan men out of the corner of my eye. The nearest one wore sunglasses. Both of them had on loose-fitting sport shirts worn outside their trousers, which meant they were carrying pistols.

"Go sit down," I told Isabella. I then stood against the wall by the door so the first man through would not see me immediately. There was a cook and waitress behind the counter, and a lone patron at a corner table.

The door swung open and the man in sunglasses stepped in, looking at Isabella. He was of medium build and slightly shorter than I.

I struck him in the side of the head with a backfist, all my torso and arm in the blow, and he dropped as if shot.

The sunglasses were twisted and broken, but still on his face. I grabbed his body and pulled him to the side, feeling for his pistol. It was a heavy .45-caliber automatic, stuck in the waistband of his pants. I jerked it off him as the door opened again.

His partner walked in. I smashed his face with the .45, staggering him, but he recovered and dodged, blood spattering from the cut on his cheek where the pistol had hit him.

I couldn't remember how to say hands up in Spanish, so I said *"¡Halto!"* and pointed the big pistol at his chest, cocking the hammer. He was dazed by the blow, but charged me anyway, fumbling for his pistol under his shirt. I hit him again with the .45, smashing the steel automatic against his temple.

The man fell, and I got a glimpse of the waitress and cook gaping at me, their mouths open in surprise.

The man with the broken sunglasses opened his eyes and sat

up. I kicked him in the face, bouncing his body back to the floor, then kicked him again so hard in the groin I moved his entire body. I couldn't have either of them in any shape to stop me.

Isabella was watching in horror. "Please," she said, "please don't kill them!"

I looked at her, then back at the two unconscious men on the floor. There was a spreading puddle of blood under the scalp wound of the man I had hit with the pistol. Neither of them was moving. I realized I was aiming the .45 at them as if I intended to shoot them where they lay. I lowered the weapon.

"I have to get to my plane," I said, and told Isabella where it was. She was horrified by my attack on the two agents and now seemed to be scared of me.

"Goddamn, I'm not going to hurt you," I said, and she moved, motioning me to follow her out through the cook's exit from the restaurant.

We went down the stairs to the lower airport level. "You have to go there," she said, pointing toward a hallway. I could see a Boeing 707 at the dock through the window.

I dropped the pistol in a garbage can.

"Go and tell them I escaped," I said. "Tell them I've left the airport to go back downtown."

"Yes, yes," she said.

"Will you be all right?" I asked her.

"You have to go now," she said. "The cooks will have called the guards."

I nodded, and didn't know what to say. She had to stay behind. I thought she was very brave. It was an emotional moment.

"*Vaya con Dios,*" she said, as I walked away.

Two days later I delivered my film and notes to the British in the resort city of Montego Bay, Jamaica, where the beaches were scenic, the sea placid, and guerrilla wars and Isabella seemed far, far away.

CHAPTER ELEVEN
Massacre in Lebanon

Paul Johnson, who first trained at Merc School in 1981 and later became my executive officer, began his combat duty in Lebanon. While serving as a mercenary with the Christian Militia under Saad Haddad, he witnessed the massacre of the Palestinian refugees at the Sabra-Chatilla camps near Beirut. I debriefed Johnson on his return to the United States. I later wrote the following account of what he told me. What follows is my best recollection of the oral report he gave me, just as he recounted it in the first person.

September 1982: Massacre: Beirut, Lebanon

It all started off as routine. We were told to report for duty, and crewed up two tracks and drove northward toward Beirut. Both of the track crews were Arabic except myself and a Canadian, so I couldn't talk much to them.

The drive north from Marjioun to Beirut was a long one, and we were on the road all day, going through Israeli roadblocks. When we finally got to our destination I didn't even know where we were. Nobody tells you anything, but maybe if I had spoken Arabic I would have understood more.

We were at the south end of a refugee camp. This camp was made of shacks and some old buildings, and was surrounded by barbed wire. Our mission was to provide security while a unit from the Phalangists went in to search the camp for hidden weapons and PLO disguised as refugees.

The Lebanese wanted the regular Palestinian people out of

their country now that the PLO had lost the war for southern Lebanon. The Palestinians in these camps had been forced out of their homes either by the fighting or by direct arrest from the Israelis and Phalangists, and now they were being held in these barbed-wire compounds.

Sure, there were weapons being concealed in the camps. Searches were going on all the time and all kinds of weapons were turning up. But what was really bad was that the new president of Lebanon, Bashir Gemayal, had just been killed by a bomb, and the Phalangists were mad. Gemayal was well liked.

The first funny thing I saw happen was the Phalangists putting on our (Christian militia) shoulder patches. I knew those weren't our guys. We had a patch that hangs off the epaulet of your shirt, so you can change it from uniform to uniform. The patch is a printed reproduction of the Cedar of Lebanon on a blue background, so it's easy to identify.

Next, a truck showed up. It had yellow Israeli license plates on it. About sixteen Israeli soldiers got off the truck, and they did some changing too . . . putting on Phalangist shirts and hats, so they would look like the other Phalangists. The Israelis left their Galil rifles with the truck and took Kalashnikovs, which were what the Phalangists carried. I thought they might have been Israeli Special Forces or intelligence people who were going to observe the searching so there would be an accurate account of the operation. The Israelis don't trust the Phalangists.

It was getting dark, so flares began going up from supporting Israeli units around the camp to light the search. These were little hand flares, not big ones.

The Phalangists opened the gates and went in, with the Israelis mixing in with them. I was trying to rest outside on my track.

Nothing special happened for a couple of hours. I heard a few shots from time to time, but that's common and nobody pays any attention.

Suddenly there was an outbreak of small-arms fire from inside the camp. It didn't sound like a massacre, it was the kind of fire you hear in a firefight—you know, fire and return fire. We jumped up in the track and locked and loaded. Nobody knew what was going on, and we didn't want to get surprised by anything.

The firing continued, but now it sounded like a one-sided

fight. The firing was heavy for an hour or so. The first clue I had to what was really going on was when I saw the people in the camp begin to run to the wire. They were running this way and that, running into each other. They were screaming, "I have no weapons, I have no weapons," in Lebanese. I understood that much.

The soldiers were firing on the people, shooting them down as they ran. This was a big camp. I couldn't even see the other end of it from where we sat. The Phalangists were shooting civilians inside their houses, in the alleys, in the streets.

There were children in that mess. They couldn't get out because of the wire, and they were shot along with everybody else. I couldn't believe what I was seeing.

Because of the size of the camp and the fact that it was dark, the Phalangists had to hunt down a lot of the people who were trying to hide from them. They kept finding people and shooting them for hours. There was continual screaming. The Phalangists were rousting the refugees out of the backs of the shacks and lining them up against the walls and shooting them.

After about six hours, we got a radio call. I think Major Haddad had gotten word about what was happening. The message said to get out of there and come back to Marjioun *now*.

We left, just started up the tracks and took off. We had that long ride south and we took the highway road down through Sidon.

We had no trouble getting back. They let us through the roadblocks okay and we finally made it back to base. Nobody said anything to us or asked us what happened, but the very next day all of us who had been on track duty at the massacre were assigned to duty up along the Syrian border.

I didn't like the fact that the Phalangists massacred those people, but it wasn't a surprise. You'd have to live in the Mideast for a while to really appreciate how those people hate each other.

The Israelis who went in dressed as Phalangists probably couldn't do anything about it once the first shot was fired. Hell, if they'd tried to stop it, *they* would have been shot. The only thing that really puzzles me is why those Phalangists put on our insignia before the massacre. Were they the ringleaders, with plans to blame it on us?

21–27 September 1982: Hasbia, Lebanon

We were then on duty in the mountains. The duty was back to boring again—roadblocks. It was even slow roadblock business. Not too many people came up our way.

Firefight

Hassad, who was one of the militia people on duty with me, and I decided to break the monotony of the roadblock with a trip up the mountain to a local village. We had done night duty together, so a bit after ten in the morning we hitched a ride from a civilian to the closest village, hoping to get a beer and something to eat.

We hiked into the village from where our ride dropped us off. I had my M16, and Hassad had his FN. Main street into town was a gravel road, and there were few people outside their homes. I realized we were being shunned, making it all seem a little like the old western movies where the townspeople stay away from the strangers because there's going to be trouble.

We stopped at one shop for a beer, but were told they had none. About the only sound in town was some Arabic music playing at the mosque across the other end of the village. When another store said they had no beer, I began to get suspicious. We bought a 7-Up instead, and the shop owner there treated us to a cup of coffee.

When we left his shop, he followed us out and locked the place up. That was strange too . . . especially when I saw a local boy come to the shop door and try to get in, not understanding why the shop was closed.

Hassad and I began walking out of town. It was just about eleven-thirty now. There was *nobody* on the streets.

A sniper opened up full auto from our left front.

Hassad spun and fell, dropping his weapon. He was hit and I didn't know if he was dead or alive. I leapt toward an embankment, bringing my M16 up and spraying at the sniper, who was on the roof or the balcony of a building just in front of me.

I jumped off the road down the embankment, thinking I

heard a weapon fall and hit the road from the building. Maybe I had hit him. Before I was down the bank, another automatic rifle began to blast away at me, hitting all around the embankment where I had been.

The cover in the ditch at the bottom of the embankment was pretty good. The guy was hitting short and long of the hole I was in. I was *low.*

I returned fire by holding my rifle out of the ditch and shooting blindly with it, trying to make noise and keep him busy, but I only had two thirty-round magazines with me.

There was nothing to do but wait. If I came out of the hole he had me.

The roar of an armored personnel carrier from down the hill broke the silence. It came closer, racing up the road toward me.

The track charged into town, the .50 hammering, then braked and ceased fire. I heard voices yelling in Hebrew. I held my M16 over my head and slowly came out.

There were two PLO bodies. I had hit one of them with my first burst, and he was wounded. The guy hit by the .50 was cut in half.

Hassad was wounded, hit in the upper chest. The wounded PLO, Hassad, and I were all piled into the track and driven down the mountain to the roadblock.

My team leader caught hell for letting Hassad and me wander off.

2 November 1982: Marjioun, Israel: Car Bomb

I usually got up about 0600 and went to breakfast at 0630 back in garrison. My usual breakfast place was Joe's, a small shop about two hundred meters from our merc house. Joe's sold meat-and-cheese pies, soft drinks, and beer. He had a table with four chairs inside his shop, but I used to sit outside in the mornings and watch the women go by.

Today I wanted to do something different. There was another shop in a different direction I had been intending to check out. They sold falafels, a change from my daily meat-and-cheese pie. I picked up my M16 and walked to the new shop, and bought a falafel and a beer, and sat down outside to eat.

Something big exploded near Joe's, boosting a huge cloud of smoke into the air and throwing rubble everywhere. I was about four hundred meters from the blast.

I ran for Joe's, seeing burning pieces of a car scattered in the street. Families were screaming and people were mobbing the road. When I got to Joe's, there was a terrific amount of confusion. Shops were on fire, ambulances were trying to maneuver in to get the wounded, and there was the frame of a car with the tires, engine, and body blown off it laying in the street.

I could tell where the car had been parked before it exploded —it would have been almost directly in front of Joe's, where I usually had my breakfast. The front of Joe's little shop was burning, knocked in by the bomb.

The building beside Joe's, the storage area for a hardware store, was caved in as well. The fruit-and-vegetable market across the street was blown away. There was fruit all over. Other buildings on the street were badly damaged. The ambulances were loading people as fast as they could.

I heard three people were killed and nine injured by the car blast. If I had been sitting there eating one of Joe's pies, I would have been dead. That was a hell of a car bomb.

There were no military targets on that little street, just working people and vendors.

I left for Tel Aviv and a plane back to the States a couple of days after. It wasn't soon enough.

CHAPTER TWELVE
Private Operator

The phone rang one night in the spring of 1983 while I was working late on some paperwork in The Bunker's office. I recognized an ex-Special Forces officer's voice when he gave me his customary, booming hello. He was an old friend, but I hadn't heard from him for some time.

He wanted to know where he could get quantities of small arms, preferably M16's, saying he had a secure foreign buyer for them. He still had the Special Forces in his blood. I could tell he was serious by the way he described his prospective deal, and I agreed to meet him so we could discuss the details face to face.

A few days later, in a restaurant not far from his home and also near the Anniston Army Depot, he outlined his project to me.

He was working with Larry Dring, he said, who was a close friend of his from Vietnam and the Special Forces. Dring was working in Lebanon now, the Phalangists employing him as a training and procurement officer. The Katibe, an assembly of Lebanese forces that included the Phalangists, wanted to replace their Soviet bloc AK-47's and AKM's with something that looked more like a free-world weapon.

They favored the M16, but felt Israeli prices for them were too high, as were the prices for Israeli helmets and webgear, which they also wanted. Colt would not sell to the Katibe directly, since they were not the actual Lebanese army, and an end user's certificate from a recognized government that the U.S. Department of State would honor was necessary for such a deal.

After thinking the situation over, I told him there was a means of getting the M16's, if the quantity was sufficient to justify the trouble. We could buy unfinished weapons receivers in

Taiwan, and shop out the rest of the parts from various European
sources, all except for the barrels, which would have to be figured
out later.

He said the eventual quantity would exceed ten thousand.

It was enough to take the trouble, I told him.

They also wanted 9-millimeter submachine guns, he said,
with silencers. That dovetailed perfectly with the M16's, because
I had recently seen a hybrid CAR-15, which was chambered for
9-millimeter parabellum, while on a trip to the Frankford Arsenal Works outside Miami. Colt was coming out with a 9-millime-
ter CAR-15 as well, but the Frankford Arsenal model was already available, and it could be fitted with a sound suppressor.

I had ordered one out of Miami as a sample, and called my
friend in mid-May, after it arrived, so he could arrange a meeting
at Dring's home for all of us.

July 1983: Larry Dring

Dring's job with the Special Forces had been in the same
highlands country in Vietnam I had prowled through on long
range patrols, Pleiku and Kontum provinces. He had been a
medic and, like my friend, had more than his share of wounds
and medals. He now lived in South Carolina, near the old military school of the Citadel, with his wife, whom he had met in
Pleiku in the TET offensive of 1968. She had been with a religious
mission there as a nurse. Dring had been dragged into her hospital, badly wounded.

We drove from Anniston to visit Dring in July, between the
Fourth holiday and the midmonth upcoming Merc School class.
We worked for several days, clarifying the details of the actual
numbers of rifles, shipping, payments, and port of entry. The
novel 9-millimeter CAR-15 impressed Dring, and he thought it
would make a good weapon for the Special Forces group the
Katibe was trying to organize.

When we left, I had made a friend in Dring. I promised him
answers to the logistical questions of the M16 project for his next
trip to Lebanon, which he planned for late August, the soonest he
would have a new load of equipment ready for the Katibe.

The Chinese Connection

The M16 project was big. I phoned, wrote, or telegramed all the right sources for parts. I collected price quotes, delivery dates, and other specifics, relaying the information to my friend, who told Dring.

My inquiries brought me into contact with something interesting. A U.S. firm named Tron-Tech, based in Atlanta, Georgia, had recently gone to the People's Republic of China and secured an agreement with the P.R.C.'s Ministry of Defense to sell Chinese-made weapons. Tron-Tech had the means to sell anything, from Type 56 Assault rifles (AK-47's) all the way up to the Red Arrow (Soviet Sagger) wire-guided missiles, and the HN-5, China's copy of the Soviet SA-7 Strela shoulder-fired, heat-seeking, antiaircraft missile. The company signed me to represent them in Central America, an advantageous position, since hardware like missiles can open many doors.

Military Intelligence

I was sitting on my side of the steakhouse restaurant booth, a Tokorev pistol in a shoulder holster under my windbreaker. I did not initially trust the two men who had asked me to dinner.

Tokorev's have a guide ramp system that eliminates most feeding jams and no safety at all, unless you count the halfcock notch on the hammer gear, which was where my hammer was at the moment, just clearing the firing pin. There was a steel-core, high-velocity round in the chamber and seven more in the magazine, capable of punching through a body armor vest that might stop a 9-millimeter or .357 Magnum slug.

The phone call that made me borrow the Tokorev out of the Merc School armory had come only a few days earlier. The man who wanted to buy me dinner said he was with the government, and he wanted to meet and talk.

Since the affair with the FBI in 1970, my dealings with the government had been minimal, just the Cuban escapade in Miami and the intelligence report from El Salvador.

Earlier in the evening, I had driven to a specified hotel in town and was met in the lobby by a man in casual clothes who recognized me although I didn't know him. We drove to the restaurant in his rental car, looping a few side streets to discourage tails, to meet his partner.

Once we were in the privacy of the high-backed booth and dinner was ordered, they showed me their identification. It was for U.S. Army counterintelligence, a branch of M.I., or Military Intelligence. They said they had been aware of the Merc School and had planned to talk with me for some time.

The two agents were polite, nonchalant, and friendly, with a disarming off-duty attitude. We talked easily, our subjects weapons, world hot spots, and Vietnam. There were a few probing questions in the conversation, drawing me out, gently testing.

By the time we had eaten, I had heard their proposition. They wanted me to act as an asset for them. My travels and involvements could possibly add corroborating pieces to official intelligence pictures. "We want to create sources of intelligence outside the system," they told me. "It keeps everybody more honest."

The agents explained there was an effort not to duplicate the distorted intelligence reports that caused so much of our trouble in Vietnam. I could agree with that. It seemed an invisible bond existed on the organizational charts, a parallel network for intelligence and operations, and the "other army" had places for people like me. The official term for us was *private operators*.

"What if I break the law doing this?" I asked, when our conversation drifted to weapons smuggling.

"I break more laws in a week than you'll break all year," one of the agents said. "Nothing goes into hard copy."

We left the restaurant and went to another hotel where they had a room booked, for the formality of my reading the papers they had brought for me. My signature was required on a binding document related to the National Security Act, if I agreed to work with them. I read the agreement carefully. I thought about my AWOL, the grillings M.I. had given me, and the military prison. Part of me did not want to have anything to do with the army. Part of me recognized the importance of the opportunity.

I signed. The army and I were reunited.

Over the next few months I was in and out of several low-profile meetings with various agents until I had a permanent case officer, understood my ground rules and knew the drop addresses, signals, and contact phone numbers. From this page on, my M.I. contact will be called Brooks, who is quite featureless and was actually different men at different times.

After all, it's my signature on the document.

My appointment as Tron-Tech's sales rep for their Chinese weaponry and my contracting with the agency Brooks represented was one of those rare right-place/right-time coincidences.

The U.S. government was searching for a source of missiles for a covert operation that was going to be run by the National Security Council and the CIA. This operation would eventually lead to the Iran/Contra fiasco of 1986. It may seem like I'm getting ahead of my chronology, but this chapter is the place to tell the story.

In the summer of 1984, during a routine lunch meeting I had with Brooks, I mentioned to him that I had Chinese weapons, including missiles, to sell for Tron-Tech. Brooks was immediately interested, and asked me not to tell anyone else—government agency or "commercial" customer—of the availability of the arms.

Hindsight tells me Brooks was on the lookout for some missiles because through channels he knew they were desired. Specifically, large numbers of tactical missiles were needed for a covert sale to Iran. I did not know that at the time. Possibly, even Brooks knew little of the overall operation, but he did know missiles were needed.

Brooks asked me to provide him with all the information I could on what weapons I could sell. I did, giving him color brochures on the missiles, printed in English and French. I presumed that any sale I made would be for covert purposes, otherwise the U.S. and China would simply sit down together and arrange a deal on their own.

Tron-Tech was pleased I might have a buyer, Brooks seemed pleased I could provide missiles, and I was pleased in anticipation of making the sale and banking the commission, so we were all happy.

I arranged a meeting later that summer among Brooks, Tron-Tech executives, and myself to begin serious discussions about a sale.

My first surprise as our negotiations went on was that the government wanted missiles in far larger quantities than I expected. My impression from the outset was that our intelligence people wanted a small quantity of Red Arrows or HN-5's for testing or for training purposes.

I also had thought the HN-5, being a small heatseeker, would be the missile of primary interest for covert purposes, possibly to be given to the contras or Afghan rebels.

When I learned the Red Arrow was the main missile wanted, and wanted in quantities starting in the hundreds and going into the thousands, I was puzzled.

The Sagger-type "Red Arrow," or in its official Chinese designation "Hong-Jiam 73," is primarily an antitank missile.

It is about a meter in length, and 73 millimeters in diameter, with stubby little tailfins. It is fired off a small portable launcher, and as I mentioned earlier "wire guided," meaning a thin control wire unreels from the rocket in flight, connecting it to a hand-held joystick.

The gunner guides the missile right to its target. I was told the range of the Red Arrow was about three thousand meters.

Our "TOW" missile (tracked optically by wire) is very similar, although the TOW II is supposed to be superior. Stories of TOW's that "went ballistic" (out of control) or that launched and actually came back at the gunner made me wonder.

Egyptian use of the Soviet-supplied Sagger, the Red Arrow's twin, stopped Israeli armored attacks in the short Egypt-Israeli 1973 war, contributing heavily to the Israeli losses. The Sagger type was obviously capable.

We were talking about combat loads of Red Arrows, not research or training quantities.

"Where are these things going?" I asked Brooks one day.

"Mideast, I think," he said without elaboration.

Two thousand Red Arrows or more seemed to me to be too many for the Afghans, and the only other conflict in session of any size was the Iran-Iraq war. I wondered which side we would be supporting.

The president of Tron-Tech knew major arms sales didn't normally take place in hotel rooms and was understandably uneasy about some of the aspects of the details of the transaction, so a brief meeting was set for the Tron Tech exec with FBI agents in Birmingham to vouch for Brooks and his official status, improving relations all around.

Much information had to be obtained from the Chinese—

not a talkative bunch—and Tron-Tech needed to keep a flow of technical descriptions, numbers, and other requested facts coming via phone and Telex out of Beijing.

By late summer and into the fall of 1984, as I was finishing with the Panama operation and just about to enter the Sikh one, problems with the Red Arrow sale were beginning to emerge.

Tron-Tech wanted too much for its missiles, something I tried to tell the company, since I was in the middle between buyer and seller and knew the private complaints of both sides.

Second, the government was beginning to doubt Tron-Tech's reliability. Would, or could, Tron-Tech keep the sale a secret? One of the company's executives was clandestinely taped, in a fit of anger, threatening to expose me (to the government of Panama) "as a CIA agent." He didn't know my actual affiliation.

His anger was over how I had represented Tron-Tech's interest during my trips to Panama. He felt justified, but I could not explain my actions to him, what I was doing in Panama was classified.

There were outside pressures on the National Security Council and CIA in the planning to make the missile sale to Iran. The two worst were time and money. Arabic middlemen were involved as cutouts and, to them, the pricing and delivery schedule of the missiles was critical, because vague promises had already been made by them to Iranian officials.

For a variety of reasons, by January of 1985, Tron-Tech had been eliminated as a source of missiles. U.S. stocks of TOW missiles were then moved out of the Anniston Army depot in quantity.

By taking TOW's out of U.S. stock, the National Security Council could get them cheaper ($3,500 vs. $8,000) than from Tron-Tech, and an assured quantity was on hand.

The deal would go bad on the Reagan administration and the Arabic middlemen. The administration would suffer the exposure of a sensitive covert operation seen as defying Congress. Key NSC officials would be indicted. The Arabic middlemen would lose face and money, and incur personal risk.

What began as a true black operation with Tron-Tech, using foreign missiles and no direct link to the United States, became a sloppy transfer of traceable TOW's.

Critics of the exposed operation would accuse the U.S. of

using the missile sale as "baksheesh" (Arabic for bribe) or as ransom to get American hostages back.

The administration would defend the operation as a covert foreign policy attempt to establish relations with Iranian moderates.

But let's get back to 1983.

September 1983: Casualties

Dring was delayed on his return to Lebanon due to a money-and-ticket transfer hitch, which was to my advantage since it allowed me to get the last of the M16 project information to him.

No M16 parts had to touch U.S. ports on their ways to the Katibe-held port of entry, where they would be assembled.

Early September started a hot, snake-infested two weeks of Merc School along the Warrior River, and when I was out of the field on a supply and communications run at the end of the first week, the message was waiting for me that Larry Dring was dead.

Dring had died of natural causes while at home. He had been only days away from leaving for Lebanon. His wife knew nothing of the liaison arrangements through the Katibe for delivering my information on the rifles.

Two of the key Lebanese in the arms deal had also died recently, in combat in Lebanon. It was a disastrous coincidence. The M16 project was thoroughly disrupted, as dead as the men who had made it go.

I took the news of Dring's death to the grim, dirty Merc students, who were cleaning their weapons at the time. Larry Dring had been well-known in the small world of hired soldiers, and the men were silent as they listened to my announcement.

When the Merc students graduated, the traditional Legion toast that ended our dinner was dedicated to Larry Dring, and I think it was given with the most feeling I had heard in a long time from a tired but proud group of new Recondos.

CHAPTER THIRTEEN
The Nigerians

I slid the long thirty-two-round magazine of .380 ammunition into the pistol grip of the Ingram M11 submachine gun, seated it with a firm slap of my palm, and pulled the bolt back to the cocked position. The folding stock was extended and locked.

The man getting out of the Ford sedan in the dark didn't know I was there. He was tall, black, and wore a suit. He carried a large revolver in his right hand.

I could see he had a partner who waited in the car, behind the steering wheel. I gripped the M11's sound suppressor and waited, watching the man with the pistol walk from the remote end of the parking lot toward my office building.

They thought I was in it, alone.

But I was in the high grass that edged the parking lot instead. It was nine-thirty at night. The lot and buildings were deserted.

They were obviously Nigerians, part of the coup faction. I had told Khaki John the damn coup group was dangerous, and they would probably try to kill us if they were double-crossed.

As the man neared the building, he assumed a crouch and raised his pistol.

"Drop it!" I shouted.

For an instant he was stunned, but then he pointed his pistol toward me.

I fired the Ingram. It had a cyclic rate of over twenty shots per second. With the suppressor, the sound was muffled to hissing violence.

The gunman leapt backward, stumbling, running for his car. I fired again, trying to graze my bullets across the pavement. I thought I heard some of them ricochet.

The headlights of the Ford came on, starkly illuminating the grass where I was concealed. I put my last burst across the front of the car, trying to shoot out its headlamps.

The man jerked open the car door.

I quickly pulled the empty magazine out of the M11 and reloaded. The Ford accelerated toward me.

I took careful aim at the windshield, the stock of the M11 tight against my shoulder, methodically pulling the trigger, placing my bursts just above the bright headlamps.

The Ford veered, and I put holes into the passenger's door. I saw the silhouette of the gunman drop in the window, then the Ford was rocketing past me.

I tried for the rear window as the car slid onto the main road, but after one shot, the Ingram's bolt slammed on an empty chamber.

It was cold in Alabama, and Christmas of 1983 was near. I had been involved with the Nigerians since March, on a spring day when Khaki John had come into the gunshop and asked about buying quantities of pistols.

March 1983: Khaki John

Khaki John was tall, young, handsome, and lived by his wits. He was always on the lookout for a fast, painless way to make money.

He had graduated Mercenary School in 1982, and I knew he was resourceful. He had earned his nickname because of the khaki trousers he had worn during his training.

Khaki John came to me with an odd story. He claimed to have a buyer for large quantities of pistols and ammunition, and possibly this buyer might want to hire graduate Recondos for overseas employment.

Not surprisingly, he would not reveal any details about his request, but we did search through some firearms catalogs at The Bunker to price various types of cheap, small-caliber pistols.

"Can I get a lot of these, I mean a *whole* lot, and not have to fill out the paperwork?" he asked about the pistols, which was a typical Khaki John question.

"John," I said, "you have to fill out the forms if you only

buy *one*. If you buy a hundred or so, you've got to fill out more forms. There's the Multiple Firearms form, the—"

"But can't you fake it somehow? Can't you tell the government they were lost, or stolen?"

"No," I said. "What in the hell do you want them for?"

"I can't say just now. I promised I wouldn't. Let me go back and talk to my contact, okay? I'll get his permission."

"Okay," I said, putting away the firearms catalogs.

John was obviously up to something devious.

---

3 May: Ravens

When Khaki John came back to The Bunker, he was more willing to talk, but what he had to say seemed to come out of the usual bag of incredible stories he used whenever he was trying to fool someone out of their money.

"I've got some foreigners who want the guns and the mercs, and they have the money to pay for them," John said.

"What foreigners?" I asked.

"I can't say right now."

"What do they need mercenaries for?" I asked.

"For a job in their country," Khaki John said, which didn't tell me much.

"What kind of guns do they want?" I asked.

"They want Ravens," he said.

I almost laughed. A Raven was one of the cheapest .25-caliber automatic pistols in the world. They were not even made of steel, but cast of zinc.

"Why Ravens?" I asked.

"I don't know," Khaki John said. "Maybe they want to use them as throw-aways."

"How many do you want?" I asked.

"I can order fifty now," he said, "and fifty more as soon as that bunch gets in. I know they'll buy three or four hundred like that." Khaki John was serious. He thought he was going to really make some money.

"What's the word on the mercenaries?" I asked.

"My contact says he needs a six-man team to begin with. I knew I could get the guys through you. How about it?"

"Sure, we can get six men, but I have to know a few things first. I can't advise anyone to take an operation without some information about it," I said.

"Well," Khaki John said, "they'll be going to Africa."

"For combat or what?" I asked.

"As trainers," he said. "That's all I know."

"What about money?" I asked. "How are you going to pay?"

"Cash," Khaki John said. "My contact will give me cash for everything."

"All right," I said. "I'll order the pistols, but when I tell you to get over here with the cash, you do it."

"No problem, Frank. These guys have the money. They really do," he said.

23 May: The Smugglers

The case of fifty Raven pistols was resting on the concrete Bunker floor. I telephoned Khaki John to come and pay for the load. To my surprise, he agreed immediately and said he would see me within the hour. I was waiting in the office when John arrived. He had the cash in his pocket and paid me for the entire shipment. I was astounded.

"See?" he said. "I told you I was good for it."

I counted the money while John examined the pistols and ammunition.

"I need to take one with me," he said, "so they can see what they look like."

I made him sign a form to take possession of one pistol, and explained to him I would have to prepare the rest of the paperwork so the entire shipment could be released.

Khaki John was smiling. He had his case of pistols and hadn't even tried to delay payment, argue me out of the agreed price, or do anything except hand over the cash.

"John," I said, "I believe you. Let's get this operation going. I'm not going to try and take anything away from you. I want to help. You make money and I make money. How does that sound?"

"Great," Khaki John said. "Okay, I'll tell you what's happening. You know I'm working with this import-export guy named Chivers. He's British."

"Go on," I said.

"Well, one of his clients is African. I've met him a few times, and he wants to buy a lot of different things to send back to Nigeria," Khaki John explained.

"Like what?" I asked.

"Shotguns, pistols, field generators, you name it. I think the guy's in the black market or something."

"Why does he want mercenaries?" I asked.

"I don't know. It's really a friend of his who wants the men. Their family is really important in Nigeria. I think one of them was a past president or something of the country."

"Are these pistols going to Nigeria?" I asked.

"Yeah," John said, "but you don't have to tell anybody."

"Are you crazy?" I asked. "If Customs catches you smuggling weapons they'll throw you in jail, twenty-five autos or rocket launchers!"

"No, I've got a safe way out for them!" John protested. "These Nigerians control the Customs in Lagos, where the ships dock. They smuggle things in all the time."

"This is trouble," I said. "If those guys are approaching you for weapons, they've already approached other Americans. It's possible their whole operation is already infiltrated, and you'll get carted off to jail when they are arrested."

"No, Frank, no one knows about—"

"John! Think for a minute! They talked to you, and they don't know who you are!"

He sat down, depressed, because he knew I was right.

"Look, level with me," I said. "Tell me what these Nigerians are doing. Maybe there's a way to stay clean and get their money too."

"Okay. I should have told you from the start," he said. "I've been working with Chivers. He was a security adviser to Libya. He said he was a mercenary. He actually threw Kaddafi in jail once."

I could appreciate Chivers, and nodded my head approvingly.

"Paul Atueyi is the Nigerian I know; he's been doing business with Chivers. He wants to buy these guns and ship them to Nigeria."

"What do they need guns for?" I asked.

"To sell them, I think," Khaki John said. "They can get an amazing price over there, but they want bigger stuff too."

"Such as?"

"They need a lot of submachine guns," he said. "Their family is involved in some type of coup."

"They told you that?" I asked, disbelieving he would have been taken into their confidence, but then again, Khaki John was good at fooling people.

"Yeah. But I don't care about a coup," he said. "I just want to sell them guns. I need the money."

"Are the mercenaries for the coup?" I asked.

"Probably," John said. "They might need the guys to go into the jungles and train the rebels."

I had to stop and consider for a moment. Coup stories are common. Almost everyone I met from a Third World country had a coup on his mind, but the actual purchasing of weapons, even throw-away .25's, was a bit of solid evidence something was happening.

"I don't want you going to jail," I told Khaki John. "Let me ask a few questions and check this out."

"Okay, Frank, but whatever you do, don't ruin my deal. Let's make some money off these guys, because they've got it."

"Well, that agrees with our information," said George Barns, an agent from the Federal Bureau of Alcohol, Tobacco, and Firearms (BATF). "We've been getting tips that Nigerians were buying pistols in order to smuggle them out of the country."

"Any reason why?" I asked.

"Looks like they're selling them in Nigeria," Barns said.

"Any hint of the use of the firearms in a coup attempt?" I asked.

"You mean to use the little gun to get a bigger one?" Barns countered.

"Yeah."

"No. Nobody has said anything to us like that. That wouldn't be our concern here anyway. All we do is make sure they buy or ship the guns legally," Barns said.

I told him of the purchase of the Ravens and of John's Nigerian contacts.

"Well, you better talk to that boy," Barns said, "and get him working with us, because smuggling firearms is a serious offense."

---

24 May

When Khaki John came back to The Bunker to pick up the other forty-nine pistols, I explained that BATF already had some knowledge of Nigerians buying pistols in our area.

"If I were you," I told him, "I'd make a deal with BATF and buy the guns for the Nigerians, take their money, and let them go to jail."

"Okay," Khaki said, "I'll do it, but please, let's milk this thing. These Nigerians have too much money to just let them get away."

"What's the word on the coup?" I asked.

"Well, Peter Atueyi lives in Birmingham. He told me his family is part of one of the tribes that lost out in the last election, and the government there now is really down on them, taking their land, cattle, and so on."

"Is there any way I can meet Chivers or Atueyi?" I asked.

"Sure," Khaki John said, "I can arrange it when the time is right."

Khaki John carried the case of pistols out to his car and drove away. I didn't know it, but BATF agent George Barns himself was parked across the street in his sedan, watching John leave.

Barns and a backup chase van pulled into traffic behind him, intending to follow John to his destination with the pistols.

Khaki John drove east on Interstate 59 from The Bunker to Birmingham, realized he was being followed, and as he was passing the exit ramp to the Federal Building downtown, suddenly took it.

Barns was forced to cut across several lanes of traffic to continue the pursuit. At the bottom of the ramp, once he had confirmed there was a chase car on him, Khaki John drove into traffic and stopped at a four-way intersection.

Barns followed him, and as the light changed, John made another surprise move. He accelerated, leaving Barns locked in traffic. To add insult to injury, Khaki John smiled and waved at the agent as he regained the ramp back up to the interstate. Barns had simply been embarrassed. I had been fooled. John was already planning to ship the pistols out of the country. He had built a false-bottom packing crate that contained a cooker-boiler, and hid the pistols and ammunition inside the crate. He then took the crate to a shipping firm at the airport and sent it to Lagos, Nigeria.

The first shipment of pistols was on its way.

---

28 May

John returned to The Bunker, again all smiles. "I need that second order of fifty pistols," he said.

"What did you do with the first ones?" I asked.

"I've got them in storage," he lied, knowing I wouldn't agree to help anymore if I knew he had shipped the pistols.

"Okay," I said. "How many this time?"

"Fifty more Ravens."

"Any word on the mercenaries?" I asked.

"Oh yeah, that's the reason I came over," Khaki John said. "I had a talk with Atueyi. He said the tribes in the south of the country seem to have a pretty tight plan for their coup, working with the military and all . . . but they need shotguns and submachine guns, to arm the tribesmen."

"Twenty-five-caliber Ingrams?" I joked.

"No, this is serious. I told Peter you could get all the submachine guns he needed. You can do that, can't you? This will make us rich," John said.

---

6 June

Khaki John drove to The Bunker, paid in cash, and took delivery of the second fifty Raven pistols.

About a month later I received a phone call at The Bunker from a man who identified himself only as "a friend of the people I was doing business with in Africa." He asked if I would meet him in Atlanta to discuss a matter of possible mutual interest. I agreed and made a note of his arrangements for me to meet him. He asked me to come alone.

The Coup Liaison

The caller had instructed me to check into a certain hotel and wait to be contacted. I was not informed in advance where I would meet him.

I was then called at the hotel and told to go to a nearby restaurant. Waiting inside, at a corner table, were two black men dressed formally in business suits. They nodded to me.

I walked to their table, and they stood when introducing themselves. They used only first names, saying they were Michael and Thomas, and they were Nigerian.

"I understand you have done business with some of my countrymen," said Michael. He seemed to be the senior of the two.

"Yes," I said. "I'm helping purchase merchandise for Peter Atueyi."

"Mr. Camper, we have been told about you and your special training facility in Alabama. We are interested in people such as those you train. I think we can do business."

Michael's English was impeccable. Both of the Nigerians were well dressed, their suits expensive, nails manicured, and all the right details were there, such as properly folded pocket handkerchiefs and genuine gold cufflinks.

"I'm not usually so blunt," I said, "but I understand you may need help with a coup attempt."

Michael looked at Thomas, then back at me. "Yes, that is the reason. I was not aware Peter had already told you," he said quickly.

"Not Peter. It was my friend John," I said.

"Well, in that case, perhaps we can dispense with some formalities," Michael said. "Yes, we do oppose the present government in Nigeria. It is corrupt, and it is ruining our country. Are you recording this?"

"No," I said, standing. "You can check if you like."

Michael smiled. "That is not necessary. I know you have

been supplying the pistols to my friends. I believe we can trust you."

"What we need are weapons," Michael said. "They will be distributed to the tribes in the south in order to gain their support."

"These would be nine-millimeter submachine guns?" I asked.

"Yes, and perhaps some shotguns for the tribes that prefer them."

"Of course," I said.

"Yes," Michael said, "but we still need a number of men who can train the tribes in the use of firearms."

"I have them," I said.

"Would you be willing to go to Nigeria yourself?" Michael asked me.

"That would depend on my schedule," I said. "When would it be necessary? When would you need the men, or the weapons?"

"Very soon," Michael said.

"I'll have to get back to Birmingham and contact you," I stalled.

"That is good," Michael said. "We can meet back here in Atlanta."

After handshakes, I left the restaurant and drove back to Birmingham. The next day I met with Khaki John at The Bunker. He was not aware of my meeting in Atlanta.

"John, those guys are dangerous." I said. "We're talking about the overthrow of a government here. If you try to play with these people, they're liable to kill you."

Pressured, his better sense prevailing, John admitted to shipping the pistols out of the country, and told me how he did it with specially made crates.

I shook my head in disgust. "That's both a Customs *and* a BATF violation! I told you to keep yourself clean," I said.

John was undaunted. "Nobody can prove a thing," he said.

"Prove it?" I asked. "Hell, all they have to do is come and ask you for the pistols. When you can't produce them, you've had it."

That worried John, but not enough. "I'll think of something," he said. "Anyway, if I don't go along with the Nigerians, they'll get suspicious."

"We've got to go to the BATF and get you off the hook," I said.

"How?" John asked.

"You've got to agree to work for them," I said. "It's your only chance."

I introduced John Martin to Bureau of Alcohol, Tobacco, and Firearms agent George Barns first on a telephone call, so Barns could assure John that the moment he came into the office he wouldn't be arrested, then arranged for them to meet.

John went to be interviewed by Barns and took the shipping papers on the false-bottom crate with him. He had personally given the second order of fifty pistols to Peter Atueyi.

During his interview with Barns, Khaki John said nothing about the coup, because I had warned him it was not a BATF responsibility.

In the summer of 1983 (about the time I was being recruited by Brooks), Khaki John disappeared, and I didn't see him for months. He hadn't requested that I purchase more pistols, and I had no further contact with the Nigerian coup organizers in Atlanta.

Then in September John surfaced. He came to me in serious trouble, confessing he had stolen over $10,000 from the Nigerians, and they were threatening to have him killed.

He had been accepting money from them to buy weapons, and he had simply taken it and delivered nothing.

"Why did you do that?" I asked, totally amazed.

"I thought they would leave the country," Khaki John said. "Who the hell could they tell? They're more illegal than I am!"

"Good God, Khaki!" I said. "Those people are serious! They'll be after your ass for sure."

"Well, they think you're working with me," John said. I could have shot him myself.

"There's one chance," John said. "If you'll go with me to meet Chivers and tell him you'll make up for the pistols, maybe he can convince the Nigerians to leave us alone."

"John, this is insane," I said. "You didn't even let me know what was happening. Those bastards might have come looking for me, and I wouldn't have had any warning."

"Frank, you have to help me!" he pleaded.

I thought about it. This was my chance to meet face to face

with Khaki John's local partners in international crime. With the
threat of Nigerian assassins, I was now into the operation on a
very personal basis.

I met with agent Barns and made an employment agreement
to penetrate the Nigerian weapon-smuggling scheme. I formally
notified my M.I. contact that I was doing it and told him I would
pick up all the information I could concerning the coup plot.

John Chivers was growing old now. He was in his middle
sixties, with white hair. His manner was classic British, and the
officer he had once been was very evident in his demeanor. For
years he had been a security adviser to Libya, finally forced to
leave as Kaddafi took power.

Now Chivers occupied an office in downtown Birmingham,
where he operated his import-export firm. I sat in his office, facing him and Peter Atueyi, the young Nigerian who had been
buying the Raven pistols to smuggle into Nigeria.

Atueyi was refined, educated, and well dressed—very much
like the Nigerians I had met in Atlanta.

John was there as well, squirming in his chair as Chivers and
I talked, comparing figures on how much it would take to make
up for what Khaki John had stolen.

Atueyi was quiet, commenting only occasionally. He didn't
even look at Khaki John. Atueyi seemed to be relieved to have
met me.

I told Chivers directly that Khaki John had simply stolen
the money and made no effort with me to buy any more pistols.

Chivers suggested that Atueyi continue to do business with
me, but with a suitable discount granted by me for the next ship-
ments of firearms until the money stolen by John was matched.
Peter Atueyi ended the meeting by placing an order with me for
150 more pistols and asked me to return to Chivers's office a
week later and pick up the money.

As Khaki John and I left the building, I waited until we
were well away before I asked about Chivers and the coup.

"He doesn't know anything about it," John said. "Peter's
never told him. For God's sake, don't mention it around him."

10 October: The Sting Begins

In Chivers's office, Peter Atueyi paid me a cash deposit in advance for the pistols he wanted. I knew then that he trusted me. Chivers and Khaki were there, watching and smiling.

I wanted to approach him about the coup, but didn't dare at the time, until I felt he was ready to confide in me. To enhance our relationship, I invited Peter Atueyi to my office to inspect the concealment of the pistols and ammunition into water tanks, for smuggling into Nigeria.

21 October

Peter Atueyi drove his silver Volvo to my office, and met Khaki John and me there. BATF agents were waiting in a van in the parking lot outside, photographing Atueyi. I had the water tanks, tools, and welding torches displayed for Atueyi to see, plus a tall stack of Raven pistols still in their factory boxes. He was very happy with the arrangements.

When Peter Atueyi left the office, John told him he would meet him later in the day, on my direction to discuss the coup. When John came back, he was not cheerful. Atueyi had told him "his friends" wouldn't trust him anymore, because he had stolen the money.

"If you could get the addresses of the other Nigerians working with Peter, would that help?" John asked.

"That would be perfect," I said.

"Well, in Chivers's office, he has a file with a list of Peter's friends in it. I know some of them have to be in on the coup attempt," John said.

"Where does Chivers keep the file?" I asked. John had seen him take it out many times, and told me precisely.

27 October: Video Evidence

The BATF agents came to my office early and set up their videotaping equipment in the storage area above the offices so they could see down the length of the entire warehouse bay.

Chivers and Peter Atueyi were coming to visit so Chivers could see the water tanks and stacks of pistols and Atueyi could pay me for his current order of pistols.

Chivers and Atueyi arrived on time and inspected the welding tanks, pistols, and cut-open water heaters.

The videotape silently recorded the money changing hands.

As soon as Chivers and Atueyi were gone, the agents confiscated the cash and left.

31 October: Illegal Entry

It was Halloween night, the time of evil spirits, and I was preparing to go out into the dark and into Chivers's office.

I had noticed a reconstruction project on the back side of the building and seen that it was possible to enter the building from the alley by climbing the scaffolding.

Dressed in black trousers, sweater, and jacket, I drove downtown in my VW, carrying my Tokorev in a shoulder holster under my jacket, a thin-bladed knife, and a small flashlight.

I parked on a side street near the building and walked down the alley to the construction site.

The scaffolding was easy to climb. I went up several floors before I reached the windows, sheets of plastic hanging over them as weather protection. I brushed aside the plastic, pushed open the windows, and ducked inside the building, not using my pocket flashlight, feeling each step across the floor to keep from bumping into anything.

I had memorized the building layout, and after a few cautious minutes found the door to the stairs, and hurried to the floor where Chivers's office was located.

The building was old, and its office doors were unsophisticated, made of stained wood and translucent glass. The locks were simple. I only had to push against the door properly to force it away from the jamb, then slip my knife blade against the bolt so the blade could be rocked until the lock released itself.

Once inside the office, I shone my light on the file cabinets until I found the one I wanted, opened it, flipped through the files, and removed the Nigerian folder.

Then I closed the office door, hoping my exit from the building would be as easy as the entry. I moved faster now, eager to get out, and after going down the stairs, climbed out again on the scaffolding.

At home, I read through the documents and found many names with business and personal addresses in Birmingham, Atlanta, New York, and New Jersey.

I had what I needed.

I telephoned Chivers at his office and told him the lie that the pistols and ammunition had disappeared from my office warehouse and that John had vanished, which was true. I had first thought John was simply staying low for a day or so, but he had not come back.

30 November: Assassins

Sitting in Chivers's office, I again wore a body recorder for BATF and discussed the loss of the money and the pistols with Chivers and Atueyi. Chivers said the Nigerians were going to send hit men after John if he did not return both.

Peter Atueyi was afraid. He said his own people might kill him, just for dealing with John.

16 December: Warning

Chivers called The Bunker, with Peter Atueyi and another Nigerian in his office. I could tell by the tone of their voices they were having a serious meeting. The Nigerian whom I did not know spoke to me. He was threatening, telling me I had to correct John's thefts and pay Peter back the money, or I would be held responsible.

John had not returned. He was in more immediate trouble

than myself. The coup faction knew him personally, and would want him first, or so I thought.

---

19 December: Attack

I returned to Chivers's office, my Tokorev under my jacket, and talked to Chivers and Peter for the last time, as a delaying tactic.

Peter was distraught. Chivers said if Peter returned to Nigeria, he was a dead man.

The Nigerian hit men's attack on me came only a few days later.

I believed I had hit one of the assassins, by the way he had fallen into the Ford, but there was no way to be certain; .380 bullets don't penetrate car doors too well.

I went back into the office and reloaded my empty M11 magazines, my fingers slightly unsteady. My nerves were only now reacting to the firefight.

---

1 January 1984: The Coup

I was in New York City, my face stung by the winter cold, when I noticed the front page of the *New York Times*.

A coup had occurred in Nigeria over the New Year, and the government had fallen. There was temporary disorder, but the new leadership was rapidly reorganizing things, and there had been little violence. Only a few military officers and politicians were dead or jailed.

---

19 March: Resolutions

Peter Atueyi pleaded guilty. John Chivers was found guilty by the court. Both were ordered fined and deported from the United States.

John had left Alabama, on the run from the Nigerian hit men, moving through Georgia and then north to Michigan. They never found him, and BATF did not prosecute John because of his cooperation.

After the one violent attempt at revenge, the Nigerians left me alone. They had wars and problems to deal with, and in 1984, so did I.

CHAPTER FOURTEEN
Panama

The Soviet Mi-24 Heavy Attack Helicopter, code-named by NATO as the HIND, was a flying weapon of awesome statistics. It could carry loads of rockets, guided missiles, infantry troops, rapid-fire cannons, and machine guns, all at the same time.

It had a pressurized crew cabin to fly at high altitudes, was fully armored against ground fire, had missile-jamming electronics, night-vision equipment, and a radar and laser-aimed weapons control. It also held the world's airspeed record for a helicopter of its class, being able to accelerate to over two hundred miles per hour and sustain it.

The Nicaraguan didn't have to keep telling me about how fearsome the HIND was. That much I already knew. What I needed were the manuals and parts he wanted to sell from the HIND's he claimed Nicaragua was going to receive, and we were bargaining for the price.

Our meeting was in a Holiday Inn hotel room in Panama City, Panama. North of us, in Nicaragua, the anticommunist contras were battling the Sandinista army, which was trained and armed by Cuba and the Soviet Union.

What had brought me to Panama had begun several months earlier, with a letter.

---

10 February 1984: The Bunker

The letter was from a firm in Panama. It said a special unit in the Panamanian Defense Force wanted to test a commando vest I had designed that was being advertising in several military magazines.

The vest was unique in that it combined the features of a bulletproof vest with the capability to carry all of the basic equipment a soldier would need in the field. The firm requested a commando vest for testing, plus other items for the special counterterror unit in the Panamanian Defense Force called the UESAT, or *Unit Especial Seguridad Anti-Terror* (Special Anti-Terror Security Unit). They wore only the color black. The UESAT needed black uniforms, caps, boots, and jackets, and other combat load-carrying equipment.

23 June: Panama City, Panama

I was met at the airport by Carlos Sanchez, a strongly built Panamanian who had retired early from the old Panama National Guard after badly injuring his back in a parachuting accident. Carlos was now a civilian purchasing agent selling to the Defense Forces of Panama.

The title National Guard had been dropped in favor of Defense Forces, because Israel had been helping Panama to organize and train and Israel called its army the IDF, or Israeli Defense Force.

The UESAT had tested my commando vest, and it had passed, the first one to do so from many other vests tested.

"It stopped the bullets," Carlos said, "but it knocked the man down."

That comment surprised me. They had actually tested the vest on a man. What had happened to the wearers of the vests that had failed? My first few days with Carlos were typical of new business. He took me on a tour of Panama City, with its sixteenth-century ruins of coastal forts and cities and its modern shopping areas and slum tenements. I saw the tropical countrysides where farmers still used burros and oxen and, of course, the Panama Canal.

The United States was giving the Canal Zone to the government of Panama. President Carter had signed a treaty in 1980 with Panama for the transfer of the canal, after threats by General Torrijos, who was then military director of Panama, to destroy the canal.

Carlos drove me past empty U.S. military barracks behind the fences of the Canal Zone, and I saw moving vans parked at some of the private homes of the American workers. Carlos told me as each section of the Canal Zone came under the ownership of Panama that under the 1980 Carter-Torrijos Treaty, the soldiers and civilians in it had to get out, and if they were not gone by the assigned date, everything they had on the premises would be confiscated.

Carlos and I also drove out in his Toyota from Panama City to Flamenco Island, which was off the tip of the old Amador U.S. Navy base. On the island was a massive World War I artillery position, a fortress in concrete, mostly below ground. It was now the home of the Anti-Terror unit.

---

27 June: Unit Especial Seguridad Anti-Terror

The UESAT base, or Garavito's Island, as the troops called it after the commander of UESAT, Lieutenant Garavito, was a beautiful place, with beaches, lush tropical fronds, palm trees, and cooling sea breezes.

The men lived in the underground barracks that were once for the gun crews of the heavy shore artillery. They had offices, their infirmary, and an armory in the rooms surrounding the fortress.

The Anti-Terror base was accessible to vehicular traffic from the mainland only by a long narrow roadway raised just above sea level, with a .50-caliber machine gun covering the road from a bunker on the hill behind the base.

UESAT was made up of one hundred men, divided into three groups, with bodyguards, headquarters staff security, and anti-terror assault responsibilities. The unit belonged to General Noriega, successor to General Torrijos.

Noriega had established the UESAT himself when he had been a lieutenant-colonel. His position in the Panamanian intelligence service had given him the leverage to propel himself to de facto ruler of Panama after Torrijos's assassination. He had done it with a combination of spying, betrayals, elimination of enemies, and large-scale, successful cocaine dealing.

The UESAT served its security functions but was also Noriega's private army. It received the best equipment, financing, and personnel.

Carlos knew Lieutenant Garavito personally, and we spent days at the base with him, changing the design of the commando vest to suit the needs of UESAT.

Each night, Carlos and I would meet for dinner, and I sensed he was making decisions about me. Whatever he wanted to propose, I estimated he would approach me before I left Panama.

The subject came up the night before I was scheduled to leave.

"You are a businessman like me, is that right?" Carlos asked.

"Sure," I said.

"We have to make our business anywhere we can, don't we? Sometimes it is very hard to make a living."

"Of course," I agreed.

"Do you think you could arrange to sell some equipment and not have to tell your government about it?" Carlos asked.

"It would depend," I said. "Is it weapons?"

"Oh, weapons are not necessary. What about uniforms and insignia?"

"Yes, I could get uniforms and patches, things like that," I said.

"Do you care if this equipment goes to Nicaragua?" he asked.

This was the opening I had been waiting for.

"Not as long as they pay their bills," I said.

Carlos admitted to me he had a contact with a Nicaraguan diplomatic representative in Panama that needed U.S. uniforms and insignias, and possibly bulletproof vests and special weapons such as Ingram submachine guns.

I didn't know if Carlos was working with the Sandinistas or simply had the chance to make a sale to them, but either way, it was an advantage to me.

I left Panama, flying back to the United States with an order to deliver fifty commando vests to the UESAT and equip them with black caps, uniforms, boots, and other items.

* * *

I met Brooks, my M.I. contact, in a restaurant and described what had occurred in Panama.

"Do you think Carlos is an agent for the Panamanian government?" Brooks asked.

"I'm not sure," I said.

"Well, is he working for the Nicaraguans?"

"Maybe," I said, "but he could be an independent."

"Yeah," Brooks agreed. "Let me tell you what they want with our uniforms. We've had reports of units of communist guerrillas in El Salvador and Guatemala, dressed in U.S. uniforms. They wear them to fool the local people, even the army, and make them believe they're part of the government."

"That figures," I said. "They also want the proper insignia. What should I do?"

"Make the arrangements for the sale," Brooks said, "but you're taking a real chance with Carlos. He could compromise you a half dozen different ways."

15 July: Miami

I met Carlos in Miami. He was there on a business trip, and we stayed in the same hotel near the Miami airport so we could collect and reship the large boxes of vests, boots, uniforms, and other equipment coming to me in Miami before we flew together back to Panama City.

"I showed your vest to the Nicaraguans," he said as we arrived in Panama. "They want some like it. They also want the uniforms. Will you talk to them?"

"Sure, when do we do it?" I asked.

"We can go now," he said. "First we have to meet a man. You understand, this is security."

"Sure, I understand," I said.

The Nicaraguan agent waited for us near the memorial of the old tower, part of a church that had been burned by the English pirate Morgan over four hundred years ago, when the entire city and fortifications had been destroyed.

The ruins were somber and beautiful, tropical flowers growing out of the gaps in the ancient stone walls, empty windows, and doorless portals. The sky was darkening for the afternoon rain as we parked off the highway.

I saw a lone man sitting on a bench near the tower, wearing a loose white shirt and tan trousers. "That's him," Carlos said.

The man was very casual, smiling at us as we approached him, and to an observer, he could have been any visitor enjoying the scenery.

"Ah, Señor Camper," said the Nicaraguan, extending his hand, "welcome to Panama." I returned his smile and firm handshake. We sat on the bench, at ease with each other.

"I understand you have military items for sale," said the Nicaraguan. "Perhaps we can make a deal."

"Good," I said. "What do you need?"

"We should discuss business at my office," he said. "Can you come there tonight?"

"Sure," I said. Carlos nodded also. I was noticing how Carlos responded to this man, and it was with respect.

"We'll be there," Carlos said to him in English.

I met Carlos that evening in front of the hotel. He seemed to be in a bad mood, and I wondered if everything was going smoothly.

"I don't want anything to happen," Carlos said. "I need to make this deal."

We parked two blocks from the Nicaraguan's consulate building and walked to it, entering through the front gate.

The building had once been a private home. It was tastefully furnished. I was admiring the heavy furniture, rugs, and art when I saw two things that reminded me we were on business. Prominently hung on the wall were framed photographs of Fidel Castro of Cuba and Daniel Ortega, President of Nicaragua.

Our friend from the park came out of a doorway, still dressed the same, and flashed his disarming smile. "I am glad you could make it," he said. "Please come back to my office. I have ordered coffee for us, genuine Nicaraguan coffee, the best in the world. If you like it, I can send some back with you."

There seemed to be only a few people in the building. The typewriter on the secretary's desk was covered, and the side offices were dark. We followed the Nicaraguan—who had still not given me his name—down the hall to his office.

He did not go behind his desk, but sat on one of the leather-upholstered chairs circled around a coffee table and motioned for us to do the same. The coffee was brought in by a servant, served on a silver tray, and we drank it, observing a traditional custom, revolution or not.

I knew microphones—if not a videotape—were probably operating somewhere. I stayed relaxed. Carlos did not seem to be doing as well.

"As you know," said the Nicaraguan, "we are being forced to fight a war with your country that we do not want. How do you feel about this?"

"I think Somoza was a dictator and he should have been overthrown," I said.

The Nicaraguan smiled even more broadly. "Thank you," he said. "Not many Americans understand. All we want is peace and the opportunity to restore our economy. That is why we are dependent on purchasing items from abroad."

Now Carlos smiled.

"We need uniforms for soldiers," he said, "and certain military insignia, such as rank and branch of service. Would this be a problem for you?"

"No," I said.

He asked me about the types of uniforms and insignias I could obtain, and how much they would cost. I told him I could get anything he wanted, the price determined by condition and quantity.

He opened a drawer and produced several insignia of the Salvadoran Army, and asked if they could be reproduced. Again I agreed, knowing a small company in the States that made police and military insignia. I used them to make my own Recondo Black Lightning patches.

"There are actually many things we need, often of a specialized nature. Carlos tells me you also sell bulletproof vests."

"That's right," I said.

"And the submachine guns, the Ingram type. They are very small. I am also interested in them," he said.

"The Ingram is a good gun," I replied, "but can't you get the Czech Skorpion, or the Soviet Stechkin?"

"Yes, of course," he said, and I knew then he was familiar with weapons, "but I really prefer the Ingram. I would rather have the nine-millimeter cartridge."

I nodded.

"Would you be able to come to Nicaragua to do business?" he asked.

"Yes," I said, "but I would need to do it very confidentially, without any stamps in my passport. I don't want the American government knowing my business."

"We can arrange for that," he said. "When will you be returning to Panama?"

"I should be back in two weeks," I said.

"That will be fine. Just tell Carlos, and we will arrange everything." He stood, and I knew the meeting was over.

Carlos exposed his politics entirely on our way out of the embassy.

"After the revolution," he said, "I can live in a house like this."

HIND Mechanic

I had a room-service breakfast, read the newspaper, and tried to watch some local television, but didn't have my heart in it.

Finally the room phone rang. It was Carlos.

"I have this guy here, and he wants to see you," he said. "Is it okay to come up?"

As soon as Carlos knocked on my door, I opened it. A nervous young man followed him in.

"I have something special for you," Carlos said, much more confident this morning than he had been last night. I shook the man's hand and he appeared somewhat relieved.

"Sit down," I offered, "and order some breakfast if you like. Who is this?"

"Just call me Benito," the young man said. "It is the name my friends use."

"Good to meet you, Benito," I said, as Carlos called room service. "Do you work with Carlos?"

Benito looked to Carlos for the answer, who frowned at him. "He works in Managua," Carlos said, "and he would like to make a deal with you."

I leaned back in my chair and raised my eyebrows. "Okay," I asked, "what is it?"

"I am an aircraft mechanic," Benito said. "I work at the airport near Managua City."

"Okay," I said.

"He has something to sell," Carlos said.

"What is it?" I asked.

"I am being trained to work on helicopters," Benito said. "And now we have a special project. We are going to receive some military helicopters, and I am going to be trained to service them."

"Nicaragua already has military helicopters," I said.

"Yes, but only the Mi-eight type. We are going to receive the Mi-twenty-four."

"Is that an armed helicopter?" I asked, as if I didn't know.

"Yes, it is armed with many different types of weapons," said Benito.

"What do you want to sell?" I asked.

"We have manuals for the Mi-twenty-four. I believe they might be valuable. Would you like to buy some of them?"

I had to answer carefully. Carlos could be setting a trap for me, or if Carlos were dumb enough, perhaps the Nicaraguans were using Benito to trap the both of us.

"I don't know," I said. "What would I do with helicopter manuals?"

"You could sell them to your government," Carlos said.

I knew our intelligence people would pay for almost anything off a HIND. We didn't know much about them except for the fact that they were flying terrors.

"Maybe," I said, "but I don't know. They probably have all they need about the Mi-twenty-four."

"No," said Benito, and began a long description of the HIND and its systems, telling me the Cuban and Soviet technicians who were training him had said everything about the helicopter was secret.

"How much would a manual cost?" I asked.

"Each one would be a thousand American dollars," said Carlos.

"I can get some spare parts," Benito said, "but they have to be small ones."

"Can't you get into trouble by trying something like this?" I asked.

"Oh, no one will ever know," Benito said. "My friends control all of the manuals and the parts. I can get as much as I need."

"Are the helicopters there now?" I asked.

"No," Benito said, "they will come later this year. We are training now on the engines, transmissions, and electrics. We have everything in a hangar, and it is guarded, so it cannot be photographed."

The news that HIND's were going to be introduced into the war was important. They could make a serious difference with their ability to attack the contra camps.

"I really don't know," I said. "I'll have to go home and ask some questions. Can Carlos get back in touch with you?" I asked Benito.

"Yes, anytime," he said.

Breakfast came for Carlos and Benito, and they ate as I drank coffee and pretended to read the paper. I was impressed with the variety of covert projects Carlos was able to produce.

I thought now I had him figured. He was part hustler and part spy. He made his money from whatever quarter he could.

An interruption came that temporarily closed some of the government offices and even took the time of General Noriega himself. A Defense Force infantry patrol, searching the border area between Panama and Colombia, discovered a large drug processing and storage station hidden in the jungle and destroyed it.

Reinforcements for the patrol were moved in, and the size and importance of the event grew as the infantrymen increased their tally of captured cocaine almost hourly.

General Noriega flew to the site with his staff to inspect it, and walked among the soldiers busy chopping down and torching huts and equipment that had belonged to the Colombians.

The incident was a near disaster for Noriega, one Castro would later have to fix for him, as a middleman. The site actually belonged to the infamous Medellín cartel in Colombia, and Noriega had been paid to secretly protect it. The attacking patrol had acted without knowing that. The cartel was furious.

Then, a few days later, the Colombians counterattacked.

A large raiding party of well-armed Colombian guerrillas, part of the Medellín cartel's private army, crossed over the border and boldly attacked the military headquarters of the region of Panama that touched Colombia.

They shot up the army and police station buildings there, and withdrew after inflicting many casualties.

The Defense Force went on full alert, asked for and received military assistance in the form of helicopter support from the Americans, and placed dozens of large patrols along the border as a blocking force.

About twelve Colombian guerrillas were captured as they tried to make their way back across the border. What happened to them became a military secret.

I flew home, knowing I had to talk to Brooks again.

I met with him in a hotel room in a small town outside Birmingham, and we talked about the possibility of obtaining HIND manuals or spare parts and about making the sale of uniforms to Nicaragua.

"This is tricky," Brooks said. "I know we need the manuals and parts if we can get them, but this doesn't agree with any intelligence I've seen. Are you sure he's talking about HIND's? We don't have anything that indicates that Mi-twenty-fours might be going to Nicaragua."

"It was Mi-twenty-fours," I said. "I didn't misunderstand him. He said they would be arriving later this year."

"Well, if they do, this is the first we've heard of it," Brooks said.

"Do I agree to buy the manuals or not?" I asked.

"I don't know. They may be trying to trap you. You're dancing on this one. Don't take any risks."

As Brooks walked out of the hotel room, it was clear he didn't believe me about the HIND's. I felt a chance had to be taken to gain this intelligence, and knew if the opportunity came, I would probably take it. I was on my own again.

---

12 August: The General

General Noriega was playing both sides against the middle, working with the U.S. and with Cuba. Through Noriega, intelligence on American military operations, positions, and technology was leaking to Cuba. This had caused the U.S. Military Group in Panama to cut American-Panamanian military cooperation to a minimum while not appearing to do so, and the Panamanian Defense Force had withdrawn as well. Neither side communicated with each other at all on matters of intelligence.

Adding to Noriega's drug smuggling and ever-increasing bribe takes, he was a tolerated liability to the United States, not an asset. Of course, he commanded all of Panama's troops, but the UESAT was his personal guard.

Since I was able to get close to UESAT, right inside the gate, I decided to gather as much intelligence on the Flamenco Island Base as I could.

I arrived back in Panama on 12 August with that goal, as well as the risky HIND project, in mind.

Carlos met me at the airport, and we spent the morning at the G4 (logistics) office downtown, discussing more equipment purchases.

The business of the next day was to go back to the UESAT base and help them conduct tests of bulletproof glass and compressed fiber glass armor.

The testing involved photography and many different calibers of weapons, and took most of the day. Every step I took, every sign over every doorway, I memorized.

I wanted to know their schedules, routines, unit breakdown, locations of arms rooms and communications—everything, including creating an accurate plot of the camp in my head.

I even mentioned to Carlos that Lieutenant Garavito should send some of his men to Mercenary School. Carlos interpreted this for me to the lieutenant, who thought it was a good idea and said he would select some of his men for that purpose. Evaluating its men in my own environment would get me even closer to UESAT.

During the noon meal that day, as I was eating with the troops in the newly completed mess hall inside the base, a man wearing sport clothes entered the room and sat at Lieutenant Garavito's table.

"That is the Israeli Defense Force liaison officer," Carlos said to me, looking down at his soup.

I ate and watched the Israeli watching me. I knew UESAT had support from the IDF and sent a number of its men every year to train in Israel. By now the Israeli had to know who I was.

After chow, as we were all leaving the mess hall, I paused to see if the Israeli would speak to me.

"So you did come to Central America," he said as he met me by the door.

I nodded, trying to appear casual.

"We heard you were out here with UESAT, doing some kind of business with them. That is the extent of it, isn't it?"

"Just routine," I said.

"These are my boys," he said, glancing at the UESAT troops. "I wouldn't like any trouble."

"No trouble."

"No? Well, I have a big Jewish nose, and I smell trouble. You're dealing with Carlos Sanchez, and he, my friend, is not kosher. You might appreciate the information."

"I do," I said.

"Then shalom."

We walked away from each other, he out the gate to his blue four-wheel-drive Nissan jeep (its fully enclosed cab air conditioned, to judge by the sticker on the rear window) and me to Garavito's office.

I had been warned and knew it all the way down to my toes.

I flew back to the States again to check on more UESAT equipment and to write another report for Brooks. It was mid-September when I returned to Panama.

12 September: The Condeca Group

Carlos met me at the airport with two of the bodyguard groups from the UESAT. "You have to go through the Customs line," he told me, "and have your baggage searched."

I had no choice, and carried my suitcase to the passenger line, wondering what was wrong. Carlos waited silently as I was checked. They did not find the small .380 pistol I had in my luggage.

"We have problems," Carlos said as I cleared Customs. "Two American mercenaries came down on this same flight from Miami two days ago. They smuggled in weapons and ambushed a car of men from the UESAT. All six men in the car were killed."

The two UESAT members with Carlos had 9-millimeter Browning Hi-Power pistols under their light cotton windbreakers, and they eyed the passengers suspiciously.

"The UESAT men were undercover. No one knew who they were. Do you remember the officer you met from headquarters who owned the turbo Saab? It was him," Carlos said.

"Where did it happen?" I asked.

"In town," Carlos said. "The car was hit with a rifle grenade fired from a shotgun fitted with a telescopic sight. The UESAT has the weapon. One of the mercenaries was caught, the other escaped. The prisoner is being questioned now."

"I'm sorry," I said. "Is that why I was searched?"

"Everyone is being searched," Carlos said. "Come, I'll take you to the hotel."

In my room at the downtown Holiday Inn, Carlos and I talked. He was depressed and could not hide his feelings. "This is a terrible thing," he said. "The UESAT suspects everyone, but I think I know what happened."

"What?" I asked.

"The Colombians paid for the mercenaries because the army burned their drug station on the border."

That made sense to me. The cartel took such things seriously.

"Will Garavito still send his men to Merc School?" I asked.

"I don't know," Carlos said, "he hasn't told me." Then, moody, worried, he left me with the promise to call the next day.

Waiting for Carlos was not a total waste of time, since something very interesting had developed at my own hotel. A special meeting of the Condeca Group, military and political leaders from all over Central America, was convening there to discuss the war in Nicaragua.

All nations of the Condeca Group were present except Nicaragua, which was represented "unofficially" in the speeches and meetings.

I listened to the officers and diplomats in the hotel lounge and restaurant. By luck, I heard something valuable.

Both Costa Rica and Honduras assured Nicaragua they would deny their countries as refuges to the anticommunist contras, in a good-faith agreement that Nicaragua would expel its foreign military advisers, meaning the Cubans and Soviets.

The agreement was intended to demonstrate that Nicaragua

wanted peace and that the nations of the Condeca Group could settle their problems among themselves.

It was an important bit of information for me, since Paul Johnson, my executive officer at Merc School, and some of the Mercenary Association members were cooperating with Tom Posey's "Civilian Military Assistance" group of Decatur, Alabama, and planning to go to Honduras to get into the war in Nicaragua.

Civilian Military Assistance (CMA) was supposed to be a charity organization created to donate and distribute clothing, food, and medical supplies to the contras.

CMA was secretly shifting from charity to warfare and, while publicly denouncing mercenaries as evil souls, was willing privately to accept all the help the people from the Mercenary Association could provide.

I would later learn that CMA was one of the organizations the National Security Council was indirectly using to resupply the contras, which perhaps explained that behavior.

Carlos brought the two sergeants that Lieutenant Garavito was sending from the UESAT to Alabama for Mercenary Association training to my hotel. They were young and very respectful of me, saluting and standing at attention.

Carlos interpreted for me as I described what the training would be like. They listened avidly, asking questions often. They were happy to be the ones selected, but some apprehension showed through as we talked about the full-contact hand-to-hand, the use of the high-velocity pellet rifle on the students, and the constant day-and-night struggles where the students attacked each other with CS and fighting sticks.

So warned, the two men were driven to the airport and sent to Birmingham, where my cadre would pick them up at the terminal there. For the next two weeks at least, I would feel safe, having two UESAT members as potential hostages, trading material to get me out, if need be.

The Tower

Carlos called me the next day, and we set out again about our business with the logistical section of the Panama Defense

Force, taking orders for equipment, going to meetings, and in general doing nothing but routine commercial transactions.

I was wondering when Carlos would make his move, and one afternoon at lunch he finally did.

"The helicopter mechanic, he is in town now, and he has something for you," Carlos said.

"Okay," I said, "I suppose I can meet him, but he's not that important. When will we go back to the Nicaraguan office to finish our business there?"

"Soon, but we must meet the mechanic tonight."

I shrugged. The mechanic was my test, he was the bait. If I bought the HIND manuals from him, Carlos and his boss—probably Nicaraguan counterintelligence—would know I was not just a businessman.

The bait, those HIND manuals, was too good to lose just on a guess, so I told Carlos that I would see the mechanic, but I had to make time, and to call me at the hotel after dinner. Carlos agreed and left.

In my hotel room, I studied a map of Panama City and devised a plan. If the meeting with the mechanic was a trap, I wanted to be able to get out of it.

When Carlos called, I told him to arrange the meeting with the mechanic near the old church tower beside the sea, at 11:00 P.M., and that I would take a taxi there.

Carlos readily agreed again. I had a private dinner in the hotel restaurant, browsed through the magazines in the gift shop, and went back to my room and changed clothes.

I put on soft, rubber-soled shoes, black slacks, and a dark jacket. I concealed the pistol under the jacket and went downstairs to locate a cab, two hours earlier than my appointed meeting time.

The taxi took me to a spot near the ruins, and I paid the driver and watched him drive away. I walked the few hundred meters past the other ruins to the tower.

It was four-sided and was about fifteen meters high, now hollow, with no floors or ladderways up. I could see the stars through the open roof.

I slowly climbed up the stone wall, placing my toes and fingers in the deep niches, and soon reached the first window. Its sill was almost a meter wide, due to the thickness of the walls, so

I pulled myself onto it and found a comfortable position where I could lean back and blend with the irregular, broken stones.

I could see down outside and inside the tower, and no one could see me, an almost perfect position. I began my wait, looking at the luminous dial of my Porsche watch. The Pacific Ocean was calm, its waves lapping ashore with tranquil regularity. I watched the sky and hoped it would not rain.

For insurance, I unsnapped the strap on my holster and loosened the pistol so I could pull it out quickly.

The highway traffic near the ruins was frequent, and I passed the time by watching the headlights go by. It was the same as an ambush vigil.

Then, as I was looking back out to sea, interested now in the faint lights of a ship, I heard doors from an automobile open and shut. I looked at my watch. It was barely past 10:00 P.M.

There were voices, and people were walking toward the tower. I knew no one had seen me climb the wall, so I was not concerned, but obviously something was happening.

When I could see the men, I noted they were in common street clothing. They stopped on the flagstone walk just under my window, and the tone of their voices revealed they were there on business.

There were three of them. One was giving orders, pointing and directing the other two, who walked away. The leader watched them go, then lifted his shirttail and checked his own pistol, a large chrome-plated automatic.

Then he too walked away to somewhere in the shadows near the tower.

I was glad I had come early and avoided the rush.

The men were either police or intelligence agents, and they had only one reason to be there.

At a few minutes before eleven o'clock I heard another car brake, then turn off its engine. It did not sound like Carlos's Toyota.

I saw a lone man walking toward the tower. When he was close enough, I could see it was Benito the mechanic. Carlos was not with him. That made me suspicious.

He stopped on the flagstones, looking to the left and right, his hands in his trouser pockets.

Benito simply stood there for a minute, then walked toward

the tower doorway, and I lost sight of him as he was almost directly under me. I could not warn him of the agents.

I heard him come inside the tower, his feet softly crunching the pebbles, but he did not stay, turning instead and going back out to the flagstone plaza.

Two of the men rushed out of their concealment, grabbed Benito by his arms, and forced him to the ground so quickly that he went down without a protest. I heard the metallic ratchet sound of handcuffs and saw the men jerk him to his feet.

The leader walked out of his shadow and stood talking to Benito in a low voice, probably warning him not to cry out.

I put my hand on the grip of my pistol, worried they might look up.

Benito was quietly replying to him. After a short exchange, the three men led him away, back to their waiting car, and I heard its doors close, the engine start, and the car drive away.

Was Benito genuine? Whom did the agents work for? Had they made an error by jumping him? Didn't they want me too?

An hour passed before I resnapped the strap on my pistol holster and eased down the wall, feeling slowly in the dark with my toes and fingers for secure holds.

I walked out of the ruins down the coastline until I reached the highway, where I stopped a taxi.

There was no message light on my phone back in my room, so I laid the pistol on the stand beside my bed, took a shower, and went to sleep.

The next morning Carlos called me early from the lobby and said he would meet me in the restaurant. I hid the pistol and went down.

"I'm sorry I could not come last night," he said. "I had to stay with my daughter, who is sick. How did it go?"

Carlos was lying. He had not come because he knew there was going to be an arrest. He had set me up, and it was a lame excuse.

"No good," I said. "I went to the tower and waited for Benito, but he never came."

Carlos seemed puzzled. "Perhaps he had some trouble," he said. "Maybe he will call back today."

"Well, I don't really want to deal with him," I said. "Trying to buy and resell those manuals is too much of a risk. That's not my business. I don't really care about them."

"Okay," Carlos said, "you stay here this afternoon and I will call you back."

He left and I ate breakfast, thinking the situation through. Everything was blown. Brooks had said to be careful, but I had taken the chance.

Was Carlos going to arrange for the gunmen who were at the tower last night to come to the hotel? Could Carlos even arrange some trouble for me with the Panamanians?

I had two of their men at Merc School, and instructions with my cadre about what to do if I was jailed or went missing. Maybe that would buy me the time to get out of the country.

Before noon I was on a Delta flight to Miami. My commercial business with Panama was cut off totally, but a good amount of intelligence had come of the trips.

The September course of the Merc School was ending just as I returned to Alabama, but I did manage to preside over the awards dinner and hand out the diplomas.

Our two Unit Especial Seguridad Anti-Terror sergeants graduated, beaming with pride when they received their Recondo patches and diplomas.

I personally took them to the airport and put them on the plane, and wished them well.

Postscript: In mid-October, just weeks later, a violent diplomatic issue flared between the United States and Nicaragua. Crates that were believed to contain MIG jet fighter aircraft were observed being offloaded from ships in Nicaragua.

The Reagan administration was ready to attack the ships, bomb the crates, or perhaps establish a naval blockade.

Tension over the "MIG's" was tangible for several days, until the White House announced that it had discovered the crates did *not* contain jet fighters.

They contained current Russian MI-24 HIND-D attack helicopters.

News coverage vanished, because "mere" helicopters were not the story MIG's were. Reading the papers, my pulse racing, I realized I had been right when I told Brooks the HIND's were coming. Should I gloat a bit over Brooks about reporting the HIND's, or feel like an almost-caught fool?

And what would the contras do now with those terrible HIND's after them?

There are always more questions in this business than answers.

CHAPTER FIFTEEN
The Sikhs

In June of 1984 the Indian army besieged the Golden Temple, the principal shrine of the Sikh religion and the refuge of Sikh militants. The siege was intended to suppress a growing insurrection by Sikh religious militants who were attempting to break away from India and found an independent state, Khalistan, in the Punjab.

Indira Ghandi, the Indian prime minister, had turned a deaf ear to Sikh demands since 1981. Attacks on Hindus by Sikh terrorists increased in 1982 and 1983. Martial law was established in the Punjab.

Finally, Prime Minister Ghandi ordered the troops to storm the Golden Temple and arrest the militants.

At least eight hundred Sikhs perished in the attack and fifteen hundred were arrested. These deaths were avenged with the assassination of Prime Minister Ghandi by her Sikh bodyguards on 31 October 1984.

Her son, Rajiv Ghandi, succeeded her as prime minister.

Enraged Hindus took to the streets throughout the country, slaughtering Sikhs and sometimes burning the corpses where they fell.

Sikh militant leaders and began to plot not only the establishment of an independent Khalistan but the destruction of the Indian government itself.

I was one of the Mercs they approached for help.

8 November 1984: The Bunker

The last qualification course of the Mercenary Association for the year was just over a week away, and the phone at The Bunker's front desk was frequently busy as veteran members of the association called to announce their arrival times and as new students called to ask questions.

One call wasn't immediately noteworthy. It was a man asking if he could pay a membership deposit with a credit card. He said he had four men who wanted to come to the association.

His accent sounded Indian or Pakistani, but calls from foreigners were not unusual for us. We made reservations for his four people, billed the card account, and went back to work.

On 16 November the students were reporting in, cluttering the offices and rear bay of The Bunker with their luggage and military equipment.

I was busy getting some of them organized in the bay when one of the team leaders came to me and asked for my attention.

"Frank, you'd better come up front and look at this," he said.

Standing in a group beside the front desk were four dark, bearded men wearing business suits and turbans.

I recognized them instantly as Sikhs, but *anyone* else could have. One of them wore a metal button on his lapel that read "Sikhs Seek Justice."

I introduced myself and extended my hand. So *this* was our four-man group. "I am Balraj Singh," said the eldest of the group, and he gestured toward the others. "This is Sukhwinder Singh, Avraj Singh, and Lal Singh. You see, we are all named Singh." He laughed.

Balraj was short and muscular, with a full beard and long hair. I had read Sikhs didn't shave or cut their hair, but the younger men had shorter beards and hair.

"Singh means 'lion,' " Balraj said. "We are Sikhs."

The Sikhs were thrown into the combat training at Merc School along with everyone else, but all were assigned to one team. It was on the second day of the course that Balraj approached me.

"I want to talk to you about the training," Balraj said. I nodded, and walked off with him away from the other students.

"Balraj, if you are thinking about quitting, I'd like to ask you to give yourself more of a chance. We've just gotten started—" I said.

"Oh, no, that is not my intention," he said. "I only wanted to say that we like your training very much. Sikhs don't quit, we are strong, like the lion."

"Then what is it?"

"In our country, we don't have wooded areas like this," Balraj said, "it is a more open place. What we need to know is city fighting and how to stop armored vehicles in the streets. Do you have some training like that?"

"Yes," I said, "but that will come later. We'll talk after you become more accustomed to this course. Is that all right?"

"Yes," Balraj said.

Later, during a lull in the hostilities, I walked to where Balraj and his men were resting, and sat down beside him. "How are you doing?" I asked, to be friendly. "Learning anything?"

"We need training in special techniques, such as the making of bombs, like time bombs, and how to assassinate government officials," he said. "Otherwise, the training is suitable."

I kept a straight face. Balraj had just asked for a lot. Good grief, I thought, I've got some hot ones. "Okay," I told him, "let me think about that. Just stay in the training."

Balraj gave me as stoic an expression as one wearing wet, cold underwear can manage. "Yes, we will," he said.

I looked at one of his men, the tallest of the group. His name was Lal Singh. "How are you doing?" I asked. Lal was lying on the ground, barely breathing. He shifted his shoulders and moved his face so he could look at me.

"Fine, thank you," he said.

"He is from the city," Balraj explained.

2:00 P.M. 21 November 1984:

The training operation was ready. A small group of students, the Sikhs among them, advanced out of the treeline toward a few paper grocery sacks of food set on a trail. If they wanted to eat in the days ahead, they would have to take it.

Hidden where the students could not see were snipers with pellet rifles and smoke grenades.

The students charged. A grenade suddenly rolled onto the trail near the food and began to hiss thick, cloying smoke into the air.

Shadowlike figures of hungry students dodged into the smokescreen, running for the grocery sacks. The pellet rifles opened fire, and the zip of high-velocity pellets followed by the fleshy whack of impact on human bodies began. The ambushed students were shouting in pain and confusion.

The first student reached the sacks, grabbing for them.

Booby-trapped, the food exploded, the blast knocking the student down. Cans and packages flew into the air. The smoke-screen now absolutely blanketed the area.

In the smoke, flames from the burning food sacks could be seen. The rations were on fire. The students were frantic to salvage what they could.

Pellets were still cutting through the brush. Sikhs, Americans, and Canadians were cursing in the smoke, bumping into each other, almost persuaded now to go hungry and abandon their food.

"Cease fire," Paul Johnson was yelling as the students fell back. They had lost. Most of their rations had been destroyed.

Men in camouflage fatigues were stomping out the fire and the food, the smokescreen was still hazy, filtering out into the woods, and scared students were coming out of their hiding places behind trees.

"We've got a man down!" someone shouted. "Balraj is hit!" I stood up from my position and began to walk toward the group of men kneeling over Balraj.

An ex-British-army veteran was applying a bandage to Balraj's face. "Bit of shrapnel in the eye," he said. I stopped him and examined the wound. The white of the eye, just under the cornea and pupil, was cut open, and fluid was running out of the eyeball.

"Bandage him," I said, "and I'll get him out of the field to a hospital."

6:00 P.M.: Eye Foundation Hospital, Birmingham

Balraj was upstairs with the doctors, I was sitting in the hospital coffee shop with an FBI agent, still wearing my dirty combat fatigues.

The agent's name was Fox, and he was with FBI Counter Intelligence. He was tall and athletic, dressed casually in a sport jacket that evening.

"We figured these guys were coming down," Fox said. "There's a big group of them in Canada. They may be over the border illegally. How's their English?"

"Well, Balraj speaks good English. The others didn't really get much chance to say anything while he was around. They're out with the rest of the class now; I told Johnson to buddy up to them and get some of their life stories."

"The Sikhs must have picked you because of the Sikh community in Birmingham," Fox said. "They might have checked you out and decided you were the guy to approach."

"Are they talking to other people?" I asked.

"Yeah," Fox said. "We know they've gone to some other independents in Canada, but that's about it so far."

"What do you want me to do with them?"

"Just try to find out what they want. Maybe they're going to make you an offer of some sort. By the way, how's his eye?"

"He'll be okay. I just talked to the doctor a few minutes ago. They have to stitch up the cut in his eyeball and keep him for a few days," I said.

"Okay. Make me a report as soon as possible. You'll do that, right?" Fox asked.

"What's our arrangement going to be? You know what the Bureau did to me in Miami," I said.

"I'm sorry about that, Frank. I didn't have anything to do with it. It won't happen with me," Fox said.

I had only just met Fox, but I liked him, and made the decision to go ahead.

The next morning, back in the field, I gathered the three Sikhs. Lal had taken charge of the group. "I want you to know Balraj is going to be all right," I said. "He knew you would be concerned and said I could bring one of you to visit him in the hospital if you like."

"No," Lal said. "We will stay here and finish our training."

I smiled at him, and he returned a wide grin. In other circumstances, Lal would have been personable.

As the Sikhs went back to their team, I waved to Paul Johnson for a short conference. He double-timed to me, giving a few orders to the team leaders as he ran past them.

"When are you and the guys pulling out for Nicaragua?" I asked.

"Posey is supposed to pick us up at The Bunker this Saturday night," he said.

"Okay," I said, "just keep up the pressure on the Sikhs. I want them to start talking to you. I need to know what they really have on their minds."

"No problem," Johnson said. "They're doing that now. I think they're glad Balraj is gone. They seem to be having a better time."

"Good," I told him. "Maybe you should think about staying here. I might be starting a new operation with them."

"No, man. We've got this Nicaraguan thing set. I've got to go."

"Paul, I think Posey's outfit is going to be trouble," I said.

"We can take care of ourselves, we're Recondos," Johnson said, and slapped me on the shoulder for emphasis.

On my next visit to check on Balraj, I found him awake and uncomfortable but willing to talk.

I congratulated him on bearing the pain of the eye injury well and brought him details of how his men were doing in the field.

Balraj began to talk politics and religion with me after a while, and I sat beside his bed and listened.

He called the slain Indira Ghandi a "bloody bitch" and said her son Rajiv would be killed as soon as possible.

We talked of the events that led to the siege and battle at the Golden Temple in Amritsar in the Punjab, and he told how the Sikhs who defended the temple had died instead of betraying their faith.

I let Balraj know, with as much finesse as I could, that I would consider helping with the Sikh cause. We talked at length, he detailing injustices I didn't doubt were true, and me listening, nodding, keeping him company in the lonely hospital room.

My concern with Balraj and the Sikhs was simple. I had no trouble picturing them exporting their war to the United States, if they felt they needed to do so.

The three Sikhs in the field continued with their training, satisfied to hear progress reports about Balraj and his treatment.

Paul Johnson and the three Merc Association volunteers came in out of the field and were picked up on 26 November by Tom Posey of the Civilian Military Assistance organization, and left for Honduras and Nicaragua.

Lal, Avraj, and Suki had become friends with several of the other students and cadre, and began to talk about the conditions in India, telling of the attacks made on their friends and families by Indians after the assassination of Indira Ghandi by her Sikh bodyguards.

I removed the students from the field after Escape and Evasion training ended on 28 November and arranged for Balraj's release from the Eye Foundation Hospital that afternoon. He was feeling better, but still wore a padded bandage over his injured eye.

For the next two days, 29 and 30 November, Balraj attended the remaining classes for the graduates, watching his Sikhs learn rock-face rappel and mines, grenades, and booby traps.

Balraj said he was responsible for reporting back to his superior in New York about the quality of the training I gave, and that he thought the training was good.

He said Communist China and Pakistan were aiding the Sikh cause, providing both money and weapons as well as safe areas inside their own borders for training or hiding.

I finally asked Balraj if the Sikhs would try to attack Hindu or Indian targets within the United States. He simply told me his people would fight "wherever they had to."

During the field training, I knew Alex Ethridge, our field photographer, had managed some photos of the Sikhs, because even though they had said they didn't want to be photographed, they made no effort to get out of the way as Alex took his shots.

Copies of the photos went to the FBI. The originals and the negatives I saved to give personally to Balraj later, so he would not suspect I had kept photos of him or his men.

Finally, as the time approached for Balraj and his men to leave, he invited me to visit him in New York and meet his superiors.

He gave me a note with telephone numbers on it for himself and Lal Singh, with a written warning not to mention anything on the phone.

"Balraj," I said as he was preparing to get in the car with his men and be driven to the airport, "training and weapons are expensive. Do you have the money for this?"

"Yes," Balraj said. "Money is no problem."

Not long after the car drove away, I sat down to finish my report to Fox about the Sikhs, while the details were still fresh in my mind.

CHAPTER SIXTEEN
Nicaragua

The mission had collapsed. They had ditched the mines and explosives and, with no food, were escaping and evading out of Nicaragua.

Sandinista units were likely in pursuit, and between the Mercenary Association Recondos and the Honduran border were nothing but ambushes and enemy patrols.

To make matters worse, the Miskito Indians and the Civilian Military Assistance leadership were feuding, and already weapons had been brandished threateningly.

"If those bastards make us hit an ambush," said one of the CMA leaders, "shoot 'em."

April 1984: Decatur, Alabama

The airliner landing at the Huntsville-Decatur airport was bringing Alfonso Callejas to us. He had been vice president of Nicaragua, under President Somoza.

I waited with members of the CMA group, an independent organization of Americans who were sending aid to the Front for a Democratic Nicaragua (FDN), in support of their fight against the Marxist-backed Sandinista government.

The CMA people were there to formally meet Callejas and to provide security for him.

I waited in the lobby with Paul Johnson, my Mercenary Association executive officer, and Tom Posey, one of the founders of CMA. Posey was an ex-marine, a Vietnam veteran, and a dedicated anticommunist.

Posey was tall and spare and spoke in a slow drawl, seemingly more of a farmer than a supporter of guerrilla warriors. He worked in Decatur selling fresh vegetables and other farm produce to grocery stores.

He was hosting this meeting with Alfonso Callejas as part of a press conference and fund-raising dinner.

I had driven up from Birmingham to meet with Callejas on another matter—the proposal of the formation of a special commando-type military unit, as a ploy to get his confidence.

After escorting Callejas to Posey's home, and after the magazine and newspaper reporters had taken statements from him, I had a private meeting with the two men.

Callejas was kindly, presenting the image of a friendly uncle, even though he had been a powerful political figure as vice president of Nicaragua and was now one of the key leaders of the anticommunist rebels. He was an excellent cross-check intelligence source.

In our meeting, I outlined my concept of the special unit to Callejas. It would consist of three groups: intelligence, sniper, and raid teams. The purpose of the special unit would be to conduct missions inside Nicaragua.

Callejas protested that similar ideas had been proposed in the past, but the Central Intelligence Agency had turned them down.

I made arrangements to meet Callejas at a later date, after he had more time to think it over. I left him with a notebook full of specifics on the creation and training of the special unit, then accompanied the Civilian Military Assistance group to a restaurant where we listened to speeches and discussions of the conditions in El Salvador, Cuba, and Nicaragua.

I was not to know for sure until much later, but CMA was getting indirect help from the National Security Council. The NSC was directing some *"contra*butions" to CMA and had a liaison officer advising them. This was a good way for NSC to launder some of its aid to the FDN during the congressional restrictions on CIA and other direct help.

This liaison with NSC would also give some legal protection to CMA, and later, when FBI, BATF, and Customs began to investigate CMA for possible violations of the law, the Justice Department would act to delay or shelve prosecution.

* * *

Paul Johnson was attracted to CMA, agreeing to collect food, clothing, and military equipment for them to donate to the rebels. I allowed Paul the use of The Bunker as a headquarters.

While I was involved with other operations, Paul Johnson later told me he and Tom Posey met frequently, and Posey asked him if he would be willing to go on combat missions into Nicaragua.

Paul said yes and further agreed to ask other Mercenary Association graduates to volunteer.

As time passed, I was learning more about the Civilian Military Assistance group, but what I was hearing was making me uncomfortable.

Posey was publically condemning "mercenaries" in general and frequently the Mercenary Association in particular, claiming a mercenary was amoral while the CMA was highly patriotic. Since Posey was privately asking us for all the help either the membership or myself would provide, I thought his position to be hypocritical.

September 1984

Two CMA volunteers, James Powell of Memphis, Tennessee, and Dana Parker of Huntsville, Alabama, had been killed along with a Nicaraguan rebel pilot when the Hughes 500 helicopter they were flying was shot down inside Nicaragua.

The helicopter was armed with rocket pods, and the two Americans had taken it over the border of Honduras without authorization and into a battle where FDN forces were attacking a Sandinista village.

There were conflicting stories after the crash. One version had the helicopter flying into the fight on a rescue mission. At the other extreme, they were on a gunship-type attack.

The fact remained the Hughes 500 was the only helicopter owned by the FDN at the time and was a critical loss. The Sandinistas gained a major propaganda victory, since they had in their possession two dead American "mercenaries," a name CMA did not like.

The rest of the small CMA volunteer group that had traveled down with Powell and Parker quickly left Honduras, at the request of the FDN. Good intentions aside, the FDN had lost their helicopter, the United States was internationally embarrassed, and the U.S. Federal Bureau of Investigation began an investigation of the Civilian Military Assistance group to determine if a violation of the U.S. Neutrality Act had been committed, one of the investigations that hit a temporary dead end.

Personally, I concluded that since Parker and Powell were both Vietnam veterans, they had probably acted out of habit and taken the armed helicopter into the fight.

The FDN didn't have replacement helicopters, and the Sandinistas were better armed than most of the Vietcong. In short, Nicaragua was not Vietnam. CMA volunteers at the time were mostly Vietnam veterans, having lived as family men and factory or office workers since leaving the service. They had been away from combat for a long time. I felt they still believed they were fighting in Vietnam, but each war is different.

Paul and I talked about Posey and the CMA, and I said I was beginning to doubt them, but so strong was his desire to use CMA to get to the war in Central America, he did not want to listen.

My trouble with Paul began then, in our disagreement over CMA. I thought CMA was acting too often out of zeal, making them sloppy and dangerous, without careful consideration of the overall effect on the Contras.

I also smelled a disaster coming.

The Congress was opposed to U.S. aid to the contras, and laws were being passed to make it illegal for the U.S. to help the contras. In my experience, Congress always wins.

Working to help the contras, working to defeat the Soviet-backed, rebel-installed government in Managua was basically illegal.

So many covert wars supported by the U.S. had crashed when Congress added its weight to that of the enemy. Those of us who might be deeply involved in *this* covert war would crash with it.

I could fight the Sandinistas, but not the Sandinistas *and* the U.S. Congress.

Paul seemed to think I just didn't want him, or any of our association people, working with someone else. I also had the impression Posey's dislike of me as an "unpatriotic mercenary" was rubbing off on Paul. That made Paul's loyalty to the association a liability to him, if he wanted to go with CMA.

This resulted in a split between us, but a split I thought was manageable. I was wrong.

Paul had recruited three other Recondos to go to Honduras, and they were as ready to go as Paul, considering themselves part of CMA.

In November of 1984, while I had Balraj Singh in the Eye Foundation Hospital, I allowed Paul to leave the field early and go back to The Bunker to prepare his equipment. The other three Recondos were also assembled there, waiting for Tom Posey.

While waiting, Paul told me the CMA was going to attempt to create the special unit I had suggested to Callejas. It was code-named Pegasus. CMA wanted to use the Mercenary Association personnel to help train and organize Pegasus.

On Monday night, the twenty-sixth of November, Posey loaded his van with the four Recondo volunteers and their personal equipment. I wished them luck. They had chosen their direction.

I heard nothing more from Posey or Paul until I saw a newspaper several days later.

NEWS ITEM: 4 December 1984, BIRMINGHAM POST-HERALD
ALABAMIAN LEADS BAND TRAINING FOR NICARA-GUAN FORAY
by William Thomas, Scripps-Howard News Service
TEGUCIGALPA, Honduras A small band of Americans—private adventurers in camouflage clothing—is putting together a war party in preparation for a commando-like strike into Marxist-governed Nicaragua early next year.

They say they hope to enter Nicaragua sometime after the first of the year. Their objective: destruction of some strategic military targets.

"We know the risk," said the group's leader, a camera-dodging Alabamian known only as Colonel Flaco. "It's about 80–20 against us."

The Americans plan to spend at least a month training an elite guerrilla unit of the Nicaraguan Democratic Front (FDN), a group also known as the "contras."

By then, says Col. Flaco, the unit could include up to 30 American volunteers and 70 Nicaraguan commandos.

The unit is called Pegasus, for the mythological winged horse.

I was stunned after reading the front-page, feature headline article.

Who the hell was Flaco? I knew it wasn't Paul, because he would not be in command. Whoever Flaco was, incredibly enough, he had revealed to a newspaper reporter the existence of Pegasus and the unit's intent, code name, and size. The news articles began to appear daily after that. The next one told of a "pistol-wielding" misadventurer from Lawton, Oklahoma, "who backed out of the mission when he found he would not be paid."

This was incredible. I had been told that they only accepted "Special Forces" qualified veterans, stout patriots who would fight without promise of pay. This man was not one of my Recondos. He was pure CMA.

Now, with the embarrassment growing, the news reports did not stop.

NEWS ITEM: 14 December 1984 BIRMINGHAM POST-HERALD
NICARAGUAN REBEL GROUP SENDS AMERICANS HOME
by Michael Kelley, Scripps-Howard News Service

The Nicaraguan Democratic Front (FDN) is sending home a group of Americans who said they were in Honduras preparing for a commando-type raid into Nicaragua, an American connected with the operation said Wednesday.

"The host country [Honduras] is very angry," [Mario] Calero [an FDN organizer] said.

Civilian Military Assistance, the U.S. government, the Front for a Democratic Nicaragua, and Honduras were all reeling from the Pegasus incident.

Paul Johnson and the three Mercenary Association members who had gone down with him arrived back in Birmingham about December 16, and I talked privately with Paul.

He was amazed at what had happened, but in a form of

denial, he seemed to be searching for excuses for what had happened.

Paul was willing to go back with another CMA effort and try again, no matter what I said.

When I asked Paul who "Colonel Flaco" was, he said he didn't know, but the rank was an assumed title, the same as the other CMA volunteers were taking, with no official significance. He wanted to believe that perhaps Flaco had some hidden reason for making the disclosure that none of the rest of us understood.

In a later discussion with both Paul and Tom Posey, I told them what I had learned in Panama, that Honduras and Costa Rica had agreed with Nicaragua to either deport or jail foreign mercenaries using their soil as a launching area for combat operations against the Sandinistas.

Posey rejected the information, saying, "We have to do what we have to do. We'll just take the chance."

Paul was contacting more Mercenary Association members now, organizing them for the next trip down. I could not stop him, but told him I wanted the real situation about CMA to be explained to the volunteers. I was angry.

Seven members made arrangements to go back to Honduras with Paul, and in the middle of January 1985, they left Birmingham after grouping at The Bunker. I did not meet them or speak to them. Being opposed to their volunteering, I was "suspect," and they, like Paul, had committed to CMA.

Paul and the Mercenary Association Recondos finally did get to Honduras very late in January and entered through Tegucigalpa Airport without incident. Then they were trucked to a forward camp on the Nicaraguan border, where they set about building their own shelters out of logs and plastic sheeting.

Colonel Flaco was in charge of them again.

But there was a difference this time. The Pegasus unit was assigned to the Misura Indian rebels, not FDN. Flaco and his men were assigned to work with the Miskito tribe, part of the Misura group. The FDN would not accept them.

One day an Indian arrived at the Pegasus camp with news of a bridge in Nicaragua that was a possible target. It was approximately a forty-mile walk south from the camp, the Indians estimated.

Flaco ordered the American volunteers to prepare for the mission with the Indians.

The target bridge was described as a concrete span approximately fifty meters in length, with a steel cable suspension, over a river tributary.

The Indians made a rough drawing of the bridge and the surrounding terrain, and estimated the Sandinista troops securing it at less than fifty.

The attacking force numbered fourteen Americans, eight of them Mercenary Association Recondos, the rest CMA personnel. About forty Indians composed the main body of the group.

Colonel Flaco was the commander of the mission. "Colonel" Joe Adams, another CMA member, was the second in command.

Two FDN officers with a radio were assigned to the attack group as interpreters. Actually they were there to keep an FDN presence in Indian operations, since the FDN and the Misura were competitive organizations and in all probability would be fighting with each other if they were not allied fighting the Sandinistas.

I was later told that one of the mission's leaders told one Recondo that "we'll have casualties on this operation; then Congress can't ignore us."

The attack group was heavily armed. In addition to the carbines, assault rifles, and machine guns they carried, their load consisted of one hundred pounds of C4 plastic explosive with which to destroy the bridge and three large antitank mines to bury in the roads leading to the bridge.

On 26 February the attack group walked out of their border camp, heading south into Nicaragua. Paul Johnson was with them.

The early part of the march was very difficult, Johnson said, because the group was moving through rain forest and jungle, and the mud and swamp were treacherous.

On 27 February Colonel Flaco announced he had to return to base camp in Honduras because he had just been summoned via a radio message "for a mission." This made Adams the commanding officer of the group.

Shortly after Flaco left, Paul Johnson told me he and another Recondo became involved in an argument with the CMA leadership of the attack group. Paul and his friend were ordered back to base camp. They walked back to Honduras behind Flaco. I never learned what the argument was about.

The attack group continued on, reaching grassland and easier walking.

By night the column would stop, establish perimeter security, and cook in groups over open campfires. This breach of light discipline was a common error made by the Indians, and it was futile to order them not to do it.

The Americans were exhausted by the exertion, but the Indians, accustomed to long marches on nothing more than beans and rice, were holding up well.

Food supplies were running low by 28 February, since the CMA command had underestimated the length of the mission.

The bridge was reached on 1 March, and the attack group moved into position in the forest to the southwest to send out a recon and plan their attack.

When the reconnaissance patrol returned, the information they brought back was demoralizing. The bridge was far better defended than the intelligence had indicated.

Instead of about fifty communist troops, a garrison of over two hundred were defending the bridge. Emplaced defenses around the bridge included heavy and light machine guns, and mortars.

Military vehicle traffic from nearby towns made rapid reinforcements available to the enemy garrison, and rows of barbed wire and minefields protected all the approaches an attacking force would use.

Adams radioed Flaco at base camp in Honduras and described the situation to him. Flaco ordered Adams to attack the enemy-held bridge anyway, *regardless of the strength of the garrison.*

Adams conferred with the other CMA officers and they wisely decided not to attack. This left the entire group deep in enemy territory, out of food, with their morale ruined.

The C4 plastic explosive and mines were abandoned, and the attack group began the long march north to Honduras.

Relations between the Americans and Indians began to disintegrate, aggravated by the CMA officers' thoughtless treatment of the Indians. Arguments had even developed between the CMA officers and the FDN interpreters, who were radioing back the messages for the attack group.

The Indians shot a deer to get rations for the group, and while camped, some fish were caught by throwing hand grenades into a river, but the CMA officers ate the fish and gave only the heads to the Indians, a mission member later reported.

Finally, the two FDN liaison officers were placed under arrest by the CMA officers because of their increasing differences. The Indians took over radio communications and refused to translate for the Americans.

Feelings were so bitter between the Indians and the CMA officers by this time that the Indians were beginning to turn against all the Americans, and would not even help identify edible roots of plants as they foraged for food.

Some Indians deserted the group, walking away from it on the march, never to return.

The Indians finally ceased altogether to take orders from anyone and, in their rush to get back to Honduras, abandoned any pretense of march security. According to a Recondo who was there, this made at least one of the leaders tell the Americans to kill all the Indian officers if the Indians caused the group to walk into an ambush.

On 9 March the attack group returned safely to Honduras, with no casualties. As soon as they were all back in camp, the two FDN officers who had been ordered arrested by the CMA officers vowed they would kill anyone that tried to disarm them.

As any sort of military effort, the mission was a joke. It was a prime example of how amateurish leadership, egos, and good intentions but miserable capability could cripple a unit. It was a miracle the attack group returned alive.

While Paul and the others were being expelled from Honduras, another Mercenary Association member was on the way to Costa Rica. Peter Glibbery and his friend John Davies, both of them English and veterans of service with the British Army in Northern Ireland, had come to visit me from South Africa, where they had lived for the past two years.

Peter, a lieutenant, had graduated the Mercenary School in late 1981, when he was still in the British army. Peter and John wanted to meet Tom Posey so they could get to Central America. I made the introduction, but warned Pete about the hazards he and his friend were facing if they went with CMA.

Paul came back to Merc School during the first-week Combat Course in March. He had passed Pete and John in transit, without ever meeting them.

The report Paul brought back from Honduras was grim. The

men had to be repatriated to the United States, their airfare to Miami bought by the U.S. government but their passports canceled until the loan was repaid.

But now Paul was no longer willing to apologize for Flaco, who he now knew was actually named Jack Terrell, and also seemed to accept the combat attempts of the Pegasus unit for the fiascos they were.

Paul had given up on CMA, but still wanted to go back to Honduras in some capacity. That much I knew.

What I didn't know was the split between Paul and me was serious. He seemed to believe I was responsible in some way for CMA's failure with the Pegasus effort. He knew I had made reports to the FBI and M.I. about CMA's actions and intentions.

Paul reasoned that this might have contributed to his Pegasus unit getting kicked out of Honduras twice. That made me a threat.

In the first week of April 1985, something occurred that would have disastrous results. An ex-British soldier who had graduated Merc School in November of '84 took a trip to a friend's farm.

The friend was a licensed blaster who had explosives on hand. During that visit, the ex-soldier was given, or stole, a quantity of C4 plastic explosive.

Apparently he had about four blocks of C4. He also had made his own private connections with the Sikhs, having gone to Merc School with them.

The story has the Brit leaving Alabama that April and going to New York to meet the Sikhs, the same ones I was then engaged in an FBI operation against.

In New York, he sold the C4 to the Sikhs. Then, as again related by those who knew him, he next surfaced in Florida, on the beachfront, with money to spend.

It is highly likely that that C4 was the explosive the Sikhs later used to make bombs to destroy one 747 and to attempt to destroy another.

Peter Glibbery and John Davies had been sent by the CMA to Costa Rica, not Honduras. They wrote to me after arriving in the country and told of how they were becoming involved in combat-patrolling into Nicaragua out of Costa Rica, on American John Hull's ranch property.

On 24 April 1985 a Costa Rican military unit entered their border camp and arrested them, and Pete, John, two Americans, one Frenchman, and eleven Nicaraguans were jailed for violation of the Costa Rican Neutrality Act. They were put in a maximum security prison in San Jose. Costa Rica had acted exactly as it said it would, a year earlier in Panama.

It was at this time, the spring of 1985, that I met Sam Hall, who had once won an Olympic gold medal for swimming. Hall came to me with a proposal for the establishment of a sort of antiterrorist Foreign Legion, and he wanted me to be the training officer for it.

I had a few discussions with Hall and looked at his documentation and album of world hot-spot photos, but sensed he was too deeply into a fantasy about the unit. I knew just the place for him, and referred him on to CMA. I would not see Hall again until I recognized his photo in a news magazine in 1987. He had gotten arrested for spying in Nicaragua, but was soon released by the Sandinistas. They said he was "mentally unstable."

Hall would eventually write a book titled *Counter Terrorist* about his life and in it claim to have visited the Merc School. He didn't actually go to the field, but he did reveal in his book an informal plan I was working on at the time to provide the intelligence for the capture of a HIND gunship in Nicaragua. Hall managed to obtain some good information on Soviet helicopters and mail it to me. I give credit where credit is due.

After Hall, I was finished with CMA. Besides, at the time I had my hands full with the Sikhs.

(Almost two years later, Peter Glibbery was still in prison in Costa Rica. Senator John Kerry finally arranged for Pete's release in exchange for cooperation in providing information on activities by John Hull, Tom Posey, and others involved with the Contras.)

Posey and the other leaders of CMA were not malicious, they were simply not fully prepared then for what it would really take to conduct successful combat operations in Nicaragua. Their zeal overwhelmed their judgment.

CMA would later bow to official pressure and rename itself "Civilian Material Assistance" to avoid a paramilitary image.

I had enough of their good intentions, and stopped referring any personnel to them. Besides, at the time, I had my hands full with the Sikhs.

CHAPTER SEVENTEEN
The Gandhi Plot

I placed the telephone receiver back on the cradle. The order had finally come to hit Gandhi. I sat still for a long time. This was Prime Minister Rajiv Gandhi, an assassination of international importance.

The Sikhs' training would begin soon. There were many details to figure: who would do it, when, how, and of course, at what price.

Saturday, 15 December 1984, 6:30 P.M.: Sheraton Centre Hotel, New York City

---

I waited for the phone to ring. Lal Singh had told me he would call from the lobby when he arrived. I waited with some anticipation, since I knew I would be meeting the Sikh organization's leaders.

Outside, Christmas shopping crowds pushed their way through the streets, and the December weather was cold, but the holiday was the last thing on my mind. I had the feeling the Sikhs were going to make me a serious offer.

The room phone rang. I answered it after a short pause. There was no sense in letting my anticipation show.

"Frank?" Lal Singh asked.

"Yes, Lal. I'll be right down. Are you at the house phones?"

"Yes, we are," Lal said. "You should have no trouble. Just look for the turbans." At least he was lighthearted.

I slipped on my jacket and checked to make sure my Ingram M11 submachine gun was tucked out of sight in the desk drawer, the short sixteen-round magazine in it. I wanted it there when I came back to the room. I would sit on the bed near the drawer as I talked to the Sikhs.

Just out of the elevator, I saw the turbans above the crowd in the busy lobby. Lal had not been joking. I assumed a casual grin and walked toward him. He had a blue turban on his head. With him were two men, both obviously Sikhs.

One was in his middle thirties, with a thick black beard and full head of hair, and was about five foot six. He wore no turban. The other Sikh was shorter, older, perhaps sixty, with a trimmed white beard and handlebar mustache. He wore a white turban and stood with military dignity.

All three wore undistinguished street clothes. If anything, they were underdressed.

I shook the white-turbaned man's hand first in deference to the elder, then the turbanless Sikh's hand. Lal was happy to see me. I introduced myself to the two strangers, trying to observe basic formalities in what I hoped seemed like an unaffected American way.

We left the lobby and were soon inside my room. I sat on the bed, near the drawer with the Ingram in it. Lal took a respectful position almost all the way across the room from me. The two unintroduced Sikhs pulled chairs around to face me.

"My name is John, you may call me John," said the man without the turban. There was still no name offered for the elder. "John," I would discover later, was actually Gurpartap Birk Singh. He was employed as a computer engineer for Automated Tools Company in New York state and made over $50,000 a year.

He lived in Brooklyn, and had come to New York three years earlier after obtaining a doctorate in engineering in London. Birk held a British passport, and his wife and children still lived in London.

As I said, at the moment I didn't know any of that. I only knew that the elder had an air of authority about him and "John" was obviously educated and businesslike.

Lal Singh was a trainee compared to men like these, but he was in the right company to move up.

"Okay, John," I began. "Balraj and Lal have given me a little information about what you might need. I can arrange for weapons. Give me an idea of what you want."

"Oh, weapons are not really my main concern," John said. "But I understand you can provide some *special* weapons."

"Like the Ingram, with the silencer," said Lal.

"Sure," I said. "I brought one to show you." I opened the desk drawer and lifted out the M11, deliberately removing the magazine from it before I handed it to John. "I also have the silencers, as Lal says." From the back of the drawer I produced the sound suppressor for the Ingram, wrapped in its black Nomex heat shield.

John looked the Ingram over carefully, peering through the center of the sound suppressor. The older man gazed at it with some interest but kept his arms folded, saying nothing.

"This is very good," John said. "I believe this is the sort of thing we can use."

"I can get the nine-millimeter or the .380 versions for you," I said, putting the Ingram back into the drawer, still playing the arms dealer. "A silencer should be included with every weapon. If you'll tell me how many you want, I'll give you a price."

The purchase of any firearms would make a case. The purchase of machine guns would be better. I waited for John to take the bait. He didn't.

"We will have to discuss that later," he said. "As you know, we Sikhs are involved in a war with India. We are having to fight to get our own homeland."

"Balraj explained some of it to me," I said.

"We realize we cannot do everything ourselves," John said. "We have to have some professionals to help us. How do you feel about that?"

"That's what I'm here for," I said. "Tell me what you need, in training or in weapons. We can agree on a price." I wanted to project a mixture of sympathy and business. The elder gave no sign. Lal was still sitting across the room and grinning whenever I looked at him.

"We cannot win a military war with India," John said. "We have to fight like the guerrilla, but we believe we can defeat them."

I nodded.

"India is a very large country, and in many ways it is a very backward country," John said. "It is more dependent on its railways and farms than a country like the United States, because in

India we don't have alternative means of transport or food to spare."

I sat back and relaxed. John was warming to his subject. Perhaps he had mentally rehearsed what he was going to say to me in much the same way I had rehearsed in what ways I would respond to this very situation.

"We need to train men in how to break oil pipelines, how to sabotage steelmills, how to spoil and contaminate food and water."

"Contaminate?" I asked.

"The Punjab is a very fertile area," John said. "We grow much of the country's food there. If we poison it, then the bastards have nothing to eat."

"And the movie theaters," said the elder, "don't forget them."

"Yes," John said. "In India, the movie theaters are filled with thousands of people, not like here, where there are only a few people attending. If one were to set off a panic—"

"Such as a smoke bomb," said the elder.

"Correct. A smoke bomb would do. They will stampede and kill each other."

I reached for my notebook on the desk. "Let me take notes," I said, "so I'll know what we need to plan for in the training program."

"There is coal mining in India. We should manage a way to stop that," John said. I wrote as he talked, scribbling hurriedly.

"The hydroelectric dams are important targets," the elder said. "And the power stations."

"And the nuclear power stations," John added.

"Nuclear power?" I asked. "How many plants like that in India?"

"We have three," John said.

"If we could create another Bhopal, it would be perfect," said the elder. Thousands of people had been killed or injured in a poison gas accident there.

"Did you have anything to do with the Union Carbide plant disaster at Bhopal?" I asked.

"No, that was an accident, but a bloody good one. That's what we need, another Bhopal. There are other chemical plants in India," John said.

It was like Balraj had told me back at The Bunker after

Merc School. All they wanted to do was kill Indians. "What kind of foods do you grow, what are we talking about contaminating?" I asked.

"Oh, we have dairy farms, we have wheat, we have sugar," John said. "We want to poison it as it leaves the Punjab, so it will be going to Indians, where our people won't get it."

"And the water," said the elder. "If we could only poison the water in Bombay. They would die by the thousands. Is this possible?"

"Well," I said slowly, "if you put some sort of water contaminant in the water system for an entire city, I think it might kill some, but it would probably just make a lot of people sick."

"The water system in Bombay, oh, you should see it," John said. "It is terrible. There are uncapped pipes everywhere. It leaks badly. There is usually no pressure. It is a terrible system."

"What about just cutting the water off altogether?" I asked.

"Yes, that is possible too," John said. "The water comes from very far away. It is a terrible system."

"So far I can see you need chemicals and acids, but what about explosives?" I asked.

"We have no trouble with explosives. We have a man with the Indian army. He gets all of that sort of thing that we need," John said.

"Even the heavy weapons? Balraj told me you needed the weapons to fight tanks in the streets. I can get RPG-7's for you, and the Russian-designed Sagger missile. The weapons that I get are made in China."

"China?" John asked. "We get aid from China now. I believe we can get those things if we ask for them."

"Has Pakistan offered any help?" I asked, to confirm what Balraj told me.

"Of course," John said. "The Pakistanis hate the Indians. They do what they can. We have friends."

"I have a concern," I said. "What about your security? I can't afford to start working with you and have the Indian intelligence people know who I am."

"Our security is very good," John told me. "We have established our people into cells, and we have blinds and cutouts. No one will know your actual identity. Even the men don't always know who their leaders are. We have to be careful."

I nodded again. If he only knew who he was talking to.

"Okay," I said, pretending to study my notes. They were hot to act, but they were not too careful. "On these railroads, what do you want to do about them?" I asked.

"We must cut all the railways," John said. "India depends heavily on movement by train. If you cut the railways you have paralyzed the country. I can promise you that."

"How many men would this take?" I asked.

"I believe we should have a team of saboteurs in each state, perhaps ten men in each team," John said. "There are approximately twenty states in India where we would need to have these men."

"That's two hundred men," I said. "Where do we train them?"

"Would you be willing to go out of the country?" John asked.

"Sure," I said. "Where?"

"Some of the men we want to train here, in the United States," John said. "Some we will train in the U.K., and others in China, at our camp there."

I imagined myself at a remote Sikh terrorist camp inside Red China, a place with barren hills and cold weather.

"Do you have any objection about going to China?"

"No," I said, and I really didn't. What an opportunity!

"Can you train teams just for assassination duty?" John asked.

"Yes. Do you want street hits, or are you talking about time bombs, snipers, what?" I asked.

"We want it all," John said.

"That's no problem."

"We have a time frame of one year," John said. "I feel if the economic system of India is badly damaged, they cannot hold on to Punjab. I don't believe they can stand a year of it. Their economy is too fragile."

"John," I said, "let me write up a proposal and mail it to you. This covers a lot of areas. I have to do a cost study on it."

"All right," John said. "You may use the address Balraj gave to you. Do you have it? It is in Brooklyn." I nodded in agreement.

"In the United States—here—where will we train your men? Do you want to keep sending them to Alabama?" I asked.

"No, that is too expensive," said John. "I am arranging for

some property up here." I noticed that again he was avoiding being specific.

"When would you like to start?" I asked.

"As soon as we can put it all together," John said.

"Well, my next Merc School begins in March. I'll be busy after that."

"That should give us plenty of time," John said. "I think we could use January and February."

"How many men will we be training in the States?" I asked.

"I expect a dozen," John said. "We can train them to take their training to other men, to teach them as well."

"Perhaps we should ask about the documents," the elder said. I looked up, not understanding.

"Oh, yes, we have a need for some travel papers, things like passports. Can you get them?" John asked me. That was a surprise. I didn't have a ready answer, so I took a chance.

"Yes," I said, "but I have to make some inquiries first. I'll get you a letter about that as well. I'll have it in the mail to you next week."

"How much would a passport cost?" John asked.

"I don't know," I said. "A few hundred. I'll let you know for certain in the letter."

The elder seemed ready to conclude the meeting. It had taken only half an hour, but I realized I was in. Lal and the other Sikhs who had taken the Merc School course must have returned to New York with a favorable report.

John and the elder stood. I gave them a friendly handshake in parting.

The elder was slightly aloof and waited for Lal to open the door to the hall. "I'll have the study for you in a week," I reminded John.

I watched them as they walked away toward the elevators, the short, dignified elder with his white turban and handlebar mustache, tall, awkward Lal, walking behind them, and John Singh, dark skinned and intense and very much in control.

They were serious men, with a deadly mission.

Outside, Christmas was coming. The display windows were filled with gifts.

In my room, it had not been Christmas. We were talking about the ruining of the economy of a nation, about poisoning the drinking water for children.

I thought about the battle at the Golden Temple and what a massacre it must have been, with the Indian army's tanks and artillery blowing holes through the walls and the machine guns pouring fire through the breaches and the windows.

I thought about how the Sikhs had been run down and murdered by Hindu rioters, their bodies mutilated and burned, after Indira Gandhi had been killed by her own bodyguards.

The hatred from both sides had to be almost a tangible thing. Now I was going to become a part of it.

Dolomite, Alabama

"We're going to give you somebody to help you out," Fox said. "He's a good man, name of Donnie Morris. He was in Vietnam with a special unit, and he looks the part of a merc."

"What does he know about the merc business?" I asked.

"Well, he's got the weapons and all that down pat. You'll teach him whatever else he needs to know, give him the cover of being one of your instructors.

"Don will be in on Wednesday and stay through the weekend. Why don't you meet us at the restaurant about nine o'clock Wednesday morning?"

I waited off to the side of the parking lot on Wednesday morning, leaning on a tractor trailer rig at Bill's Farm House in Hueytown. The Farm House is one of those dependable little Southern restaurants where they always have iced tea, and automatically include grits with breakfast.

At almost 9:00 A.M. precisely, I saw Fox's government Ford drive into the lot and park. Fox stepped out of the driver's side door, and a slim man of medium height came out of the passenger side. They were both looking toward the restaurant as I walked toward them, away from the truck.

Fox noticed me as he and Morris were approaching the restaurant door. "What's this, a countersurveillance technique?" he asked, in good humor.

I got my first close look at Donnie Morris. He was lean, about forty years of age, and I noticed he had a pronounced limp.

Fox was right. Morris had none of the usual federal agent appearance about him.

Inside the Farm House, we had breakfast and discussed the coming operation over fried eggs, biscuits, and coffee. Fox had briefed Morris on the events up until now, and I supplied the details.

"How'd you get the limp?" I asked Morris. Between us, it wasn't a personal question. It was something I might need to know.

"Vietnam," Morris said. "We were out on a patrol, down in the delta. We got into some shit, and I was hit. One of my buddies pulled me out. I took a hit from an AK-47. It did a lot of damage to my knee."

His limp was the only distinctive thing about him. The people in the restaurant around us that might have noticed Don Morris wouldn't remember him in an hour.

---

10 January 1985

"Hello, Frank? This is John," Birk said. "Do you have a moment to talk?"

"Sure, go ahead," I said, sticking the suction-cup microphone on the earphone and switching on the recorder. The call was a surprise. I held the suction cup with my finger.

"I have your letter here," he said, "and we are considering the proposal. Thank you for getting it to me so promptly."

I looked down to make sure the tape was turning. "Good," I said.

"I have a little project for you right now," Birk said. "We have a man who has been caught and thrown in jail in India. We would like to get him out. Do you think that is possible?"

"Tell me what the situation is," I said.

"This is a very important man to us," Birk said. "The Indians caught him smuggling weapons into the country on the China border. We really need to get him out."

"When did this happen, John?" I asked.

"Last week."

"Do you know where he is being held?" I asked.

"That information is coming to me," he said. "An operation like this, how much would it cost?"

"I don't know offhand." I stalled. "I have to know what will be involved, how much time we have. I need to know how many men we'll need."

"We have the people," Birk said. "You can have your pick."

"I have to see if I have men available," I said, to gain some time. "You know most of my people are in Nicaragua right now."

"Yes, of course, I understand," Birk said.

"When can you get the intelligence about the location of the man?" I asked.

"I have sent for that now," Birk said. "I suspect we don't have much time. I don't know how long he might last in the hands of those bastards."

"John," I asked, "is this the man you described to me as being able to get all the . . . military . . . items you wanted?" I was refering to explosives.

"Yes," Birk said. "I am afraid so."

That was an advantage to me. It took my competition out.

"I'll call you back in a few days," Birk said, "after I've received the information."

"Okay," I said. "Thanks for calling. I think we can help your man."

As soon as Birk hung up, I rewound the tape, listened to some of it to ensure it was clear, then removed the cassette from the machine and wrote the time and date of the call on the blank label.

I met with Fox again at Bill's Farm House, discussing the rescue raid with him.

"We can't let you go that far," Fox said. "There's no way to protect you."

"Not even in England?" I asked. "We'd probably stage out of there."

"I don't know," Fox said. "It's hard doing that sort of international coordination. We can't have you over there breaking some British laws, or interrupting an operation M15 or Scotland Yard might have cooking."

"Well, what am I supposed to say?" I asked.

"Tell him you'll do it, keep him talking," Fox said. "We'll just have to get as much out of this as we can here."

I was disappointed. I couldn't see how such a potential opportunity could be overlooked, but I had agreed to comply.

___

21 January 1985

___

I turned on the recorder, the suction cup fixed securely to the earphone. After I dialed the number for the Automatic Tools Company and heard it ringing, I spoke the time and date aloud, so it would be picked up on the tape.

An Automatic Tools operator answered, and I asked for John Singh.

"John Singh?" the operator asked.

"Yes, he's on extension seventy-five," I answered.

"That's engineering. You must mean Dr. Birk," she said, and transferred me to that line. It was the first time I had heard Birk's real name.

"John? This is Frank," I began when he answered.

"Yes. Thank you for returning my call. I have some more information about our situation in India," Birk said.

"Did you get the intelligence on the prisoner?"

"Yes. We know now where he is. It is very near the border of Pakistan, which is good for us."

"Yeah," I said. "I've been thinking it over, and I've called several of my men. I have one or two that can be available."

"I don't want to do anything here," Birk said. "We will organize in London. Can you come to London?"

"Sure," I lied.

"After we meet in London and get more information, we will fly to Pakistan. My men will be waiting there."

"John," I said. "I also want you to meet one of my staff people. He spends most of his time out working, but I can get him pinned down for a day or two for a visit. He can get the items you need. I use him as my contact when I need special items or equipment."

"That will be a pleasure," Birk said.

"Okay," I said. "I'm going to be in touch with Donnie—that's his name—in a few days. I'll call you back."

I noted the time and date on the label of that tape and added it to my file.

25 January 1985

Suction cup in place. Tape machine on. Verbal note of time and date.

"Hello, John?"

"Well, hello, Frank. How are you?"

"Great. I don't have long, so let me take care of some points right away," I said.

"Of course," Birk said.

"I've talked to Donnie. He's planning to meet you and me in New York."

"I'm afraid I have some bad news," John said.

"What?"

"Our man in India didn't make it. There is nothing we can do for him now."

I paused. I had expected the news, and intelligence operation or not, I felt a touch of compassion for the prisoner, regardless of his cause. I had sat in jail before, looking at the walls, wishing for a miracle.

"John," I said, "I'm sorry."

"Yes. It is a pity. We knew he was going to talk, that was unavoidable, but we wanted to get him out anyway, if only to show the bastards we could do it."

"When will you have some time for a meeting?" I asked.

"Is this weekend all right?" Birk asked.

"Good," I said. "I'll call Donnie and make arrangements with him. Can we get a look at the training site?"

"Of course. We do need to get that arranged. We should meet early, because the drive from New York upstate will take at least two hours or more."

"Great. This will take a worry off my mind. I need to see how we are going to get electrical power, what sleeping arrangements we will make for the men, and what the land looks like. I'll bring my camera and take some photos."

"Good idea," Birk said, taking the bait.

"Okay, John, see you this weekend."

The tape went into the file.

Saturday, 26 January 1985, 9:30 A.M., New York Hilton Hotel

When Lal knocked on our hotel room door, everybody was ready. I was sitting on my edge of the bed, and Donnie Morris was leaning against the low chest of drawers beside the television.

I had scattered newspapers and maps over the bed to discourage our visitors from sitting anywhere but the two chairs we had prepared for them in a corner of the room.

A serving tray, glasses, and a pitcher of iced orange juice was set on the lamp table between the chairs. The Sikhs drank only water or fruit juices.

In the adjoining room was the FBI surveillance team, listening and watching electronically. The room was wired for sound, there was a closed-circuit television camera recording us on videotape, and Donnie wore a small tape recorder on an elastic belt under his sweater and windbreaker.

Outside, there was an FBI van parked across the street from the hotel entrance. Behind its mirrored windows were sophisticated 35-millimeter cameras with telescopic lenses.

In order to guarantee a good photo for the boys in the van, Donnie said we should personally walk Birk and whoever came along with him to the front door and say good-bye to them there, which would cause them to pause for a moment, perfect for a nice snapshot.

To top off all this, an entire chase team, consisting of aircraft and automobiles, all linked by radio and working from a command center, stood ready to follow if the Sikhs took us to the proposed training site.

I opened the door and in walked Gurpartap Birk Singh, alias John Singh, and tall, smiling Lal. Morris stood a bit more erect from his slump against the chest of drawers and managed a welcoming expression. He slumped because of the body recorder concealed under his sweater, and bending forward slightly helped create wrinkles across his sweater that made the small rectangle of the recorder invisible.

Birk and Lal walked straight to the waiting seats, and I poured them glasses of fruit juice. Almost shyly, Lal said hello to Morris and took his chair after Birk had sat down, again deferring to Birk's superior rank.

"John," I said, "this is Donnie, the instructor I've been telling you about. He made this trip especially to meet you." Birk rose slightly from his seat and reached forward to shake hands with Donnie, who maintained his slight slump as he leaned toward Birk and took his hand. Lal nodded to Morris.

"Don can get you things you need," I said. "He's got the contacts for the plastic explosives, the Ingrams, and the passports."

"Well," Birk said, "it is very useful to know such a man."

In his jeans, sweater, and black cotton windbreaker, Donnie looked perfect in his part of mercenary.

I began the meeting with my price quotes for conducting the training Birk wanted, and questioned him concerning details of lodging, feeding, and transporting his men.

Birk had answers ready for me, and I learned there were going to be fewer students than I had expected. He was now talking in terms of a dozen or less men and a course that would extend for only a few weeks rather than three months.

To keep our business arrangement realistic, I had to calculate, refigure, and bicker for the dollars.

"Can we get a ride up to the training site?" Donnie asked. "We need to see it before we make plans."

"That is not necessary now," Birk said, sipping his orange juice. "I have made other arrangements. That property up in the mountains is still covered with snow. We cannot even reach it by car right now. I didn't realize this condition would exist when I bought that land, so I have begun to look for something closer."

On the bed I had a large-scale map of New York state, positioned so I could just turn and casually refer to it and allow Birk to point out the general area of his upstate property, but now it apparently didn't matter.

And if we were not taking the trip upstate, the entire caravan of cars, helicopters, and light planes would not be needed. I could imagine the agent in charge of the chase detail sighing in relief.

With that matter settled for the moment, I moved on to another critical subject—the false passports. "Donnie gets some of the traveling papers I need," I said. "Don, John wants some U.S. passports. Do you still have that friend who can get them?"

"Yeah," Morris said, "but it depends on how many, and on how fast. What exactly do you need?"

"Oh, not so many," Birk said. "I don't have an actual count right now, but possibly a half dozen."

"For six, I think I can get them for three hundred dollars each. I need some advance notice, though," Morris said.

Birk considered the price and seemed to like it. "I would like one for myself as well," he said. Morris shrugged, to indicate it would not be a problem.

"You'll need to get the photos and the names you want in each one," I said to Birk. "The photos have to be the passport-quality type."

"Now, I have a consideration," Birk said. "In June, here in New York, there will be a special fair for India. It will be displays of art, foods, and culture.

"We even have word that the biggest bastard of them all, Rajiv, will be coming."

"You wouldn't want to hit Gandhi in the United States, would you?" Morris asked.

"Oh no, we wouldn't want to embarrass our host country," Birk said. "We would like to have good relations with the United States."

Morris appeared thoughtful, as if he were making decisions about becoming any more deeply involved. "You told Frank you were looking for explosives," he said. "Do you mean like C4?"

"That's the U.S. military explosive," I explained.

"Yes," Birk said. "Since our man in India has been jailed, it has been very hard for us to get what we need. How much C4 can you supply?"

"Well, I don't know right off," Donnie said. "I have to go back and talk to my source. How much do you think you'll need?"

"I suppose it would depend on the power of the explosive as to how much we need," Birk said.

"What do you want to blow up?" Donnie asked.

"We have one building, it is like a hotel," Birk said, and asked Lal something in Punjabi. Lal answered, then Birk turned back to us. "A large hotel and a major bridge."

"Railroad or automobile bridge?" I asked.

"Just automobiles," Birk said.

"That's a lot of C4," Morris said.

Lal spoke again to Birk, reminding him of something. "We

can get a bomb aboard an Indian naval vessel. We would like C4 for that as well," Birk said.

"Aboard a naval vessel?" I asked. "That's pretty tight security! How can you get a bomb big enough past the guards?"

"You don't understand," Birk said. "We don't have as much security in our country as you do. The naval ships are not even guarded at times, and even when they are, we have many Sikhs who work on them or on the docks."

"You need over a hundred pounds of C4 just to start with," Morris said.

"Can you get it?" Birk asked.

"I'm going on a job and I won't be finished for a couple of weeks, but I'll get the answers about the passports and the C4 and relay them back to you through Frank," Morris said to Birk.

Birk was satisfied. He stood, and Lal collected the orange juice glasses and set them beside the pitcher. All of us left the room together and walked to the elevators, and rode one down to the lobby.

Donnie pushed the glass door open, and we filed out onto the New York street. I could almost feel the camera focus on us.

"I'll call you," I said to Birk as he and Lal walked away. Birk smiled and waved at us.

Morris was wearing a smile of his own. "I think we got 'em," he said.

To Kill Gandhi: Mid-March 1985

The phone rang. I answered it and recognized Fox's voice instantly.

"Frank, we've got a hot one," he said.

"What?"

"Birk just told Donnie that he now has permission to hit Gandhi."

"Is that right?" I asked.

"This is *the* Gandhi, do you know who I mean?" Fox asked.

"Rajiv," I said. Of course I knew who he meant.

"This operation is a lot bigger than it has been," Fox said. "This is a matter of international importance. We can't let a bunch of crazies kill a head of state here in the United States."

"Remember in New York?" I asked. "Birk told us there he didn't want to embarrass the United States."

"Well, he's changed his mind now. He's talking money with Donnie now. He'll be calling you next."

"What's Donnie saying?" I asked.

"Nothing right now. He's listening. We have to be careful with this."

"What do you want me to say when he calls me?"

"Stall him, tell him you're thinking about it. Try and pull anything out of him you can. We need some time," Fox said.

"I suppose they want to do it in June during Gandhi's visit?" I asked.

"Yeah. We could ask State to change Gandhi's schedule around, or to postpone it. We have to do something."

"Where has Birk been?" I asked.

"Well, he told you he was on vacation, but he just told Donnie he had been in London for a Sikh World Council meeting."

"Then that's where he got the order to kill Gandhi," I said.

"Right. The old boy is serious too. He told Donnie he wanted the hit while they were driving out to take a look at the new training property."

"Where's it going to be?"

"The place is in southern New Jersey, just a wide spot in the road. We need to get together and have some coffee. I'll draw you a map. You're supposed to know where it is, in case Birk starts asking questions."

"Fine, just give me the time and place to meet," I said.

I would later learn Donnie had been taping Birk when Gandhi's hit was discussed, but it had been while riding in a 4×4 truck with heavy, lugged snow tires. The roar of the tires on the pavement ruined the clarity of the tape, and an important piece of evidence. Even the famous FBI lab couldn't clean up the tape.

Delaware, New Jersey: Sikh Terrorist Training Camp

It could have been a local sheriff's worst nightmare. Just off New Jersey's Interstate 80, on Highway 46, near a little town named Delaware, Gurpartap Birk Singh had established the site for his camp.

It was not far from the Hunter's Lodge Motel and the Delaware Truck Stop, both small local business concerns.

Across Highway 46 from the truck stop was a group of houses. Behind the houses was a wooded area that sloped down to a small creek.

The Sikhs were planning to use those houses and the wooded area.

Imagine what could have happened if a police or sheriff's car had responded to a call to the houses. Even a SWAT team would have been outgunned and unprepared.

As I said, it could have been a local sheriff's worst nightmare. International terrorism, something Americans expected to see only on television, would have been in their own backyard.

The Raid Plan: Late April 1985

The raid to arrest all of the Sikh terrorist trainees was planned for approximately 8 May, two days after the "training" course had started.

Donnie and two other FBI agents, all pretending to be Mercenary School cadre, would be at the Delaware site to greet the incoming students.

There were different raid plans to cover different situations. In one plan, Donnie would escort the Sikhs into a nearby wooded area near the training site's building under the impression they were going to attend a class.

At the wooded area, contraband weapons and explosives would be ready for the supposed training. Hidden in the forest around the training area would be the FBI teams, with video cameras as part of their equipment to record the actual raid.

A second—and preferred—option was to begin the training and then at night, while the students slept, move in the raid teams and arrest all of the Sikhs quietly and efficiently.

I could not be present at the training site. It would reveal my cover, and at that time, a good deal of care had been taken to keep my participation and position secret.

Fox told me to make an excuse to Birk to miss the very start of the training. During the last week of April, while Donnie was visiting with Birk to settle some of the final details before beginning the training, Donnie called me and after a short, faked discussion, handed the phone to Birk.

I told Birk I could not be on time for the training because my son had injured his arm in a motorcycle accident, and I needed to be home for a few days.

Birk wasn't happy but he accepted the excuse.

When I put the handset down on the cradle, I thought that the next I heard about the Sikhs would be on the national news.

24 April 1985: The Veracruz Connection

A member of the Mercenary Association traveled to Birmingham to meet me and offer a proposal for an operation. He was Antonio Velez, a Mexican-American mercenary. The information he brought concerned a very powerful drug dealer who lived in Veracruz.

The local police couldn't arrest him because of his political connections, and they feared and hated him because he often had his critics or opposition killed.

A rival drug dealer also wanted the man dead. The police and drug dealer made a pact to have the man arrested and sent to Mexican federal authorities in Mexico City.

I knew the Sikh operation would not last much longer, and agreed to get to Mexico as soon as possible.

Saturday, 4 May 1985: "The Sikhs Are at The Bunker!"

I was packing my suitcase, deciding what I would or wouldn't need for Mexico. The trick was in not carrying anything that would seem to be military. My bag had to look like a *tourista*'s, everything intended for a holiday.

It was about 10:00 A.M. The sun was shining outside, I was looking forward to Mexico, and I was relieved that very shortly the Sikhs would be in the bag and I would be paid.

I heard my son's motorcycle outside, and he came into the house in a hurry.

"The Sikhs are at The Bunker!" he cried.

I stopped packing. My first thought was he was joking.

"Are you sure?" I asked.

"Yes!" Barret said. I could see he wasn't joking. "They're talking with Paul right now."

"How many of them are there?" I asked, wondering what was happening, what had gone wrong.

"Just a couple, that's all I saw."

"Are they friendly?" I asked.

"Yeah. It's Suki and another guy. Paul told me to get over here and let you know."

"Did they see you?" I asked, since my excuse to Birk had been that I couldn't get there for the first few days of the course because of an arm injury Barret had in a motorcycle accident.

"Yeah," Barret said. "Suki asked me how I was feeling."

"Get back over there, don't leave Paul alone with them," I said. "Find out what the hell they're up to, and let me know."

Barret left. I knew something was terribly wrong. No Sikhs were supposed to be in town at all.

I was on my way to start another mission. This had all the earmarks of a possible disaster.

I telephoned the downtown FBI office and asked the switchboard operator to call Fox at home. As it was the weekend, he was off duty. I told the operator it was an emergency and to give have him call me as soon as possible.

Just on the off chance things might stabilize, I went back to packing, sorting the colors and types of shirts, trousers, and socks I would need.

The phone rang. I answered, and it was Fox.

"There are Sikhs at The Bunker," I said, and began to explain what I knew so far. As I was doing that, Barret came back, hurrying to the bedroom where I was waiting.

"They want Paul to go to New Orleans and kill somebody," Barret said. "They want guns. Paul's just driven them to Tim's so they can buy a pistol from him."

I relayed the information to Fox.

"Let me tell you something," he said. "We got a Telex from the CIA saying there was going to be a minister of the Indian government traveling to New Orleans for some kind of medical treatment, and there might be an assassination attempt against him."

"And?"

"Well, Birk recently asked Donnie to provide a hit man and

a weapon to do it. I didn't pass that along to you, because Donnie didn't think it was important, and he's been really tied up getting this raid ready."

"That's why they're here," I said. "They must be on their way to New Orleans."

I was keeping my reaction to myself. I couldn't believe Donnie would try to cold-shoulder Birk on something as serious as an assassination request, and to top it off, nobody had warned me.

"What kind of weapon did they want?" I asked.

"A silenced pistol," the agent said. "We had one with the silencer welded onto it and the firing pin filed down that we had ready to give them if they had insisted, but Donnie really didn't want to do it."

A quick vision of the Sikhs trying to test fire the FBI-supplied pistol came to my mind. If they had tried to shoot it and it failed, they would have become instantly suspicious.

"Yeah, but giving them a pistol that can't fire would have—" I started to say, but Fox interrupted me.

"We couldn't give them a real one," he said.

That was true. I had to set my agitation aside and get back to business. I questioned Barret about what type of automobile the Sikhs had, exactly how many Sikhs were there, and what they were wearing, while Fox could hear me. He told me to stay where I was and he would call me back.

After I put the phone down, Barret explained that he and Paul had been sleeping late in the rear of The Bunker, and there had come a loud banging on the large steel bay door. Sleepily, wearing only a T-shirt and jogging shorts, Paul had walked to the bay door and pushed it up. Squinting into the sunlight, he was confronted with two Sikhs.

For a moment, Paul didn't know if they had come to kill him, if they were looking for and wanted to kill me, or if for some chance they were just dropping by on a visit. He knew the raid was set for the beginning of the week.

Suki—Sukhwinder Singh—a graduate Merc Association student, was one of the two there. Neither Barret nor Paul knew the other man with him. The stranger was wearing a camouflage bush hat and was dressed in wrinkled sport clothes. He had a heavy beard and long hair.

I would discover later that Suki's partner was none other than Gurpartap Birk Singh himself.

"Paul said he'd get back as fast as he could," Barret said. "The Sikhs were asking for you. Paul told them you were out of town."

It sounded like Paul was doing a good job. He was obviously delaying the Sikhs to give me a chance to coordinate with the FBI.

As I was still questioning Barret and taking calls every few minutes from Fox, Paul was selling a pistol to Suki and Birk. Suki had originally asked Paul for a pistol, silencer, and grenades, if they were available. When Paul said the Merc School was out of all those items at the moment, Suki settled for just the pistol. The pistol in question belonged to Tim Arnold, a Mercenary Association graduate, whom the Sikhs had met during their training course.

Suki haggled with Tim over the price. It was a stainless-steel Astra .45-caliber automatic, a copy of the U.S. service automatic. They settled on $220.

Paul, Tim, Birk, and Suki drove to a garbage dump to test-fire the pistol. Suki offered Paul and Tim the job of riding to New Orleans with them and killing their target. He said they would be back in Birmingham by the next day.

At first Suki offered Paul $1,000 for the hit, but when Paul said no, he upped it to $1,400, refusing to go any higher, mistaking Paul's reluctance for an effort to raise the price.

Paul then drove the Sikhs back to The Bunker, so they could leave.

When I next called Fox, he told me police protection was being arranged in New Orleans for the Sikhs' target, Bhajan Lal, chief minister of the state of Haryana.

The Sikhs had left Birmingham about 1:00 P.M. in a dark-gray Chevrolet Celebrity. The six hours it would take for them to drive to New Orleans would be enough for the authorities there to prepare for them.

Bhajan Lal, The Sikh Target, had arrived in New Orleans on 29 April for a lens implant in one of his eyes, which he had at the Louisiana State University Medical Center. He then moved to the Meridien Hotel and was staying on for two weeks of outpatient treatment.

The Indian government had indeed cautioned the U.S. State

Department that Lal's name was on the Sikhs' hit list. He had been outspoken against the Sikhs, and his state was near the Punjab and the center of trouble.

The warning call from the FBI in Birmingham to the New Orleans FBI office was relayed to the New Orleans police department, and they were advised to strengthen their guard.

Before that, Bhajan Lal had only a single Indian security guard to protect him, but after the call at least fourteen New Orleans police department personnel were assigned to the job.

Lal didn't seem much concerned about the threat. The police advised him to change hotels and cancel a dinner appointment he had planned for that night with a friend. He refused.

The police provided him with a guarded limousine and a tailing security car. He left for dinner at 7:30 P.M.

Birk had spoken very little while around Paul Johnson. He had worn old clothes, the camouflage bush hat on his head part of his nondescript but militant image.

In his Chevrolet were two loaded pistols, a .38 Colt snub-nose revolver, Tim Arnold's .45 Astra automatic, two daggers, and a traditional Sikh *kirpan* knife religiously necessary for a warriors mission. Birk's men had studied Lal's face from newspaper photos that were also in the car, along with a city map of New Orleans with the Meridien Hotel's location circled on it.

They parked the Chevrolet near the hotel, with the weapons hidden under the seat. Birk then directed his men to make a walking recon of the hotel. He had three men traveling with him instead of the one Paul and Barret had seen.

In addition to Suki, there were Virinder Singh and Jasbir Sandhu Singh.

Jatinder Singh Ahluwalia, who lived and worked in New Orleans as a cab driver, waited to meet Birk. Jatinder was acting as the local liaison for Birk, there to give him assistance. He had apparently been watching Bhajan Lal for several days and could take the hit team directly to the target's doorway.

Police lookouts outside the hotel saw the Sikhs as they walked past the building and radioed their numbers and positions to the command post.

There had been a short-term disagreement among the New Orleans police officials before Birk had been spotted. One side said the Sikhs should be arrested as they actually tried to kill

Bhajan Lal so there would be unquestionable proof of their intentions.

The bolder New Orleans police officers said the Sikh hit men had to be stopped as soon as possible, because they were too dangerous.

With Birk and his men actually on the street outside the hotel, the decision had to be made. It was no longer academic.

Armed police and plainclothes officers moved quickly onto the street against the Sikhs. Birk and his men surrendered without resistance. Their weapons were still in the Chevrolet.

It was approximately 10:00 P.M. in New Orleans. The police had only four Sikhs in custody. Ahluwalia, the cab driver, had seen the police coming and escaped. He apparently went as quickly as he could to a telephone, and called New York or New Jersey and reported to the Sikhs there that Birk had been arrested.

Word of the arrest spread quickly among the waiting group of terrorist trainees. They grabbed their belongings and escaped into the trackless Sikh underground communities in New York and Canada.

Lal Singh was among those who vanished.

With the Sikhs also went any intelligence on the C4 they had reportedly bought from the Brit merc.

Like the Sikhs, the C4 was now probably over the border in Canada. We just didn't know about the C4 then. We just didn't know.

The FBI imposed an immediate news blackout on the arrest of Birk and his men, in the hope of keeping the action secret from the Sikhs. Apparently they were not yet aware that Jatinder had already issued a warning.

In interrogation, one of Birk's men revealed who Jatinder was and where he lived, but still the FBI did not want to arrest him, for fear word would spread to the Sikh community.

It even was suggested the day after the arrest that Birk and his men actually be released, without letting them know that the wider Gandhi plot had been penetrated. Birk and his people could then be recaptured at the training camp.

On Monday, 6 May, about twenty U.S. government security and intelligence officials arrived in New Orleans for an emergency strategy session that lasted two days.

They agreed that Birk's failure to return to New York had probably already compromised the training camp and the raid that was to follow.

The FBI sent a car and a few men in on a reconnaissance to the New Jersey training camp site, to the house on the property that was to be used as a classroom and barracks. No one was there except a couple of Sikhs who hadn't been identified in any earlier investigation. They were simply maintaining the grounds, and claimed innocence and ignorance.

The Sikh cab driver was arrested at his home by FBI agents on 12 May, his arrest left until the day prior to the public announcement on the thirteenth by William Webster, head of the FBI, that his organization had foiled plots by Sikh terrorists to assassinate both Haryana Chief Minister Bhajan Lal and Prime Minister Rajiv Gandhi.

The New Jersey raid, with all its anticipation and planning, did not happen, but I was in Mexico and didn't have time to worry about it.

News Item: 14 May 1985
FBI Foils Sikh Plot to Kill Gandhi
New York: U.S. authorities say they have foiled Sikh plots to overthrow the Indian Government and to kill Prime Minister Rajiv Gandhi during a visit to the United States next month.

The FBI said five Sikhs had been arrested in New Orleans and two others who were implicated were still being sought.

CHAPTER EIGHTEEN
Mexico

My sniper put the rifle to his shoulder and sighted on one of the bodyguards protecting the drug baron inside his ranch house. The raiding squads were ready, somewhere behind in the night.

We had been in Mexico almost a week, stalking our target.

I gave the order to fire.

7 May 1985: Birmingham Airport

I drove Paul to the airport, questioning him on the way to ensure he had his expense money, tickets, and reservations in order. He was flying to Veracruz ahead of me as a security measure.

"Antonio'll be waiting for you at the airport in Veracruz," I said. "He'll have the rest of the expense money there. Remember what I said to do if you have to abort before I arrive."

"I'll escape and evade out and meet you either in Mexico City or back here in Birmingham," he said.

Repeating details might seem redundant, but basic procedure required we resolve any potential misunderstandings before they happened. It was planning for the problems that ensured an operation would work.

Our operation was a dangerous one. We were being paid to take an important drug dealer prisoner and deliver him to the Mexican authorities.

The police would not try to arrest him on their own. He was far too powerful, and therefore too dangerous for that. If the arresting officers failed, or if he was released or could escape, all of them he could identify, plus their families, were as good as dead.

Antonio had described some of the drug dealer's exploits to me, and he seemed to be a man of such arrogance, riches, and important friends that he was nearly untouchable.

I let Paul out in front of the airport, and he swung his bag off the car seat, smiling. "See you in Mexico, partner," he said, and waved as he walked away.

I drove back to The Bunker to finish my own packing. I had a trunk with a false bottom almost finished. Under the panel was part of my own kit, a small 7.65-millimeter automatic pistol, a silencer, cans of CS gas, and special soft-nose ammunition for the sniper rifle Antonio had waiting in Mexico.

In the trunk I stashed my clothes, shoes, and a pair of two-way headset radios disguised as Walkman-type cassette tape players, complete with belt carry cases and music tapes.

8 May: Customs, Mexico City

On the way south to Mexico City, I read through Gayle Rivers's *The Specialist,* a book offered to me by another passenger, which was about a British mercenary who made his money performing assassinations and taking political prisoners. It was an entertaining book, and though I had no way of personally verifying it, some of it struck me as authentic.

The passenger who owned the book was an American basketball coach going to Mexico City for a series of international games. When I asked him his opinion, he shrugged and asked me if I thought events like Gayle Rivers described actually happened.

I told him that sometimes they really did.

We reached Mexico City just before midnight, and only about thirty passengers disembarked with me. The rest were continuing on the flight.

I walked with the sleepy passengers to the baggage claim, picked up my trunk on the carousel, then went to the Customs stations. As soon as I saw there were almost as many Customs agents as passengers, I sensed trouble. An agent motioned for me to bring my trunk to him.

I laid it on the table, unlocked it, and he reached inside, pushing the contents around. I was ready to close the lid, relock the hasp, and move on to the waiting area. My next flight was not until well after dawn.

The agent knocked on the false bottom and looked at me.

"Open it," he said in English.

I hesitated. This was taking on the shape of a major disaster. "Open it," he said again.

I was thinking very quickly. I decided to bluff him. "That is my equipment," I said.

"Please open it, sir."

I reached inside, felt for the finger hole, and pulled the bottom up. The agent saw the pistol and silencer.

He looked at me with amazement. I assumed a stern expression. "Go get your supervisor," I ordered. He dashed away. I stood beside my trunk as if I were irritated with the delay.

In two minutes, several guards had arrived. They wore the white shirts and green trousers of the Mexico City airport security, their silver badges very prominent.

The Customs agent returned and again reached inside my trunk. I grabbed his hand. "Get the supervisor," I said as more security personnel arrived.

Finally the supervisor came, a Smith & Wesson automatic pistol on his belt. The crowd parted to allow him through, and cautious and curious, he walked up to me.

"Is this yours?" he asked, pointing to the trunk.

"Yes," I said. "We need to go to your office to talk."

"Come with me," he said, and I followed him, one of the security guards behind me carrying my trunk. The group of Customs and security agents also followed, wanting to see what was going to happen.

Inside the office, the supervisor took out the pistol and silencer, then examined the ammunition. "These are unusual items," he said. "Are you a policeman?"

"I am a weapons dealer and antiterror instructor," I said. "I am traveling to Veracruz to begin training the police department there. You can call the training officer in Veracruz if you like; I'll give you his telephone number."

"You will do training for the police in Veracruz?" he asked.

"Yes, I will. Please be careful with my equipment," I said.

"Why don't you carry this equipment differently?" he asked.

"Because of reactions of Customs agents," I said, "and because of the threat of theft. I am responsible for that pistol and the rest of the equipment."

"Do you sell weapons?" he asked.

"Yes. I am authorized for automatic weapons."

"Do you have any proof?" he asked.

I reached inside my briefcase and produced a catalog of military equipment from The Bunker. "This is my company," I said. He took the catalog and flipped through the pages slowly. "I will be presenting this equipment to the chiefs of police in Veracruz and Tabasco."

"I believe I understand now," he said, "but I know I cannot telephone this time of night. The only thing I can do is issue you a receipt for this equipment and ask you to come back tomorrow and claim it. Is that all right?"

"Of course," I said, and had to stifle my relief.

I stayed the rest of the night in the Holiday Inn near the airport, minus my pistol, silencer, CS gas, and ammunition. It had all been replaced with a sheet of paper and an apology from the supervisor.

I rose on time in the morning and carried my trunk out to the airport shuttle van, knowing precisely how lucky I was to be traveling now and not greeting the day in jail.

The flight from Mexico City to Veracruz was brief, taking me over the mountains and down to the seashore. The sky was clear and the tropical blue of the water was beautiful.

We landed and taxied to the terminal. A stair ramp was pushed to our plane, and I stepped out of the cabin air conditioning into the warmth of the sea breezes off the Gulf of Mexico, then followed the passengers across the airstrip into the terminal building.

Antonio was waiting just inside the door, and he extended his hand, clasping mine firmly. "How are you, sir?" he asked, smiling.

"Great," I said. "Where's Paul?"

"He's at the hotel, waiting for you."

"Okay, let's get my trunk and get out of here," I said.

I explained to Antonio exactly what had happened in Mexico City as we drove to the hotel, and he shook his head in astonishment. "That was close," he said. "You were very lucky."

He stopped in front of the Villa del Mar, a beachside hotel used mainly by the local people, and I carried my trunk inside our room.

Paul was sitting at the table near the door, the curtains opened so he could watch the gulf as he studied diagrams and photographs. "Hi, Paul," I said, placing the trunk on one of the room beds.

"Hey," he said. "Glad you made it."

I quickly told him the story about Mexico City, while Antonio grinned and watched Paul's expression. The incident was almost a joke now, since nothing serious had happened because of it.

"Jesus," Paul said. "Well, at least we can get along without the pistol. Looks like Antonio has this all figured out."

I sat down beside Paul, examining the notes and photos of men and houses. Antonio had done most of the intelligence before I arrived. That would save time. "Have you eaten?" I asked them.

"No," Antonio said, and opened the door. "We can go to a little restaurant near here." We carefully locked the room door, walked across the beach to a patio café, and ordered a tray of tacos. I had a Coca-Cola while Paul and Antonio drank Tecate beer laced with lime and Tabasco sauce, Paul drinking two to Antonio's one.

"This is the situation, Frank," Antonio said. "The guy has three houses. Two of them are his girlfriend's, right here in town. The other is his ranch in the country. I have watched them all, and I see two good possibilities."

"Which are?" I asked.

"We can try for him at one of his girlfriend's houses, because of its location, or we can go to the ranch. Either place is good."

"Is the rifle ready?" I asked.

"Yes," Antonio said, "but we need to take it out for a few test shots to make sure the telescope is adjusted."

"Does the Russian silencer work okay?" I asked.

"It is perfect," Antonio said.

"Have you seen the target?" I asked Paul.

"Just his photo," Paul said. "The guy looks like a snake."

"What kind of security does he have?" I asked Antonio.

"Sometimes a carload of his men, with AR-15 rifles. Sometimes he only has one bodyguard."

"Do they do a good job?"

"No," Antonio said. "They don't know how. They are there only to stop someone from running up and shooting him with a pistol. They know nothing about sniper fire. When the first bodyguard goes down, they will all run."

"When does he have the least security?" I asked.

"Maybe on his ranch," Antonio said.

As we ate, I wondered if the target knew we were in town and if his men might be planning to come to our hotel and shoot us, perhaps at such a moment as this, while we were armed with nothing more lethal than forks and table knives. Our business was a sword that cut both ways, and Paul's drinking was not helping his alertness.

I read the file on the target. He was Felipe Lagunes Castillo, forty-three years of age and a cousin of the governor of the state of Veracruz, Agustin Acosta Lagunes. In addition to his drug business, Castillo was a rich cattle rancher and was an important man in the Cattlemen's Association. I was beginning to understand why the locals would want Castillo out of the picture. I also understood why they were afraid of him.

The man was tied to the Colombian Medellín Cartel, the cartel I had first learned of in Panama. That association alone was enough to make him an untouchable, and he acted as if he were bulletproof. The Medellín Cartel was incredibly powerful and widespread, having even the heads of governments in its pocket.

Castillo had ordered the execution killings of a well-known local newspaper columnist, Manuel Buendia, and journalist Javier Vasquez, for their critical reporting of him.

Once Castillo had sent his men to steal the automobile of the chief of police of Veracruz, and then told the chief if he wanted the car, he would have to come to his ranch personally and get it.

His ranch was named El Cocal and was near Veracruz City. Antonio had marked the ranch on one of the maps and the entrance and exit roads to it.

Antonio's arrangement with the Mexican federal authorities was to deliver Castillo to Mexico City. When Castillo was secure in jail there, all of us would be paid.

Nothing was clean about the operation. Castillo was being taken out because he was too violent and too powerful.

11 May: The Weapon

Antonio's rifleman was a young Mexican police officer who spoke no English. His name was Felix, and Antonio told me he had used him before on serious missions.

"Fine," I said, "let's see him shoot."

Felix lay down behind the rifle. It was a modified 7.62-millimeter, bolt-action hunting rifle. The stock had been cut to fit the length of Felix's arms, and a special brace had been attached to the butt to secure the rifle to his shoulder so it would not move as he worked the bolt for rapid shots.

A large telescopic sight was fitted over the receiver, and the bolt handle had been custom-made so Felix would not strike the sight with his hands as he fed and ejected the cartridges.

The barrel was supported by a bipod, and screwed onto the end of the muzzle was a prize item, a Soviet *Spetsnaz* (Special Purpose Forces) sound suppressor.

Using the suppressor would quiet the report, of course, but it would also prevent the movement of grass or bushes near the weapon because there would be no muzzle "blast." The flash associated with a fired weapon would be reduced as well, so for night fire, no one could easily determine the position of the sniper.

We were on a remote hilltop in the mountains, about an hour's drive north of Castillo's ranch. Paul paced off two hundred meters down into the valley to set up a large bucket we had found abandoned beside the road. He was wearing the headset radio I had given him, which was voice activated, so no manual controlling of the radio was necessary.

"That's good," I said into the lip mike of my headset. Paul stopped and securely planted the bucket.

"Am I coming in clear?" he asked.

"Perfect," I said. "Now move off to the side about ten meters and spot these rounds for us."

Paul walked aside, waving at me. Felix pulled the stock of the rifle into his shoulder, squinted through the scope, and fired.

The report from the Spetsnaz suppressor was not the thunder of a high-powered rifle. It was more like that of a small-caliber pistol, and without the sharp sonic frequency that travels from a shot. I was watching the suppressor, not the target, and saw there was no raising of dust at the muzzle.

"Damn, that thing's really quiet," Paul said to me over the headset, "down here it sounds like a *pop.*"

"Where's he hitting?" I asked.

"On line but low. Bring it up slightly."

I told Antonio, who translated to Felix, who clicked in one notch of elevation, worked the bolt, and fired again.

"You got it," Paul radioed.

"Okay," I said. "Now give me three rounds rapid fire, and I want all hits," I said to Antonio.

Felix checked the rifle magazine to insure he had three more shots, poised his body and focused all of his attention on the distant bucket, and fired three shots that almost sounded as if they were coming from a semiautomatic rifle, his right hand flying as he jacked the bolt.

"Good shooting," Paul radioed. "That's three hits!"

"Bueno," I said to Felix, and reached down and shook his hand. "This is a hell of a rifleman," I told Antonio.

While Paul walked back, Felix talked with Antonio about the rifle. "He says the shoulder brace works well, not allowing the stock to move as he operates the bolt, and the suppressor seems to eliminate much of the recoil of the rifle."

"Keeps it pretty quiet too," Paul said as he arrived, sweating from the climb. "Honest to God, it don't sound like a rifle down there."

After dinner and more cans of Tecate beer, again too many for Paul, in my opinion, we went back over the details again. Antonio and I agreed that Castillo was best taken at his ranch.

The plan took shape as we worked over it late into the night. A recon team consisting of Paul and me would move to the house after dark locate and identify the target and his bodyguards. The sniper would move forward on signal from the recon team and take his position. The recon team would dash into the house after the sniper had shot the bodyguards and eliminate any remaining opposition. Then the support group would move in and take custody of Castillo.

If the plan failed, and Paul and I were killed or captured, the others would be able to get away. It was a big risk, but that was what we were being paid to do—take the chances for the local police.

"Do you think we ought to try a night recon of the ranch?" I asked.

"That's not a good idea," Antonio said. "If we are seen, we ruin our chances of coming back again."

That made sense. "When's the best time to pull the raid?" I asked.

"Sunday night," Antonio said. "They will be very lax then."

"Okay," I agreed. "Then we'll just get some rest."

"How about showing me the cantinas down here?" Paul asked Antonio. "I don't want to sit all night in a hotel room."

Antonio looked at me. I shrugged. "Okay, *amigo,*" he said to Paul, and I lay down to read as they left.

Sunday Morning, 12 May

I was asleep when someone knocked on the door. It was just light outside.

"Yes?" I asked, stepping to the door.

"Come on, open up, it's me," said Paul. He sounded drunk.

I unlocked the door and he came in, unsteady and grinning. "I'm beat," he said. "Antonio went back to his hotel about midnight. I had the prettiest li'l senorita. She wrote me a poem. Can't read it. It's in Spanish," he said.

This was my first time on an operation with Paul.

"You've got to get cleaned up," I said, "we might have work to do today."

Paul washed, changed clothes, and lay down on his bed, telling me Antonio wasn't coming back anyway until later in the day.

I let him sleep, and walked to the local restaurant for breakfast. As I ate, watching the beaches begin to fill with sunbathers and swimmers, I decided we were ready. We could do the raid that night. Paul would be sober by then. I spent the rest of the day trying to relax but wasn't too successful.

Antonio and Felix came to the hotel an hour before sundown, with weapons and equipment inside nylon bags Felix carried. By then Paul had been awake for hours himself. He had eaten, drunk a six-pack of Tecate, and was becoming anxious.

Antonio handed me a bag I knew contained a Magnum revolver and handcuffs. He had one for Paul too, but noticed Paul was not really sober. He frowned at me.

"Come outside for a moment," Antonio said to me. Paul waited in the room while Antonio and I went out to his car.

"He is still drinking," Antonio said. "He can't go. He's not reliable."

"It's your operation," I said.

"We can't take any chances. I wish he wasn't even here. He knows too much now. If anyone catches him, he'll talk."

"I've got an idea," I said. "Tell him we've got a delay, give him some more *cerveza*. He'll go to sleep."

We went back inside. "We've got a problem," I told Paul. "I can't explain it now. I'm going to a meeting with Antonio. You wait here until we get back."

"Just wait?" Paul asked.

"It'll be awhile." I said. "Get some chow, take it easy. This whole thing might be scrubbed." I gave him the money he'd need. At least Paul didn't question me. He slept the night of the raid, believing there was a delay.

Sunday Night, 12 May: The Raid

Two pickup trucks of armed men were waiting off the road in the dark exactly in the spot where Antonio had promised. They all had pistols and Colt AR-15 rifles. It was a serious group, and they talked briefly with Antonio while Felix and I got out of the car. My weapon was a .357 magnum revolver.

The trucks left as Antonio walked back to us. "They know to come when they hear the first shots," he said.

"How long will they wait?" I asked.

"As long as necessary," Antonio said. Felix prepared the rifle, screwing the sound suppressor onto the muzzle and clipping the bipod to the barrel.

I handed one radio to Antonio and put on my own headset,

whispering in the lip mike to test it. Antonio nodded, adjusting the fit of the earphone to suit himself.

Felix led off, and I followed him, walking slowly and carefully, with Antonio behind me as tail gun. He was keeping a good watch over his shoulders, the same as on a combat patrol.

Felix knew his route, and after an hour of weaving through underbrush, climbing over fences, and pausing to listen in the stands of trees, we knelt together.

Antonio pointed toward a low hill. "That's where we have to go," he said. "We can see the house from there." It was open ground to the low hill, and we crept across it, crouched forward, trying to be lower shapes in the dark.

We crawled to the crest. The large, traditional ranch house was near us, less than fifty meters away. There were lights in the windows, and several automobiles and pickup trucks parked out front. It all seemed very peaceful and unsuspecting.

"The patio is off to the other side," Antonio said, "From this side you can see into the front room and one of the bedrooms."

"Good," I said.

"Okay, I'm going around to the patio," he said.

Antonio vanished in the darkness. I lay still to give him enough time to get clear of me before I moved. I looked over my shoulder to where Felix waited, giving him the signal to stay in place.

"You okay?" Antonio radioed.

"Fine," I said, and began to crawl down the hill, keeping flat.

"They're in the house," Antonio said. He was whispering when he spoke to me. Sometimes just the sound of breathing would activate the lip mike, because we had the sensitivity set on maximum.

I was getting close enough to the house to see into the curtained windows. I could make out shapes of people and hear voices. I wondered why there were no outside guards.

"I'm in a good spot," Antonio said. "I'm looking through the patio door. Castillo is in there."

"Who else?" I asked.

"Two or three men. I know one is a bodyguard because he's wearing a shoulder holster. One of the men is too old—hey! I see a kid."

"Kid?"

"A little boy. About twelve . . . and there's a woman, could be his wife."

"What are they doing?" I asked.

"Just talking. Can you see anybody?"

I watched the windows and saw a man move across one.

"I got a guy with a white shirt," I said, "might be coming your way."

"I see him. He's a bodyguard too," Antonio said.

"Weapon?" I asked.

"Can't see one."

A half hour passed while we watched and listened.

"I think this patio side is the best," Antonio said. "Bring Felix with you."

"On the way," I said.

We crouched together in a thicket, peering through palmetto bushes at the patio, and I agreed the position was good.

I clearly identified Castillo, who was sitting in an overstuffed chair, drinking liquor from a glass kept filled by one of the bodyguards.

There were only three other men in the house with Castillo that I could see. The two younger men were obviously guards. One wore the shoulder holster Antonio had reported, the weapon in it probably a .38 Special.

The other man was about Castillo's age and was engaged in active conversation with him. I saw the boy only once, when he walked through the room.

The sniper rifle was awkward in our cramped location, the sound suppressor making the barrel even longer than usual. Felix set it down beside him and looked to me.

I pointed to the patio door. *"Dos hombres,"* I said to Felix, pointing to the bodyguards, and drew my finger across my throat.

"Sí," he said.

"Uno momento," I told him, then turned to Antonio.

"When he shoots the two guards, all of us will charge the house. We're going in through the patio doors."

"Okay," Antonio said.

Felix lay down, shouldered his rifle, and put his eye to the telescopic sight. I heard his thumb click off the safety. Legally, I must deny everything that followed.

I pulled my pistol. I wished I had my M11 submachine gun.

Or an Uzi. Even a Browning Hi-Power. Anything but a wheel gun.

Castillo was laughing. The woman was standing near his chair. The bodyguard with the shoulder holster was leaning toward Castillo, as if emphasizing a point in the conversation.

Felix fired.

In the stillness, the sound suppressor seemed loud, the bullet blowing a small starred hole in the glass patio door, sending fragments out like diamond dust. The guard with the shoulder holster went down.

Felix slammed the bolt back and forth and pulled the trigger again, and a second tiny hole burst through the glass, dropping the other guard, who pitched across the table, sending Castillo's drink to the floor.

"*¡Asalto!*" I said, and the three of us leapt from the palmettos and ran toward the patio.

I shattered the glass door with the barrel of my pistol and rushed over the bodies of the two guards. Castillo was still in his chair, his mouth open. Antonio ran past me, covering the hallway.

The woman did not scream. The boy ran to her, and Felix started yelling at them in Spanish. I grabbed Castillo by the arms, locking my handcuffs on his wrist. He seemed too shocked to resist.

Felix threw the woman, boy, and older man against the wall, covering them with the rifle. I pointed my .357 Magnum into Castillo's face. He seemed to be on the verge of a heart attack.

When the boy tried to speak, Felix shouted, "*¡Silencio! ¡Silencio!*"

Headlights shone suddenly through the windows and I heard a truck braking. I jerked Castillo out of his chair just as the support team entered the house. I was surprised they were wearing masks, but I should have expected it.

I shoved Castillo into the support team's hands. AR-15 flash suppressors dug into his belly as the men pushed him out the patio doorway, over the broken glass.

Antonio, Felix, and I walked out behind him. Castillo was forced into the bed of one of the trucks, his rumpled shirt hanging from his trousers, the glaze of amazement still in his eyes.

"*Finito,*" I said to Antonio and Felix, and we walked away

from the house, up the road to where our car waited, not looking back.

Antonio and Felix drove away from the hotel. I went into my room, and without talking much to Paul, undressed, took a shower, and lay down to sleep away what was left of the night, my pistol beside my bed.

13 May: The Morning After

I had my bags packed when Antonio knocked on the room door. Paul opened it.

"Good morning," I said to Antonio with a slight smile. Paul was packing quietly, placing his clothes into a travel bag. He still didn't know the raid was over, only that we were to leave.

"Are you ready to go to the airport?" Antonio asked.

"Sure are," I said. "How about some breakfast?"

We locked the room and walked to the little restaurant near the hotel, and ordered coffee and food for us all.

"That was good work last night," I said, when Paul walked to the cigarette machine. "Tell Felix for me he did very well." Antonio nodded.

"When will you meet us in Mexico City?" I asked.

"I have to go to the employer first," Antonio said. "You know, he left the state while all of this was happening. He was afraid."

"Well, when is he going to be back? I want to get paid," I said. Paul returned to the table and sat down.

Breakfast came, and we ate, talking about many things, but no details about the operation. When we were finished, we walked back to the hotel, and Antonio paid the bill while Paul and I loaded our bags into the car. On the way to the airport we made our plans about communications and meetings.

There was still enough expense money to last the next few days, and we already had return airline tickets back to the United States.

Paul and I boarded our flight to Mexico City with the traveling families and businessmen. Antonio shook my hand at the gate and said he would see me soon.

Two hours later, leaving Mexico City airport, Paul looked at me and smiled. "You plan to go to Customs and get your stuff?" he asked.

"Sure," I said. "You take this receipt, go to Customs, and ask for a pistol and silencer. Be sure to tell them that you're me."

"Bullshit," Paul said, almost believing I was serious.

We took a taxi downtown to a hotel.

NEWS ITEM: 14 MAY 1985 THE NEWS—MEXICO CITY
VERACRUZ: CATTLE BOSS FATALLY SHOT
Jalapa, Veracruz: A wealthy and powerful cattleman reportedly related to the governor was found dead of gunshot wounds here Tuesday in the latest instance of escalating violence in the state.

Lagunes Castillo's wife reportedly told police that her husband had been forcibly abducted from his El Cocal ranch near Veracruz City by a heavily armed group Sunday night. She said their vehicles bore the markings of the Veracruz State Police.

15 May: Mexico City

"Antonio!" I said, holding the newspaper article as I spoke into the phone. "What happened?"

"They must have killed him, Frank. I didn't know about it," Antonio said. He was still in Veracruz.

"What happened to the boy?"

"I don't know. This is not good. I don't believe now they intended to let Castillo live, but they never told me."

"What about getting paid?" I asked.

"The employer, he has not come back. Because Castillo's dead, he is terrified. His deal was to have him taken alive."

"When will he be back?" I asked.

"I don't know, Frank. He is afraid for his own life."

"Well, we can't stay here. I have to get back to the United States."

"Perhaps we will still get the money," Antonio said. "We did our job. I am very sorry, I will talk to the employer as soon as he comes back."

"Okay," I said, "you take care of yourself."

17 May: Birmingham Airport

Paul and I left the plane with the rest of the passengers, and while Paul watched the baggage return for our luggage, I went to the phone and called home to see what had been happening while I was gone.

I discovered the Birmingham newspapers were full of stories about the Sikhs having attended Merc School and that I was being publicly named as a trainer of terrorists.

Tired, disgusted at the killing of the man I had gone to such effort to capture, and angry at not being paid for my work, the news that everyone was being falsely told I was a terrorist was bitter.

Paul walked to the phone where I stood, the bags slung across his shoulders, and asked what was going on.

"The usual," I said, and took my bag. As we walked out of the airport, I began to explain.

CHAPTER NINETEEN
Air India Flight 182

The electronic baggage monitor at Canada's Toronto airport had broken down, and some of the luggage being loaded aboard Air India Flight 182, a Boeing 747, had been hand inspected.

Flight 182's destination was Bombay, with a stop in London.

Counting the crew, there were 329 people aboard the Air India jet. It flew first to Montreal, where three suspicious bags waiting to be loaded with other luggage were kept off the aircraft. After being examined, they were found to contain nothing harmful. The inspection of luggage was routine for an international flight.

Flight 182 did have an unusual feature. It was carrying a *fifth* engine, one being transported back to India for service. The engine was mounted under the port wing, not an extremely uncommon procedure.

Once off the ground in Montreal, Flight 182 headed east, for its five-hour trip to London and a scheduled refueling. The passengers aboard the flight were mostly Middle Eastern, both Sikhs and Indians, but many of them held Canadian citizenship.

There were wives, sons, mothers, and fathers on Flight 182. Meals were served, a movie in Hindi was played, passengers read, and children played in their seats and in the aisles. The aircraft was at 31,000 feet and in radio contact with air traffic control at its destination airport near London.

They were just off the coast of Ireland, preparing to descend. Touchdown was in forty minutes. Flight attendants were walking the aisles, checking the cabin and passengers, preparing them for landing. It was 0719 hours GMT.

An explosion in the forward baggage compartment of the 747, under the decks of the passenger section, ripped a hole out through the side of the fuselage.

The passengers would have looked up in fear, seeing the flight attendants grabbing for support on the nearby seats. In a howling rush, the cabin air would have blown out of the twisted aluminum where the bulkhead and deck joined, paper and loose clothing flying in the incredible hurricane of escaping air.

The cabin lights should have flashed, flickered, and gone out. Screaming, shouting passengers would not have been heard above the shrieking wind.

Oxygen masks would have automatically dropped from the overhead compartments. Some of the passengers may have grabbed for them.

Flight 182 then rolled and dived, its electrical systems burning out. The air crew could not have known what was happening to them. The bomb had been right beside the electronics bay.

In moments, many of the passengers probably died, killed by explosive decompression as their lungs and blood vessels ruptured from the instant loss of pressure. Blood and water freezes at six miles up, and for a short time, there would have been frost on the skin of the doomed.

But not all would be dead. Some of the passengers would only be unconscious, unaware that they were falling toward the ocean. Investigators would later estimate the fall to have lasted two to four minutes.

The 747 would have hit the cold Atlantic salt water, shedding parts and sections of its alloy skin as the huge jumbo jet crashed across the surface.

When the splash and foam from the impact subsided, the wreckage of Flight 182 sank, the fuselage broken open, and over a hundred corpses floated to the surface, along with bits of their belongings and floatable pieces of the aircraft.

The ocean was 6,700 feet deep where Flight 182 settled. Its two flight recorders, witnesses to the disaster, began to send out a consistent radio signal. This would be the only grave marker many of the passengers would have, and in a month the signal would go silent.

On 10 July 1985 Scarab I, a robot submarine, retrieved the

voice recorder. It was the first time a recorder had been salvaged from such a depth.

The voice recorder tape was examined by Air India. According to a statement they released, the tape revealed only normal cockpit conversation, a dull or muffled sound, then silence.

I was sitting at home in Birmingham on that Sunday of 23 June 1985, in the late afternoon, when I saw a television news report of the loss of Air India Flight 182 and the death of the 329 people on board. A videotape clip showed bodies in the water. *Sikh extremists were claiming credit.* For a moment I was sick.

The Sikhs were showing us they were still in business and could reach out and kill if they wished.

Fifty-five minutes before Air India 182 vanished off the radar screens, a powerful bomb exploded at Narita International Airport, near Tokyo, Japan, killing two Japanese baggage handlers and seriously wounding four others.

The baggage containing the bomb had just been removed from Canadian Pacific Flight 003 from Vancouver, Canada, which had landed at Narita only forty minutes before the explosion, with 390 people on board.

The bag that exploded was thought to be in transfer to another Air India 747, Flight 301, from Tokyo to Bombay.

Obviously, the bomb timing was miscalculated by its makers, and was intended to destroy Air India Flight 301. It would have exploded as the aircraft left the coast of Japan.

Had that happened, two Air India 747's would have been downed at almost the same time, with a combined toll of over six hundred souls.

Japanese investigators at Narita found parts of what they believed to be a timing device made with sophisticated electronic chips embedded in the body of one dead baggage handler along with chemical residue of plastic explosive on the luggage.

The type of explosive used at Narita is important, because probably the same type was used in both the Narita and Flight 182 bombs, on the logical assumption the bombs were made at the same time, to do the same type of job, by the same Sikh bombmaker.

The Japanese, who have excellent evidence-analysis capability, released the information that they found residue of a *plastic*-type explosive. Was the C4 plastic explosive the ex-British soldier took to New York and sold to the Sikhs in April of 1985, as his friends said he did, the same plastic used to kill the passengers and crew of the jumbo jet and the baggage handlers in June of 1985?

Two demolition blocks of C4, each weighing about a kilo, equal about five to eight sticks of high-grade dynamite in explosive power.

Experiments in Canada with steel luggage and cargo containers, exactly like the one that had exploded at Narita, showed it took about five to eight sticks of dynamite to equal the damage done to the container at Narita. The British merc would only have needed to have four blocks of C4 to sell to provide the Sikhs with two identical, powerful bombs.

Some Indian and Canadian journalists even speculated that it was dynamite that did the killing, but the Japanese specifically said they had detected residue of *plastic* explosive at Narita.

Authorities in India would not even admit that Flight 182 had been bombed until about six months after the incident, and then only after wreckage from the flight had been raised that showed absolute proof of an internal explosion in the aircraft.

Reports, later denied by Japanese authorities, claimed the fingerprints of Lal Singh were found on some fragments of destroyed baggage at Narita. An "L. Singh" had been listed aboard Canadian Pacific Flight 003, but he had not gone through Japanese Customs and apparently was not actually on the flight.

There would be a reason to deny Lal's fingerprints and confuse the question of the type of explosive used.

The world press could quickly blame the U.S. as being indirectly responsible for the bombings on three strong points.

First, the Sikhs who bombed the Air India jet were likely part of the group trained at Merc School, especially if Lal Singh were implicated, as FBI wanted posters for him indicated. This made the U.S. "responsible" for the training, if someone wanted to take that view, since I only continued to train the Sikhs as part of an FBI operation.

Second, it was highly probable that the Sikhs had obtained their plastic through an unwatched hole in the U.S. operation—the British ex-soldier who illegally obtained the explosive.

And third, the U.S. operation overall to arrest the Sikh terrorist cadre in New Jersey had failed due to judgment errors by the agents involved, and those Sikhs, in escaping, were likely the ones who "struck back" in revenge.

Of course, the Reagan administration could not afford to be seen as even indirectly responsible for a major terrorist act, so a subtle shift of the blame was effected.

The press was given me as a target. Of this I have no hard proof, only knowledge of the results.

What I have to say now is also on the order of speculation. I believe the government of India, eager to prevent more rioting, killing, and the nurturing of more hate between the Sikhs and Hindus, requested the Canadian, Japanese, and American authorities to suppress information concerning both bombings, and those governments cooperated.

In the months just after the loss of Flight 182, Rajiv Gandhi was planning to sign a treaty with "moderate" Sikh leaders, some of whom had originally been present in the Golden Temple prior to the siege and attack but had left the temple after disagreeing with the extremists.

Gandhi would not have wanted the continuation of violence to mar or prevent the treaty, which was intended to bring peace and stability to Sikh-Indian relations.

Only days after signing the treaty, Sikh extremists assassinated the most important of the Sikh signators.

The Sikhs made one attempt at revenge against me. A four-man hit team—three Sikhs and a Canadian mercenary—plotted to come to Birmingham from Canada to find and kill me. All I can say about the incident is that the would-be assassins were compromised early, I was warned by the FBI, and the oncoming team was stopped.

CHAPTER TWENTY
Disavowed

There is a beginning and an end to everything. The end of my career as a mercenary began with the Sikh operation and a phone call from a distraught woman in California, who told me she was in trouble, but we will take them in order.

The first indication of trouble was from Fox, as I came off the plane from Mexico. He told me during my phone call to him from the Birmingham Airport that the press had discovered the Sikhs had been Merc School students.

While I had been in Mexico, the FBI press announcement about its breaking of the Gandhi assassination plot had been released. The announcement created a flurry of news interest, and Alex Ethridge, our field photographer, quickly sold to the press some of his November 1984 photos of the Sikh team in training.

The news media immediately assumed the Mercenary School was in the business of training terrorists. Press interest in the Merc School had always been strong. Many national, and international, journalists and a few TV and film crews had visited our course over the years, so I had some experience in handling—and being handled by—the news media.

All the major news services came at me at once for the next couple of weeks, as Alex's photos were widely published, wanting explanations why such *terrorist* training was allowed to take place in the United States.

I could not satisfy their questions because I had to protect my cover. The resulting news reports were blistering. The general editorial agreement among them was that I was as guilty as the Sikhs, but somehow had escaped the wrath of the law.

The flap had only started to die down when, on 23 June 1985, the announcement of the loss of the Air India 747, with 329 people on board, was made. Sikh radicals claimed they had bombed the airliner.

Within a few days, investigators released the names of two Sikhs who were suspected of involvement in the bombing. Lal Singh was one of them.

From Alex's identification of the Sikhs in his photographs, the press knew Lal Singh had been at Merc School, and his probable connection to the murder of the passengers and crew of the 747 became, in their opinion, my fault.

A second vengeful media assault erupted that dimmed to insignificance the one that had just barely passed. The Canadian press, their country the staging area for both the Air India and Tokyo bombings, was the worst. It demanded justice or blood. The Indian press was next, since it had been an Indian aircraft lost, and, of course, the Japanese joined in because of the Narita Airport incident.

Not far behind were the U.S. and European press, all seemingly with their minds set that they finally had a terrorist on the spot, one they could photograph, question, and exhibit.

To refuse to talk to them, in their crucifying mood, would have been worse than talking. At first, I stuck to my original cover story, that I had trained Sikhs at Merc School and knew nothing more. But as I read the resulting headlines that were denouncing me worldwide as a terrorist and trainer of terrorists, I felt forced to explain at least some of the truth—that my involvement with the Sikhs had been part of a U.S. operation *against* terrorism—without going into detail—and on the *Today Show, 60 Minutes,* and Larry King, I did.

Most reporters, journalists, and interviewers didn't want to hear anything that blunted the "domestic" terrorism slant to the story, and basically ignored the new information.

Their most commonly asked question of me was still: *"How does it feel to be responsible for the deaths of all the people on that plane?"*

In newspapers all across the United States, and in some foreign countries, indignant editorials ran about me, some complete with political cartoons crying for retribution, and they were heard.

Members of Congress demanded I be put out of business, if not jailed outright. They either did not know of my relationship to the government, or if informed by some intelligence agency, they did not care.

The Mercenary Association was targeted for destruction.

The Senate Subcommittee on Terrorism under Senator Denton launched an investigation of me, but the day they were to see me they were secretly briefed by the FBI, and before the investigators left The Bunker, we were discussing a possible operation I could perform based on drug information I had concerning Nicaragua. Indeed, a potential operation in Nicaragua did evolve out of the meeting.

Uninformed or ignorant, the Attorney General of Alabama, Charles Graddick, who had aspirations to run for Governor in mind, publicly sued me for "terrorist activities" and operating a private school without a license.

I quietly informed him of the facts, but the suit made good press, so he persisted with it, and actually increased the pressure by arranging a severe state tax audit of me.

That was not going to be all.

I was told he began to work to encourage any possible prosecution of me by the Federal Bureau of Alcohol, Tobacco, and Firearms because I owned and controlled so many weapons. The BATF, even though I had worked directly for them in the past and given them much intelligence and assistance on other matters, had apparently never trusted me and seemed only too glad to help him.

Exploiting the BATF wasn't difficult. The Birmingham office of the BATF had an apparent animosity toward the Merc School based on the fact that they had little or no notice of what operations I was involved in, so they only saw foreigners, weapons, and sometimes criminals coming and going to The Bunker.

To personally complicate things for me at the time, there were two assassination threats against me. One had a Cuban origin, out of Miami. The FBI was investigating it. The contract called for "the life of Frank Camper." A friendly ex-spook warned me that it was anti-Castro Cubans who wanted me because they thought I was working against the contra cause. That had to be a spillover from mercs who had been in Central America. Some of them had worked with the (current) Cuban 2506 Brigade.

The second threat had the Brit merc alleged involved in

obtaining the C4 out on a contract for me, with the Sikhs as his probable employers.

As serious as the death threats were, they were at least in my domain and I could handle them. The press was not.

BATF undercover agents had filtered through Merc School several times in the past, and I was to discover as I later read the BATF file on myself that I was always a potential "target" for them.

The attorney general did not stay in office to enjoy any fruits of his suit against me. Graddick was denied candidacy in his bid for governorship because of arranging for vote fraud and getting caught at it. The suit was dropped.

The most logical question at this point would be why none of the agencies for which I had worked would speak up for me. The answer is simple. Their policy forbids it. I had to ride out the anger of the press on my own.

I had once been an asset to my government. Now I was a potential liability. If I became too enraged at the press and began to talk, the government had to wonder where I would begin and where I would stop.

In the summer of 1985, following the bombing of the Air India jet, Reagan's missiles were going to Iran, and the security cap on that operation was tight. If I spoke of that, a national scandal would follow—as it eventually did anyway.

I had also learned (by late 1985) how the C4 that so likely went into the actual bombings had been obtained. Adding that information to what I knew of the Sikhs' escape in New Jersey, and explaining it to the press, would have created a major embarrassment for the U.S.

The administration was supposed to be "at war" with terrorism, not goofing up and causing it.

My own cover was now working against me. Press researchers knew I had been involved with leftists or communists in the early 1970s and the PLO in the Mideast, and the publicized cases of the 1980s had me as a possible paid killer in Miami and a weapons smuggler in Birmingham, to mention only a couple.

In this respect, I could understand the current press judgments, even if they were issued as crowd-pleasers rather than searches for truth.

Of all people, the publisher of *Soldier of Fortune* magazine took pains to condemn me. It made me wonder if he was as careless with his research on other subjects before committing himself to print.

For a last straw, a sanctimonious Baptist preacher in my own hometown told his congregation one Sunday morning, "There was no need to look across the world for terrorists—one lives right in the community."

It was bitter to take such flak for having helped prevent the possible assassination of the head of state of India and, by luck, one of the Indian state ministers.

The irony was my cover had always been based on seeming to be the same as the very enemies I fought. Now I was paying dearly for it.

The telephone call from the woman in California came as the July 1985 Merc School course was in session.

She told me a tragic story. She said she owned several private schools for small children and had been forced to fire a group of her teachers.

In revenge for their firing, she told me, some of the ex-employees had vandalized the schools, tried to set fire to her home, and killed her pets. She said she was afraid for her life and the safety of the school children.

The police had been unresponsive, saying they had to catch someone in the act before they could do anything about it. The woman wanted to know if I would at least come to California and talk to her about her problem.

By coincidence, I had a trip to Hollywood already planned at the end of July. I went to talk with an independent production studio at the Universal Lot about a possible Merc School movie, hoping to make the best of a bad publicity situation.

I never worked for individuals. I agreed to meet the woman because it was convenient, and I had sympathy for her.

I had also planned to bring a team of Merc School cadre to Hollywood to introduce to the studio executives, if it would help to make the deal.

By agreeing to investigate and possibly provide security for the woman and her schools, I could use her money to transport and employ the team, relieving a logistical burden.

So it was that I agreed, and the team came. The three men

were Jimmy Cuneo, Bill Hedgecorth (a veteran of Lebanon as a freelance merc), and Paul Johnson.

I spent a week in Los Angeles with Lee Faulk before Paul and the rest of the team arrived; they had driven cross-country in Paul's van. I was able to brief them when they arrived on what I had discovered in my investigation of the ex-employees of the private schools and assign security duties to them before I left.

Lee had flown out to visit me there, to see Hollywood, but as luck would have it, fell sick soon after arriving and spent most of her time in bed. I flew her home as soon as she could travel.

I had completed my business at Universal—interviews with my cadre were not necessary—and was planning to leave after I familiarized the men with the area and their employers. I estimated I could be traveling by Monday or Tuesday, and planned to leave at least two men behind for personal security for as long as the woman wished to keep them.

On Tuesday, 14 August, I was flying to Chicago to face more press, and Paul Johnson was driving back to Alabama. Jimmy and Bill stayed with the school owner in California. They were back in Alabama by the end of the month, to begin the September Merc School.

During September, only weeks after I got back, each one of us were called to the BATF office in Birmingham and questioned about the California trip.

The BATF agents would not be specific to me about the crime they were investigating, but it involved the burning of automobiles of two of the ex-employees of the private schools.

During the questioning, I told the agents everything I knew, but it was clear they were not interviewing me for information. They were in fact preparing a case against me.

During the rest of September, it was business as usual. *60 Minutes* taped a segment on the Merc School, and the actor Robert Duvall trained with us to prepare himself for his movie *Let's Get Harry*. He created his role as a mercenary in that movie largely by studying me.

The best laugh we got out of Duvall was when, with a gentle prod, he paraphrased a line he had made famous in the Vietnam epic *Apocalypse Now,* suiting it to Merc School.

"I love the smell of CS in the morning," he said, in reference to the scent of tear gas that always lingered at our base camp.

One thing I should have noticed, but didn't because I was

too busy, was that Paul and Jimmy had withdrawn from me slightly.

I should have been more observant.

Despite the heat from BATF, my work continued. In the last part of 1985, I was becoming involved in a developing coup against Ghana in West Africa, but the operation fizzled. I was glad to have turned it down, because all the men involved were eventually arrested on a weapons-laden barge in South America and went to prison.

I had been keeping Brooks posted on the fledgling plot, which was hard to take seriously. At least two other plots with the same goal were under way at the same time, from other directions, with better organizing and funding.

In early 1986, while on a trip to Europe, I was offered a contract against a KGB agent by a man whom the agent had once imprisoned.

I lost the job, and the FBI/CIA operation that would have gone with it, when the man backed out.

March of 1986 found me in New York, to be available to testify in the trial of Gurpartap Birk Singh as he was tried for the Gandhi assassination plot. He was found guilty of Neutrality Act violations and firearms charges.

The Nicaraguan operation that began with the "investigative" visit to me by members of the Senate subcommittee on terrorism went further. A cocaine production site near Managua City was the target. My part of the operation was to train the contra teams that would actually do the job, with DEA footing the bill.

As with most operations involving contra groups, I was dealing with diverse and often viciously competitive groups of people in order to get my job done. What began as a simple commando raid was quickly complicated by each group's insistence that its own special interest be served.

Assassinating Daniel Ortega, head of the pro-Soviet Sandinista government of Nicaragua, was the special interest of one of the groups important enough to the original operation to make me listen.

The group was vital in that they were providing intelligence. They seemed to be well placed enough to know of the drug sites and to believe they knew some of Ortega's moves in advance, and felt an attempt to kill him with sniper fire might work.

They were extremely evasive with me about the source and nature of their intelligence assets, insisting I provide equipment to them first as a show of good faith before we could make any more progress.

The "equipment" was sniper rifles, day and night scopes, and training in how to use them.

I put the equipment on my request list to DEA, as part of the overall mission to knock out the cocaine factory.

Skeptical of Ortega's would-be assassins, I had made no official report of them yet in my calls to my DEA control agent, waiting instead to have more solid information before I spoke. A representative of the assassination faction was due to visit me for a meeting in May of 1986, to answer some of my questions. The meeting never took place.

Without warning, a BATF arrest raid came on the morning of 20 May, a Tuesday. Armed agents, wearing bulletproof vests under blue windbreaker jackets with "ATF" markings in white on their backs, came to my house for me.

There was a Merc School class in progress, the course having just started over the weekend. Paul Johnson and Jimmy Cuneo were in the field, expecting me to join them shortly.

Bill Hedgecorth was at home, in Rhode Island.

I was quickly handcuffed, my rights read to me by an agent I knew personally, and a search team began to go through my desk and files. The same thing was happening at The Bunker, where bolt cutters were used to open file cabinets, foot lockers, and even padlocked duffel bags.

From the minute the handcuffs had been locked on me, I was angry. Why would the BATF do something like this? Why hadn't they coordinated with the FBI, or with Brooks's agency? I first thought the arrest was linked to my upcoming operation in Nicaragua.

Still handcuffed, I was driven to the field in the back of a pickup truck, escorted by an army of police and BATF agents.

Jimmy and Paul were also arrested and, clad in their combat fatigues, put in the truckbed with me.

Command at the school was left with my son, Barret, and

other cadre, who immediately stepped in to take Paul and Jimmy's place.

"Don't give them anything but your name, rank, and social security number," I said to Paul and Jimmy, to lighten the moment. They didn't smile.

The arrests, we quickly learned, were for the burned cars in California.

The bond hearing the next day was a long and tedious one, five and a half hours, but in spite of the federal attorney asking the judge not to grant us bail because "we were dangerous and would flee the country," we were all given low bonds.

Jimmy was released that night, but Paul and I had to wait until the next morning to complete our bail.

As we were doing just that, with our bonding agents waiting for us and our release paperwork ready, my lawyer suddenly came to me with the news that a federal order had come in that *canceled* our bond.

He was astounded and said he had his assistant already filing for an emergency hearing about it. Something was very wrong. We were being bluntly denied a normal process of law.

In the hearing, arguing bitterly against the order to cancel our bail, our lawyers got the judge to agree the order was "highhanded and unusual," but he would not overrule it, uncertain of what to do, so he let the order stand.

Jimmy was already home in New York. Bill Hedgecorth was arrested by BATF agents in Rhode Island on 21 May, the day of our bond hearing in Birmingham.

Paul and I were taken back to jail. By 27 May all of us were either in a federal prison south of Los Angeles or just arriving.

Terminal Island was the name of the prison. It was an old fortresslike compound built originally as a military prison in the 1930s, on an island in the San Pedro shipyards, linked to the mainland by a bridged road.

Paul and I were brought in and processed together.
Then we were split up, and I was taken directly to solitary confinement. It was the royal treatment for the highest-risk security cases, such as spies, traitors, and mass murderers. It prevented contact with anyone, including the press.

Cuneo, who was taken back into custody in New York, was

out in the general prison population, and in fact would soon be released again on bond.

Paul Johnson and Bill Hedgecorth were kept separate from each other, but were put in two-man cells in another part of the prison. I was the only one in solitary.

My cell was very small and narrow. Two bunks side by side would have filled it. There was a sink and toilet. The solid steel door had a small, barred window at face level and a padlocked trapdoor under that for feeding.

The wall window that might have looked out to the prison yard was covered by a vented metal plate. No view there, but some air did come through the louvers.

I wondered how many men had been held in this cell in the fifty years it had stood. The old concrete floor was cracked. Paint thickly coated the door and walls.

Some prisoners had etched names, or dates, into the walls, obviously a slow, laborious process using a bit of smuggled metal hidden from the guards.

I sat down on my military bunk. It was just like the one I'd had in basic training, except the springs had been replaced by a steel sheet welded in place.

Someone wanted me to break, that was why I had been sent directly to maximum security. But I had been through all this before, in 1968. At least I knew something about such treatment.

Having seen something of it before didn't make being railroaded as fast as possible into a dungeon any less chilling. Somewhere, something was very wrong. Even if I was actually guilty of burning two old cars in California (as BATF was saying now), it should only have been a state charge, a virtual misdemeanor. There was no sense in it.

A grand jury in Los Angeles quickly indicted all of us on a hefty list of federal charges, including arson, conspiracy, unregistered explosive or incendiary devices, use of firearms in a crime, interference with interstate commerce, and racketeering.

A major federal case was made of a state charge. The potential sentence for all the charges added up to almost eighty years. If I were not the man wearing the handcuffs, I would not have thought such a thing possible.

I would learn on 2 June, while at my "new" bail hearing at the L.A. federal courthouse, that only a few days before, on 30 May, Jimmy Cuneo had agreed to testify for the government against me for reduced charges. I was stunned. Trial was set for 22 July.

We went through the motions of a bond hearing, with the judge quickly denying my request.

So far, my attorney had not been able to slow down, much less stop, anything happening to me.

The section of the prison I was held in had the Orwellian title of Special Housing Unit, or SHU, and its small, dimly lit cells were called "houses" by the guards.

Of course, compared with the heat-lamp-baked metal box I had once spent a month inside in the army, the SHU "house" was almost plush, with its running water and ventilation duct.

On the floor above us was "B Dorm," which was the mental ward. Through the ventilation ducts I could hear the worst of what went on up there. Beyond restraint, some of the inmates would scream and beat on their cell doors, drumming violent, dislocated echoes down to my cell.

Shouts from the crazed inmates above me were like those I had heard in the Fort Campbell prison riot, the bellow of those who didn't care any longer if they lived or died.

I was handcuffed any time I was taken out of my cell to talk to my attorney on his visits to me, or even if I was just being walked down the hall to the shower.

Solitary confinement is intended to distort reason. The days I spent in the cell might have been slow madness, but I had the discipline born of years of practice. When the long view is too overwhelming, you look only to the small and immediate.

I could not let my hopes rise too high, or let depression take me down. I had to maintain a balance and live each day as it came.

The month of June was marked off my handmade calendar a day at a time, until I had broken my old military record for imprisonment in isolation.

Every day was a separate wait. The nights were the worst. They passed much slower than the days. Time almost seemed to stop then, like drifting on a dead sea, and the smallness of my cell, with its heavy, stark walls, reminded me more of a tomb than anything else.

* * *

Full control of the Merc School was now with my son, who had reorganized the course format and personnel to better function in my absence. Not one scheduled course in 1986 was missed.

I spent July 4 in solitary, remembering my independence holiday in 1968, in the army hotbox. Introspection added to the pressure. Solitary focuses mental concentration. It gave me all the time I needed to think, to examine my life, to try to decide if it had all been worth it. I had survived the years, getting older— my fortieth birthday was due in October—but perhaps not smarter.

The missions and operations were apparently all behind me now. What had I gained? Whom had I actually helped? Did the people I had hurt really deserve it? Did the people I helped appreciate it?

The basic question was why have I lived this sort of life at all?

The answer off the top of the pile, of course, is to have done it for duty's sake, but wasn't the thrill of survival, the conquest of danger, also important?

If so, the justifying argument of duty only was lame. I would have to admit to basically having done it to suit myself and lay no blame on duty.

After Vietnam, I had promised myself never to fight under anyone's flag again unless it was on my own terms. In the end, you must be true to yourself.

Right and wrong is the final question, and I was my own final authority.

I did not believe in politics or politicians. They called themselves the solutions. They were, in my opinion, usually the problem, salt in the wounds of the world.

I believed in loyalty and courage, even if for their own sake, but recognized that these two traits were used by crafty politicians to lead soldiers from war to war, in just cause or artful manipulation.

Most of all, I felt for the innocent, those who suffered so the powerful could exert their power. If I had ever done anything truly worthwhile, I wanted it to have been for the innocent, to have relieved some of their agony I had seen.

* * *

It appeared I was going to end my career in undercover and covert operations by being jailed by my own people. I had become a liability. The system was trying to bury me. Even those who knew I was not a terrorist, as the news media claimed, but an independent who worked for our own law enforcement or intelligence agencies, still wanted me out of business.

My mistake had been in assuming, if not actual loyalty, at least an earned respect and debt for services rendered, from my governmental employers to me.

Maybe I was looking for the break I didn't get after Vietnam. Maybe I was a fool for ever considering I was due anything at all.

Not one agency, not *one* that had paid me or used me, spoke up for me or made a move to come to my aid. I wrote them and received no answers.

No one knew me anymore.

I was disavowed.

With deliberation and sameness, the days wore on, closer to trial date, but in the second week of July, our trial was postponed all the way to 28 October. It was a blow. It added months to the wait, every day of it in isolation.

On what would have been our original trial date, Paul Johnson went with his lawyer to the Los Angeles federal courthouse and, fulfilling a promise he made a month earlier, pled guilty to the charges, joining Jimmy Cuneo in agreeing to testify for the government. I had been expecting him to do that.

The summer sunlight of July died on my cell wall each afternoon, filtered through holes in the window plating. August numbers replaced July numbers on my calendar.

August was a long month. I broke one hundred days straight in solitary by its end.

September added even more. Counting lost its point.

October, which had seemed so far away in July when the trial was postponed, finally arrived—but with the slowness of one check mark on my calendar per day. The actual trial date of 28 October approached with the jarring hesitancy of a square wheel, each turn a day, each day grim anticipation.

Just before the trial was to begin, the prosecution offered me a deal. Confess, take ten years instead of the possible maximum of seventy-five if I was found guilty, incriminate my codefendants, who now included twenty-eight-year-old Lee Ann Faulk, as well as Bill Hedgecorth, and I would actually be released in three years.

I said no.

Lee's unfortunate part in the whole affair was only to have visited me for a few days while I had been in California, and in fact she had left before the date of the car fires.

She had been charged on a later indictment, apparently as a pressure tactic against me, but she had at least been allowed bail while Bill and I had been held in jail.

Not long after, a shattering thing happened to Lee. There was a break-in at her psychologist's office in Mountain Brook, outside of Birmingham. The burglars came in through the room of an unoccupied adjoining office, defeated the locked interior door, and entered her psych's office. All that was taken was Lee's personal file. The psych notified the police and the *Birmingham News* carried a short piece on the incident.

Break-ins are a routine covert operations tactic. Gordon Liddy went to jail for one. I had done a couple myself, so in this case I wasn't too surprised. But Lee was devastated. I later told her that whoever took it was hoping to find incriminating or classification-breaking information I had told her and she had told her psych.

Such info couldn't legally be used in trial, but its source could be camouflaged and information in the file used to break her. The theft was wasted, however. Lee knew nothing to tell, and the file contained nothing but personal, not governmental, secrets.

Despite his cooperation, Paul Johnson was also still in jail, although Jimmy Cuneo had been released on bond soon after his "agreement" with the prosecution.

The two schoolteachers had been arrested on the same day as myself. They had also been denied bond and were put in a women's prison. They were not dangerous criminals with records. They were two middle-aged preschool owners.

BATF was keeping them imprisoned to terrify them into a confession.

The weekend before our trial began, both of the women entered pleas of guilty to conspiracy, induced by promises of release. Their "guilt" was not having committed a crime, or even knowing of a crime, but simply having called me and paid my men's expenses. There was no more to it than that. The coercion had worked.

One of the women was heavily fined and later released. The other was given seven years. Their lives were ruined, and all in BATF's effort to make a case against me.

The women were not used by the prosecution as witnesses against me. They knew nothing to say that would convict me and counted only as "kills" on the prosecutor's record.

It took two days to pick a jury, and on Thursday, 30 October, the trial began, under Judge Alicemarie Stotler.

The first move by the prosecution, without the jury present, was to ask for and have granted a motion to prevent the disclosure of any classified information during the trial and suppress my background and relationship with the U.S. government.

I was effectively gagged. My personal history of cooperation with law enforcement and intelligence agencies and, therefore, a means of establishing my reliability or believability would be unknown to the jury.

Information on the "victims'" use of drugs and their records of arrests and prostitution, which I had discovered, were all suppressed too. The prosecution didn't want the jury to know about them as they actually were, and the judge agreed.

In the course of the trial, since there were no witnesses to the crime or solid evidence such as fingerprints, it was going to boil down to who the jury believed, me or Paul and Jimmy, who said Bill and I had accompanied them on an early-morning run on the thirteenth of August, 1985, to burn the cars, with Lee Faulk knowing it was going to happen.

I testified that Paul and Jimmy had, in fact, been out alone together that predawn morning, supposedly on a security patrol of the schools, which were mostly clustered within one township, and Bill and I had been at the hotel.

The prosecution argued that Lee, Bill, and I were guilty, that I was the organizer of the fires, and my motive was simply money.

I was presented to the jury as a pure mercenary, who ran a school for mercenaries. In my defense, I could not argue back.

The motion to suppress prevented me from doing that. I had to sit and take such an allegation.

Ironically, the news of the Iran-contra affair began to break during the trial. Everyday new information came out about how President Reagan had approved a covert missile sale to Iran to try to get U.S. hostages released, and how money from the sale had been used to buy weapons and equipment for the contras.

Investigations and indictments against many operatives who had supplied and funded the contras would result. Another covert op had collapsed in on itself, taking the innocent and guilty alike down with it.

The ghost of mission after government mission taunted me in that courtroom. The prosecution was using it all against me now. My government wanted me in jail.

We were three weeks on trial.

In the closing arguments, our defense lawyers argued that Paul had influenced Jimmy to join with him and strike at the ex-employees, and now they were attempting to shift the blame, in order to reduce their sentences.

The prosecution told the jury that I was "a minor, rinky-dink mercenary" who would do anything for money and that Paul and Jimmy were my "dirtbags," even though they were testifying for the government against me.

The jury took a week to deliberate. Bill Hedgecorth, who like me had now spent six months in jail, was angry and nervous.

"I guess we've done all we can," he said to me. "If we go down, at least we'll go down like Recondos."

He was not one to quit. During his first course at Merc School, he had been captured and tied to a tree all night in freezing rain. When I found him the next morning he was so cold his eyes wouldn't focus, but he didn't drop out of the course.

Lee, who had been kept separated from me during the trial, endured it all far better than I had expected, sometimes crying silently and dabbing at the corners of her eyes with a handkerchief, but she stood by me without wavering, even facing prison.

Lee and Bill had also been offered deals to "confess" and both had refused, unwilling to accept a felony conviction based on intimidation alone.

On 21 November 1986, after almost a solid month of trial

and deliberation, the jury returned and announced it was dead-locked.

On most of the ten counts against us, their vote was widely split. Only on one, the charge of conspiracy, had it come close—eleven to one for a verdict of guilty.

That one vote was all we needed.

The judge declared a mistrial. For the moment, we had survived, even if by default.

It was back to my cell again, back to waiting.

A new trial was set for March of 1987, adding more months to the ordeal. Christmas in solitary was especially grim. My father was diagnosed with terminal cancer, and my appeal for bail to be with him before he died was denied.

That appeal was made for me by my new attorneys, Bill Wynn and Bill Delgrosso from Birmingham, Alabama. They had been following my case, concluded I was not getting a fair trial, and volunteered their time and services, because they bluntly believed I was innocent.

The second trial began on 17 March 1987.

Again the judge granted the government's motion to suppress my background and relationship to the agencies that had employed me.

The judge then also ruled out the appearance of some of my witnesses and restricted the questioning of most of the others, preventing the jury from learning of BATF's spotty and error-ridden method of making a case against me.

Wynn and Delgrosso soon found themselves so restricted in presenting a defense that on three occasions they were threatened with contempt of court for violating suppressions of evidence, so hard did they defend me.

Bill Hedgecorth's and Lee Faulk's attorneys also did the best they could under the circumstances, but the weight of the case was on Wynn and Delgrosso.

"I've never seen rulings like these," Wynn said to me during the trial. "Usually it's the defense that wants to get things suppressed, but the government is suppressing everything here. According to them, you didn't exist until you crossed the California state line."

* * *

The jury went out on 9 April and was back with a verdict on 13 April, a Monday morning.

Lee Ann Faulk was declared not guilty on all counts.

Bill Hedgecorth and I were found guilty on four of the ten counts against us. Those were generalized counts, not the specific ones of actually committing a crime. We were hit with conspiracy, weapons, and racketeering.

Whatever else, my career as a privateer was over.

Last Entry in the Journal: 1 June 1987

The Medellin cartel had threatened to assassinate me at my sentencing, so I was secreted to the Los Angeles Federal Courthouse basement on the night of 31 May, and surrounded by a small army of heavily armed marshals. I was taken before Judge Stotler the next morning.

I was given fourteen years. Bill would later get five.

From the courthouse I was rushed under heavy guard to a Bell JetRanger helicopter waiting on the high roof of a nearby parking deck. I was to be flown directly to a penitentiary.

Lee had told me she would wait. Nothing was over yet. Twenty years ago I had flown to war in clattering jet helicopters. I had survived those missions. I am determined not just to survive this one—but to win.

Postscript
Capitol Hill

On 14 July 1988, Frank Camper appeared before a subcommittee of the Senate Foreign Relations Committee. The Secretary of the Army declassified his security agreement with army intelligence, and documents from CIA, FBI, and BATF were provided to the subcommittee to verify Camper's private operator relationship and activities with the United States.

In sworn testimony, Camper told of the 1984 effort by Military Intelligence to purchase Chinese missiles of the same type and quantity that a year later would go to Iran in the form of U.S. TOWs in the Iran-Contra affair.

He also described his activities in Panama gathering intelligence on General Noriega, and the abortive effort in 1985 to capture the Mexican drug baron in Veracruz.

Camper revealed to the committee details of the bombing of Air India Flight 182, and described how the C4 plastic explosive suspected of use in the destruction of that aircraft and the 329 passengers and crew, had been obtained.

Frank Camper's appeal of his conviction, based on government suppression of facts and evidence in his case, went forward soon after his appearance before the Senate.

Return to the savage storm of VIETNAM in some of today's best novels.

__CENTRIFUGE
J.C. Pollock 11156-0 $3.95

__CROSSFIRE
J.C. Pollock 11602-3 $3.95

__GOING AFTER CACCIATO
Tim O'Brien 32965-3 $4.95

__MISSION M.I.A.
J.C. Pollock 15819-2 $3.95

At your local bookstore or use this handy coupon for ordering:

DELL READERS SERVICE, DEPT. DVT
P.O. Box 5057, Des Plaines, IL. 60017-5057

Please send me the above title(s). I am enclosing $_____.
(Please add $2.00 per order to cover shipping and handling.) Send
check or money order—no cash or C.O.D.s please.

Dell

Ms./Mrs./Mr._____

Address_____

City/State _____ Zip_____

DVT–1/89

Prices and availability subject to change without notice. Please allow four to six
weeks for delivery. This offer expires 7/89.

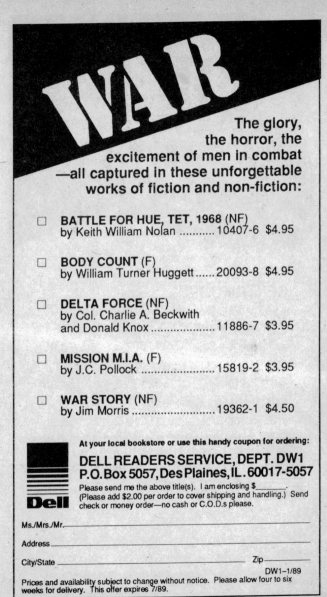